FINANCIAL SECTOR OF THE AMERICAN ECONOMY

edited by

STUART BRUCHEY
ALLAN NEVINS PROFESSOR EMERITUS
COLUMBIA UNIVERSITY

A GARLAND SERIES

FINANCIAL LIBERALIZATION AND THE RECONSTRUCTION OF STATE-MARKET RELATIONS

ROBERT B. PACKER

GARLAND PUBLISHING, INC.
A MEMBER OF THE TAYLOR & FRANCIS GROUP
NEW YORK & LONDON / 1998

332.042
PIIf

Library of Congress Cataloging-in-Publication Data

Packer, Robert B., 1963–
    Financial liberalization and the reconstruction of state-
market relations / Robert B. Packer.
        p.   cm. — (Financial sector of the American economy)
    Includes bibliographical references and index.
    ISBN 0-8153-3161-4 (alk. paper)
    1. International finance. 2. Capital movements.
3. Finance—Government policy. I. Series.
HG3881.P253 1998
332'.042—dc21
                                                            98-37933

ab

Printed on acid-free, 250-year-life paper
Manufactured in the United States of America

TABLE OF CONTENTS

Financial Liberalization and the Reconstruction of State-Market Relations

CHAPTER I

Introduction

> Accustomed to presuming a state system predominantly composed of sovereign states authorized to address and cope with change, we are unlikely to inquire whether states have been weakened and their micro components strengthened, whether the nature of force, legitimacy, and authority relations has undergone meaningful redefinition, whether the state system continues to be the prime organizer of global politics, or whether another world has emerged alongside the state system as the basis for world order (Rosenau, 1990: 39-40).

In his volume *Turbulence in World Politics,* James Rosenau pointed out a number of dramatic changes in the parameters of contemporary global affairs. Most important is the observation that the capability of states and governments to provide satisfactory solutions to the major issues on their political agendas has been reduced. This occurrence is largely the result of the emergence of issues—such as the consequences of international financial integration—that are the direct products of new technologies or of the world's greater interdependence.

While most economists focus on the effects of integration on interest rate differentials (Feldstein and Horioka, 1980; Frankel, 1991; Marston, 1995), exchange rate stability and coordination (Williamson and Miller, 1987), and open economy macroeconomics (Dornbusch, 1980; 1993), scholars of international political economy in political science have focused on the effects of integration on the distribution of power between states (Keohane and Nye, 1977; Odell, 1982; Gowa, 1983) and among societal groups within states (Hawley, 1987; Frieden, 1991).

In this study, I hope to add to the literature concerning the distributional consequences of financial integration by focusing on the rise of non-state actors within a transformed international system. In it, I argue that structural change brought on by transnational production and post-industrialization has created space for non-state actors to acquire autonomy from sovereign entities. While finance is by no means the only specialized sector to achieve autonomy, it has perhaps the most immediate impact on the ability of governments to pursue policy. The ability of individual investors, pension and mutual fund managers, and foreign exchange traders to break the bounds of state direction has yielded "governmental disintermediation," as financial asset-holders remove their savings from state-regulated institutions when the direct purchase of financial claims issued by other states and non-state entities bring a higher rate of return. The ability of financial asset-holders to circumvent the political risk created by government policies is an example of what Rosenau would call a "conceptual jailbreak," in which the dominant state-centric paradigms of world politics must be challenged in order to address changed realities.

Financial asset-holders have a vested interest in maintaining and enhancing their autonomy *vis-à-vis* the state. Financial integration, in the form of both domestic regulatory reform in the financial services industry and liberalization of capital controls on transnational capital movements, grants financial asset-holders the autonomy they desire to maximize private returns. Because financial integration has transformed a formerly oligopsonistic market for financial capital to a more competitive one, governments must devise new approaches in order to induce finance capital to remain domiciled in the state.

But this sequence of events begs the following questions: Why did governments grant finance capital autonomy to begin with? And what is inhibiting governments from reimposing controls, rather than carrying out further regulatory reform and liberalization? To answer these questions requires that we address the structure of state-market relations, as well as investigate the role of finance capital's structural power in shaping governmental policy. That is, financial asset-holders are actors largely endogenous to the state political system. Because the role of government is that of intermediator among individual and group interests, the political process is one of conflict and resolution among competing resource allocation packages.

However, unlike most consumers for state services, finance asset-holders help to provide the resources that states use to distribute. Therefore, financial asset-holders are often in an enhanced position compared to other claimants to governmental services, particularly in market economies. While both states and markets allocate resources, resolving the problem of scarcity in a society, the allocative process is different. States acquire resources largely through confiscation, either from other societies via conquest or from those under its own authority through taxes and requisitions. States distribute resources based upon the political power (determined by demographic, economic, or military capabilities) of competing claimants on resources. Markets, by contrast, allocate resources based upon the independent decisions of individual producers and consumers acting in their own (perceived) best interests without central direction. To be sure, market decisions are not wholly voluntaristic, as certain market actors may possess the ability to extract rent from other actors.

Financial asset-holders have been able to establish themselves as major players on the international stage due to the advent (in actuality, the reemergence) of global (financial) capital mobility. Capital mobility refers to the capacity of capital to cross borders, rather than to actual flows of money. Put differently, capital mobility refers to the relative absence of friction on financial flows across borders (Andrews, 1994: 195). Actual flows of financial capital at any given moment are contingent on profit incentives, deriving from differential rates of expected return in different states. The political effects of capital mobility are distinguished from many traditional political issues by virtue of being transnational rather than purely national or local in scope. Because international financial integration is a phenomenon not wholly within their jurisdiction, governments are hard-pressed to develop policies in response to its domestic repercussions. Because domestic policies are increasingly intertwined with significant international components, the compliance of national citizenries can no longer be taken for granted.

The extent to which domestic policy choices are constrained by international market forces and the political leverage of international finance capital interests has been an issue addressed by scholars in international political economy (Polanyi, 1944; Hawley, 1987; Haggard and Kaufman, 1992; Cerny, 1993; Andrews, 1994). Economic shocks are often cited as a principal cause of major shifts in foreign and domestic economic policies. Innovation and diffusion, the twin motors of change in economic systems, do not occur without underlying conditions making their acceptance possible. Both occur as a result of the failure of existing policies, and the perceived need among actors for change. The Great Depression of the 1930s revealed the shortcomings of the economic policymaking of that time. Governments were eventually shaken from their policy inertia and embraced innovation. But I would argue that the Keynesian macroeconomic policies that were adopted reflected the tendencies toward greater centralization and management that had been under way since the adoption of Fordist mass production techniques in the early twentieth century, and greater government involvement in economic affairs (both in developmental and social policy) which had existed since the latter half of the nineteenth century.

International economic shocks—such as the end of fixed exchange rates, commodity price volatility, balance of payments disequilibria, and the rise of offshore equity and debt financing—changed the basic policy agenda once more during the late 1970s and 1980s, forcing some policy changes directly (e.g., the decline of Keynesian demand management), and generally enhancing the political power of finance capital interests. As in the 1930s shock, the changes that revealed themselves in the 1980s had a gestation period of at least three decades. The resurrection of the world economy after the Second World War, under American leadership, led to the longest period of sustained economic growth in modern history. American leadership and Keynesian demand management went hand in hand in creating for European and Japanese national economies a permissive environment for state-guided growth. Capital market segmentation and regulation, the Depression-era state response to perceived market failure, provided incentives for adventurous financial market operators to create sovereign-free offshore markets of exchange. As Western societies grew rich, Fordist mass production techniques gave way to niche manufacturing and consumer—as opposed to producer-guided products and services. Large industrial capital interests, the privileged beneficiaries of financial repression[1] and market segmentation[2], saw their profit margins squeezed by the beginning of the 1970s as productivity gains began to lag increases in labor cost (Marglin and Schor, 1990). The lower rates of return available in regulated domestic markets provided additional incentive for finance capital interests to demand greater freedom from sovereign entities. Increased capital mobility, both permitted and uncontrolled, was to have a major constraining impact on state macroeconomic policy.

According to Haggard and Kaufman (1992), there are three distinct ways in which international factors impinge on domestic policy choices. First, developments in international goods and capital markets determine the availability of external resources, which in turn sets important limits on the range of policy options. Second, policy is influenced by international linkages: the transnational social and political networks and coalitions that link domestic and international actors. Finally, states are constrained by leverage: the financial, political, and ideological power exercised by finance capital interests, both directly and through the structure of the broad "rules of the game" (Haggard and Kaufman, 1992: 10).

The integration of financial markets, through both domestic regulatory reform[3] and the removal of restrictions on capital mobility, reduced the resources available to governments to pursue state-led strategies and increased the leverage of financial capital interests and "internationalist" political forces at home. Over time, international financial and ideological pressures also had the more profound (though difficult to measure) effect of transforming the nature of the policy debate itself. This last impact, that of ideology is an important one for it goes to the under-researched notion of the structural power of finance capital—that is, the ability to financial capital interests not merely to make demands on political actors, but to set the parameters of debate on policy.

The actual leverage of finance capital interests is not grounded solely on the role of domestic politics; countervailing international factors also enhance influence. These include the "high" political interests of governments[4], the difficulties in orchestrating a transnational capital control regime, and a number of peculiar features associated with the nature of international financial markets that make enforcement of capital controls difficult. One reason for enhanced leverage of finance capital interests is that potential enforcers of a capital control regime—governments—have multiple and conflicting goals *vis-à-vis* finance capital. The concern to attract capital for growth purposes, leading to the liberalization of existing domestic regulatory frameworks, can easily override the interest in enforcing an international capital control regime. This, in turn, can undermine efforts to coordinate transnational capital flows and produce quite perverse incentives. Where governments are already committed to fiscal

rectitude and current account surplus—such as Germany and Japan—
additional finance may strengthen the national currency, though such an
event was likely to occur anyway. When nonconditional resources are
made available to deficit countries —such as the United States—
finance allows the government to procrastinate, rather than pursue
needed adjustment.[5]

The depiction of financial asset-holders in the 1960s and 1970s as
actors in pursuit of escaping the bounds of sovereign-based entities
(i.e., states) is an important one. In the study of world politics, states are
accorded a privileged position among actors in the global arena. To be
sure, states have resources—particularly military ones—that are
unmatched by non-state actors. International law further codifies the
position of sovereign-based actors through its many norms and
conventions. If one accepts, however, the proposition that the
sovereignty of actors may constrain as well as enhance their actions and
effectiveness—in the sense that it imposes responsibilities and
obligations which must be met in order to preserve their authority and
which can thus divert resources and energy from the service of other
goals—then it is not so great a leap of faith to accept the proposition
that those actors who lack sovereignty may therefore be freer to
exercise the full measure of their capabilities on behalf of goals. That
is, while individual governments and the sovereign state system must
operate with agendas open to a broad range of issues, non-state
("sovereign-free") actors with narrow agendas are receptive to only
selected types of issues and can concentrate resources in pursuit of
achieving goals. When the policy issue is considered complex and
demanding of special information, policymakers are more likely to
defer to epistemic communities of "issue authorities," particularly in
times of great change and uncertainty. It is this asymmetry of attention
and expertise attached to the issue of international financial integration
by state and non-state actors that has simultaneously reduced state
effectiveness and enhanced that of finance capital interests.

FINANCE AND GOVERNMENTS

The changed relationship between finance capital and state officials is
most graphically illustrated by the difficulties faced by politically Left-
oriented governments in carrying out their preferred policies of state
intervention and income redistribution. Through the threat or actuality

of capital flight and investment strikes, finance capital interests can have a decided influence over the policies of state officials. If free movement of financial capital is allowed, domestic interest rates are tied, via Eurocurrency markets, to the "world" rate of interest (Glyn, 1986: 37). Moreover, if the future of the exchange rate is in doubt, interest rates have to exceed world nominal rates by the discount on the forward rate, which will widen as confidence declines. This confidence factor is the mechanism by which the pressure of international finance capital is channelled against the implementation of policies that challenge prevailing financial orthodoxy. Harold Wilson, Labor party prime minister of Britain in the 1960s and 1970s, recorded how this pressure was exercised during his tenure in office:

> That night we had our most desperate meeting with the Governor of the Bank. Claiming that our failure to act in accordance with his advice had precipitated the crisis, he was now demanding all-round cuts in expenditure, regardless of social or even economic priorities, and fundamental changes in some of the Chancellor's economic announcements. . . . [W]e had now reached a situation where a newly-elected government with a mandate from the people was being told . . . by international speculators that the policies on which we had fought the election could not be implemented (Wilson, 1971: 37).

This situation is a far cry from that envisioned by John Maynard Keynes and the other founders of the Bretton Woods international monetary regime. Keynes, whose thinking was shaped by the Depression, wanted the new regime to allow state officials the freedom to pursue policies of demand management, which would have a countercyclical effect on national economies. Capital mobility, which allows financial market operators to ship funds out of a state whose government's policies they did not like, would frustrate demand management. The industrial countries, thus, emerged from the Second World War with controls on virtually all types of international transactions. Many currencies were not even convertible. In such cases, all currency transactions, including those involving international trade, had to be settled through special clearing facilities. In the two decades following the war, the industrial countries began to ease restrictions on the convertibility of currencies and to liberalize international trade in goods. It was only in the 1970s, however, that the liberalization of international capital flows became a major goal. Even then, many industrial countries continued to maintain controls on capital flows. At various times in the last two decades, firms found themselves paying widely differing rates for national and international loans even when the loans were in the same currency (Marston, 1995: 1).

With international financial integration and the enhanced power of financial asset-holders, the main aims of governments changed dramatically in the 1980s. Replacing the goal of full employment, the pursuit of redistribution, and expansion of public sector transfers, the main aims of most Western governments in 1980s were to curb inflation, improve competitiveness, and to spur economic growth (Fagerberg and Skarstein, 1990: 76). In pursuit of these goals, it was deemed necessary to reduce growth in public spending, to cut taxes for higher-income households and the business sector, and to deregulate markets, especially in the strongly regulated area of finance. The argument rested on New Classical[6] logic, with a strong emphasis on supply factors. Reduced growth in government spending was assumed to have a positive impact on inflation, while at the same time making tax cuts possible. Tax cuts, in turn, would increase the incentives for work and investment, and weaken claims for higher wages. These effects, together with greater efficiency allowed by market deregulation, would boost productivity and competitiveness and curb inflation.

The essence of New Classical policies towards the financial system was to repeal some direct regulations on private bank practices (such as interest rate ceilings on deposits and restrictions on lending in certain market segments), the elimination of the oligopolistic market in the securities brokerage industry (such as the end of fix commissions on trading), as well as the elimination of restrictions on transnational capital flows and private ownership of certain classes of financial assets.

GROWTH OF INTERNATIONAL FINANCIAL TRANSACTIONS

Since 1975, international financial capital flows have grown at phenomenal rates. Cross-border transactions between U.S. residents and others, for example, have risen from 4.2 percent of GDP in 1975 to 36.4 percent in 1985, to 92.1 percent in 1990, and 134.9 percent in 1993 (BIS, 1994: 175). In the case of Japan, the growth in cross-border flows is even more dramatic: from 1.5 percent of GDP in 1975 to 121.0 percent in 1990, before ebbing with the Tokyo stockmarket crash. In Germany, international portfolio transactions grew from 5.1 percent of GDP in 1975 to 54.9 percent in 1990 (the year of reunification), and 169.6 percent in 1993. In Britain, home of the largest offshore equity and bond markets, cross-border transactions reached 1,015.8 percent of GDP in 1991.

Despite these rapid increases in the size of transnational capital flows, however, the stock of cross-border holdings remain a small fraction of total assets outstanding. This is the conclusion of a study of international portfolio diversification conducted by French and Poterba (1991). They found that investors in each of the national home markets of the Group of Five (G-5)—the United States, Japan, Germany, France, and Britain—have a significant "home bias," which limits their investment in foreign markets to less than ten percent of their assets.[7] The domestic ownership shares of the world's five largest stock markets are: United States, 92.2 percent; Japan, 95.7 percent; United Kingdom, 92 percent; Germany, 79 percent; and France, 89.4 percent (French and Poterba, 1991: 222). In a different study, however, Tesar and Werner (1992) point out that estimates of portfolio holdings are unlikely to be completely accurate because they are based on benchmark surveys that in the case of the United States are over 40 years old. Even with this *caveat*, the initial conclusion they also reach is that, despite the growth in cross-border transactions, international diversification appears to be limited. So it remains to be seen how well integrated financial markets have become.

In addition to strict controls on capital flows, since the Depression official regulations and non-official market conventions had limited the degree of competition in most national financial markets. There existed in these markets both "market segmentation" and "financial repression." Market segmentation refers to the emplacement of "fire-walls" between providers of different types of financial services. Most famous is the American Glass-Steagal Act, which separates the activities of commercial banks (which accept deposits and make loans) from those of investment banks (which underwrite securities to finance new capital investments). Financial repression refers to interest rate ceilings on deposits and loans. Such ceilings had two uses: first, to discourage competition among depository institutions for customers; and second, to ensure market access to preferred borrowers. Since 1980, many national financial markets have undergone significant regulatory reform, commonly termed "deregulation." In some countries regulatory reform was initiated by explicit government programs, while in others deregulation was spurred on by competition from new financial instruments like certificates of deposits and commercial paper. The liberalization of international capital flows also played a role in the regulatory reform process in national markets. Liberalization opened the national markets to the intense competitive pressures of the Eurocurrency markets and other international markets. Firms denied competitive pricing for loans at home could easily turn to Eurocurrency loans or to medium-term international bonds. Similarly, investors who were denied market rates of return at home could seek them in Eurocurrency deposits or other international instruments (Marston, 1995: 3).

By the end of the 1980s, it became generally accepted that international financial markets had become more open than at any time since the end of World War II—indeed, since the pre-1914 gold standard era. The post-Depression capital control regime had collapsed. Domestic financial markets were undergoing varying degrees of regulatory reform. Interest rates on many short-term national instruments became indistinguishable from those on Eurocurrency deposits and loans in the same currency. During the decade of the 1980s, secondary-trading values in the international equity market surged from less than $100 billion in 1980 to over $1.6 billion in 1989. According to Salomon Brothers, gross cross-border equity flows among the United States, Japan, Britain, and Europe totaled $776 billion in 1989 (Ziegler, 1990: 7).

Following extensive financial liberalization and market regulatory reform over the past decade or so, international capital movements have increased enormously and now dwarf transactions on current account. One indicator of the vastly increased scale of capital movements is that gross capital outflows from the main industrial countries (excluding official and short-term banking transactions) came to about $850 billion in 1993. Such flows averaged around $500 billion during the 1985-93 period as a whole, compared to only about $100 billion a year in the first half of the 1980s (BIS, 1994: 147). The freedom of financial market operators to transact international financial business, though not entirely unprecedented, has never been experienced to the present degree, even before the First World War (BIS, 1994: 147). Indeed, in some respects it is entirely novel, in that the whole pace and complexity of international capital transactions have been transformed by data-processing and communications technology, and by the financial innovation which that has facilitated.

The ramifications of liberalization and regulatory reform have spawned new systemic dangers in the increasingly integrated financial markets. Prior to the 1980s, interest rates in some key national markets remained regulated and shielded from international competition. The financial services industry has been revolutionized by competition in formerly segmented markets. It is important to realize how different markets today are from those of just a few years ago. Following the huge flows of international money are financial services firms that have been rebuilt to thrive upon volatility and risk (Ziegler, 1990: 28). As profit margins narrow, these firms have sought higher returns from trading on their own account, seeking to profit from short-term moves in interest rates and currencies. For traders, markets are most profitable when they are most volatile. As transactions costs come down, those with a vested interest in volatility can leap in and out of markets more easily. This process lies behind much of the great boom in the trading of securities during the 1980s. The task that lies ahead for sovereign state regulators is an unenviable one. It is to ensure that competition on a global scale does not endanger the capital-raising abilities of international capital markets.

PAST AS PRELUDE

In an integrated financial market, there should be no significant gap between national interest rates and Eurocurrency interest rates in the same currency. So it is possible to speak of the dollar financial market or the yen financial market as a unified whole without specifying whether financial instruments are national or international in origin. In such a world, relative financing costs are governed primarily by currency factors rather than by the peculiar characteristics of each national market (Marston, 1995: 3).

In recent years world capital markets have become more integrated than at any time since the pre-1914 gold standard period. Indeed a comparison with that period serves to bring certain aspects of recent experience into sharper focus. In a study directly comparing the integration of financial markets in the 1980s with those of the pre-1914 period, Zevin (1992) found the latter more integrated, based upon two key measures: the size of the net investment position and the percentage of foreign equities traded in major financial bourses. Zevin found that Britain's net foreign-investment position relative to GNP in 1913 was 153 percent.[8] Schwartz (1994: 152) noted that by 1913, for every £2 Britain had invested in its domestic economy it had £1 invested overseas. Zevin cited data provided by Morgenstern (1959), which revealed that 59 percent of shares traded in London in 1900 were of foreign origin, compared to 20 percent in 1987.

Zevin (1992), while claiming that the degree of international financial openness has yet to match that of the pre-1914 period, nevertheless admits to the increase in openness over the past two decades. The persistence of such sizable capital flows since the 1970s has resulted in a sharp rebound in the proportion of financial assets held by non-residents. According to one calculation, non-resident holdings now amount to around 20-25 percent of total outstanding government bonds in the Group of Ten countries other than Japan (BIS, 1994: 146). While the recent period of increased international capital mobility can be characterized as a return to historical norms there are three aspects of the contemporary liberalization effort, cited by the Bank for International Settlements, that set it apart from the pre-1914 period: the monetary and exchange-rate regime, the range of financial assets, and the role of institutional investors.

The first and perhaps biggest, difference is in that exchange rates are more flexible today than they were then. Unlike the fixed exchange-rate system of the gold standard, exchange rates today are set by market supply and demand conditions. Under conditions of capital mobility, states with financial assets offering higher-than-average real rates of return are likely to encounter large capital inflows, while states with financial assets offering lower-than-average real returns will encounter capital outflows. In current circumstances, the liberalization of capital flows has constrained the ability of national policymakers to peg the exchange rate to a fixed value, as the recent 1992-93 collapse of the European Union's exchange-rate mechanism (ERM) has shown. But more than exchange-rate stability is compromised by capital flows. The heavy capital flows of the pre-1914 period did not upset fixed exchange rates because there was much greater credibility in the gold standard commitment. Governments readily sacrificed other goals (e.g., full domestic employment) in order to maintain long-term payments balance. Because of policy credibility, only small interest rate differentials were required to finance current account imbalances:

highly interest-rate elastic capital flows thus supported the fixed exchange rate (BIS, 1994: 147). In such a situation, capital mobility helps to stabilize a fixed exchange rate regime as capital smoothly finance *ex ante* balance-of-payments imbalances.

The second difference from the pre-1914 period is the much wider range of financial assets that can be readily traded nowadays—in domestic as well as in international markets. Moreover, such assets (notably in different currencies) have yielded much more divergent real returns than during the gold standard period. Then, there was less of a need for the financial diversification and risk-hedging which lies behind the high turnover in modern securities markets. Total international securities transactions in the six Group of Seven countries that compile such data amounted to $6 trillion per quarter in the second half of 1993—about five to six times the value of international trade (BIS, 1994: 147). As a result, portfolio-related transactions in the foreign exchange market now dominate trade-related transactions. In the United States, Japan, and Britain this change had already occurred about a decade ago; in continental Europe, it has been more recent. This increased volume of portfolio capital movements has made foreign exchange markets much more sensitive to changes in sentiment in financial markets, an important factor behind the volatility in currency values.

A third difference is the much greater weight of institutional investors: insurance companies, mutual funds and pension funds. It was the diversification of institutional investors' portfolios that was a major driving force of capital flows in the 1980s. Institutional investors' holdings of foreign securities increased in Japan from eight percent in 1980 to 40 percent in 1990. In the United States, however, investment by residents in foreign securities remained relatively small, reaching only 15 percent of mutual and pension fund assets in 1993 (BIS, 1994: 147). But this figure represents a dramatic increase since the 1980s. Such holdings are sensitive to shifts of sentiment in international financial markets. As will be detailed later, enhanced capital mobility combined with flexible exchange rates to once more subject national economic policies—in particular attempts to maintain misaligned exchange rates or macroeconomic policies at variance with neoliberal precepts—to the sanction of finance capital interests. The Bretton Woods experiment with government-determined prices for financial assets has ended, and global neoliberalism has returned. The interaction of a changing international financial landscape with the distribution of power between domestic political coalitions both catalyzed and were formed by international financial integration.

INFORMATION TECHNOLOGY AND FINANCIAL INTEGRATION

"Money is information on the move," according to one popular cliché. The essence of money is not so much in its physical appearance as in the information it conveys, whether as a unit of account, a medium of exchange, or a store of value. Technology has profoundly altered the scale on which financial transactions take place, allowing financial firms and consumers of financial services to conduct a greater volume of transactions in less time and with wider repercussions than could have been imagined in earlier eras. According to Richard O'Brien (1992), international financial relationships have evolved to the stage where one can speak of "the end of geography," as financial market regulators no longer hold full sway over the regulatory territory, financial firms have a wider choice of geographic location (provided that an appropriate investment in information systems is made), and consumers of financial services enjoy a wider range of services outside the traditional services offered by local banks. "The end of geography is a challenge to all participants in the world economy, from developing to developed economies, to public and private policymakers, to producers and consumers of financial services" (O'Brien, 1992: 1-2).

The principle effect of technology for political economists is that it "democratizes" economic policymaking. In the past, financial asset-holders could never be certain about the intentions of national policymakers, and with the ability of asset-holders to hedge political risk constrained due to restrictions on capital mobility policymakers could use "information asymmetry" to extract resources from financial asset-holders. Because policymakers knew what policies they would implement and asset-holders did not, governments routinely instituted "inflation surprises" that caught asset-holders off-guard. These "inflation surprises" had the effect of inducing financial asset-holders to submit more financial resources to the state (through their purchases of government debt) than would otherwise be the case had they been privileged to information concerning future state policy moves. Improvements in technology have narrowed the "information asymmetry" between states and markets, making government-induced policy surprises increasingly difficult to pull off.[9]

With the emergent evolution of world politics, state officials have their capacity to mobilize constituents diminished as state policymaking become more decentralized, less coherent and effective (Rosenau, 1990: 119). By contrast, financial asset-holders—particularly those with transnational links—have more opportunities and inducements to act in pursuit of their private interest. Because state officials interact with, and are responsive to, the international system of which their state is a part, they become channels through which structural continuities and changes are initiated and sustained. Thus, one must focus on the organizational, bargaining, and other structural dynamics to comprehend state officials. To understand the role of financial asset-holders, as private actors, one has to look to both the structural and domestic levels, the former to understand how circumstances may provide opportunities for the initiatives of financial asset-holders and the latter to probe how and why some such actors seize the moment and exploit the opportunities.

Finance asset-holders do not, for the most part, constitute organized groups with clear authority structures and other mechanisms for sustaining the coherence and coordination of their members. Rather, such interests create a collectivity produced by the convergence of the actions or orientations of large number of individuals in the absence of organized authority. Investment strikes and capital flight are but the most obvious ways in which the orientations and actions of individual financial asset-holders coalesce into politically-relevant action.

As capital moves ever more easily across territorial boundaries, it draws national financial systems into an international web (Maxfield, 1991: vii.). In the 1980s capital flows also seem to have spread neoliberal economic ideology—from Reagan's America to Thatcher's Britain and beyond. Keynesian demand management, which dominated national policymaking in all industrial economies after the Second World War, can only be effective under conditions of nationally-segmented finance, where domestic markets are regulated, foreign exchange circumscribed, and short-term financial operations curtailed. In the late 1970s and in the 1980s there were dramatic financial regulation reform and capital market liberalization moves in countries as varied as United States and New Zealand, Britain and France; this cross-national similarity in otherwise different national contexts suggests international forces must be at work, just as in the spread of Keynesian ideas.

THE INTELLECTUAL PUZZLE: NON-STATE ACTORS AND STRUCTURAL CONSTRAINTS

One is led to study the consequences of international financial integration on national macroeconomic policymaking because its uncertainties and outcomes involve the future well-being of peoples everywhere. The policy challenges international financial integration pose stagger the imagination and raises questions about the ability of leaders and publics to manage their affairs. So it is reasonable to presume that the better the circumstances and dynamics that foster international financial integration are understood, the greater the probability that policies designed to cope with its effects can be framed and implemented.

The task of describing and explaining the policy constraints brought about by international financial integration is compelling because those constraints have thrown the world's images of political institutions and its conceptions of political process into flux. Scholarship in world politics can only advance when it offers new understandings of political relationships that are consistent with the evolving pattern of how state officials, non-state sectoral interests, and national publics perceive and interact with each other.

While it is the policy implications that immediately provoke inquiry into the repercussions of international financial integration, the subject also poses an intellectual puzzle that lies at the heart of world politics scholarship. For this we must probe beyond policy concerns into the deeper recesses of accounting for structural change, where only a wider theoretical framework can begin to offer meaningful explanations. The puzzle is embodied in the fact that international financial integration has developed largely at the sufferance of state authorities, whose very ability to conduct macroeconomic policy has been reduced as a consequence. With few exceptions, policymakers wish for greater choice of policy and instruments, not less. Stability is universally preferred to uncertainty, and yet revolutionary change has become the prime characteristic of international finance. Why? If governments, interests, and publics prefer routinized and predictable politics, we must ask how is it that these preferences have so little effect on the prevailing realities.

What can explain explosive, rapid change in world politics? More particularly, why did national policymakers decide to undertake financial market regulatory reform and liberalize capital flows? In answering these questions it is readily acknowledged that the theoretical framework presented here is founded more on inferences and interpretations than systematic data. The reason is that it is inherently difficult, if not impossible, to "know" in any true sense the intentions of policymakers. Intentions are not directly observable. We do, however, have a written record of the actions of policymakers and opposing interests, from which to draw inferences, and build a conceptual framework. Despite the shortcoming, throughout this thesis there is an underlying recognition and deference to the principles of scientific method. To quote Rosenau (1990): "To be short on evidence is not to be inattentive to the need for evidence, and the recognition that theoretical propositions must ultimately be subjected to empirical tests serves to constrain and discipline the inquiry."

The model that will be used to explain international financial integration has the following assumptions: (1) state officials choose to pursue policies that will achieve their preferred goals at the lowest (political) cost; (2) policy choice is constrained by structural parameters, that are largely beyond the scope of individual states to control; and (3) non-state actors have enhanced their autonomy by recent parametric shifts and are more assertive in defending and expanding that autonomy. Policymakers, in collaboration, create regimes that allow for control of the external environment and the joint pursuit of individual state goals. Such collaboration requires consensus on the part of policymakers as to both the goals and the use of instruments in which to achieve them. Such regimes, however, are effective only as long as the collaborative commitment to maintain them is in place, and the underlying permissive structural conditions allow for instruments of control to be exercised. A breakdown in either will render the regime inoperable.

Therefore, to make the case that international financial integration has fundamentally changed the policy environment in which state officials operate, it must be demonstrated that: (1) policymakers had clear preferences as to macroeconomic outcomes and the means of achieving them; (2) international financial integration would inhibit the achievement of policymakers' preferred outcomes; (3) policymakers, domestically and internationally, made an effort at forging a regime that would control the undesirable effects that unimpeded capital mobility would bring; (4) financial asset-holders were disadvantaged by state policy and made efforts to circumvent it; and (5) changes in the underlying structure of the world economy undermined the relationship between states and finance interests, reducing the effectiveness of policymakers' instruments and enhancing the autonomy of financial asset-holders.

The model used in this study is one of structural change, in which the parameters of state action widen or constrict, fundamentally altering the effectiveness of state action. What determines the parameter shifts is the ability of non-state actors to exercise autonomy over areas of interest to them, and thus resist state attempts to extract resources for the purposes of achieving the outcomes preferred by policymakers. To be sure, determining what are preferred policymaker outcomes is fraught with difficulties, as discussed above. However, such preferences are at least theoretically susceptible to being observed, even if some innovation in observational techniques must first be made. One's choice of method is ultimately limited by prior understanding of the subject. Since knowledge of the policy implications of financial integration is in key respects rudimentary, so must be the procedures used to trace the factors that constrain national policymakers.

This is not to say that all the evidence relevant to the policymaking constraints of financial integration is shrouded in abstract theorizing. Some of it consists of clear-cut socioeconomic indicators that depict the expansion of integration on a global scale. Deeper integration among the world's financial institutions, for example, can be readily discernible in data on capital flows or multi-market differences in common-currency interest rates. At the same time, the argument pertaining to the underlying political structures and processes also focuses on emergent structural patterns that are not nearly so manifest and thus require inferences from a skimpy and inchoate data base. The shifting pattern of authority relations between state policymakers and financial asset-holders, for instance, has weakened the state system and strengthened non-state actors. One's political antennae can pick up the emergence and spread of such attitudinal dynamics even though systematic empirical materials that demonstrate their operation have yet to be compiled.

Borrowing from the methodological outlook of Rosenau (1990), the analysis of the national macroeconomic policy autonomy consequences of international financial integration rejects classical Realism by positing a multi-centric (as opposed to a state-centric) world having evolved autonomously from one in which states alone functioned, a world in which actions and reactions originate with a multiplicity of actors at diverse system levels, all of which are motivated to maintain the integrity of their subsystems and to resist absorptions by the systems of which they are a part. The analysis also counters the hegemonic stability theses of some Neo-Realists (Gilpin, 1981) by arguing that, while the structures of the state-centric world permit the emergence of hegemonic leadership, the multi-centric world is too decentralized to support the hierarchy through which hegemons predominate. Technological diffusion and equalization of production costs, which Structuralists (Chase-Dunn, 1981) argue causes hegemonic decline, lead to changes in profit-rate differentials and results in financial asset-holders reallocating their portfolios to take advantage of greater profit opportunities abroad. One of the outcomes of this process is to reduce the incentives, on the part of financial asset-holders, to support economic nationalism within the declining hegemonic power. As the financial investments of the hegemonic core state are spread throughout other core states, so too are the economic and political interests of financial asset-holders. Financial asset-holders in the hegemonic state have an incentive to promote international financial integration, which in turn reduces the leading-sector advantages of the hegemonic state economy.[10]

The extent to which financial asset-holders have the freedom to pursue their interest will determine the speed of the hegemonic rise and decline. In addressing the importance of non-state actors in the operation of the world economy, one must direct attention to the notion of the "autonomy dilemma," which serves as the driving force of the multi-centric world just as the security dilemma constitutes a dominant concern in the state-centric world. This "autonomy dilemma" is revealed by the incidence of financial asset-holders seeking to hedge political risk through currency substitution and portfolio diversification. To the extent that sovereign states seek to maintain national policymaking autonomy, they attempt to limit the ability of financial asset-holders to hedge political risk. Because of information asymmetry, financial asset-holders are never fully certain of what state policy actions will be, so they increasingly demand higher risk premiums on domestic currency-denominated assets or employ international portfolio diversification—both strategies aimed at preserving and enhancing their autonomy from the state.

International financial integration, a structural-level process, has come to serve as both a source and product of corresponding domestic-level shifts wherein financial asset-holders are becoming more analytically skillful and technologically sophisticated, thus fostering the replacement of traditional criteria for evaluating government-market relations (i.e., "the banker's bargain") with performance criteria that, in turn, serve to intensify both the deregulatory and liberalization tendencies at work within and among states. This interactive relationship between changes in state-non-state actor relations and the changes at the international system level speaks of Gourevitch's "second-image reversed" analysis of structural change. Gourevitch reminds us that attempts to explain change at solely the system or state-levels leads to an incomplete picture of the dynamics that lead to change.

CHAPTER PREVIEW AND REVIEW

The central theme of this study is that parametric change has expanded the autonomy of non-state actors, and has reduced the capability of governments to extract involuntarily resources from their constituents. This change has profound consequences for world politics. For more than a century the field of world politics has been dominated by the intellectual outlook of *Realpolitik*, which assumes an unchanging political context where states predominate. Even the modern Realists who accept the possibility of structural change nonetheless argue that it is state-driven, with only the configuration of states—not the principles of interaction—being changed.

To be sure, states remain the most powerful actors on the world stage. Only among states does one find the military capabilities necessary to defeat one of its members. Few non-state entities can match the ability of governments in accumulating resources for purposive action, or in sustaining that action through bureaucratic organization. States, therefore, remain very important. However, the ability of national policymakers to act autonomously in the pursuit of preferred macroeconomic outcomes has been curtailed in recent decades. The postwar capital control regime has broken down, economic crisis in the 1970s fractured the policy consensus, and financial innovation has left governments reacting defensively.

The question remains as to why, and to what extent, governments have lost their earlier policy autonomy. To answer that question requires that a political economy approach be used. Implicit in such an approach is the recognition that financial relations, like nearly all other economic interactions, are inevitably characterized by relations of power. One must establish to what extent the current policy environment has corresponded to the dictates of market forces and to what extent it responded to political factors. Clearly, increasing the mobility of capital has had domestic distributional costs, both between capital and other factors, and between more and less mobile forms of capital. To illustrate this interaction of states and the international structure, consider Frieden's (1991) work on the effects of international capital mobility on domestic political alignments and states' preferences. Frieden decomposes a nation into four sectoral interest groups: import-competing producers of tradable goods, export-oriented producers of tradable goods, producers of non-tradable goods, and international traders and investors. A state's preferences emerge through competition among these interests. Moreover, shifts in the integration of global finance affect the distribution of political power among the units. For example, a reduction in the degree of exchange-rate flexibility and a move toward a "strong currency," in a world of international financial integration, reduces the cost of international trade and investment. These changes favor and enrich domestic groups that benefit from greater trade. By assumption, benefited groups become more powerful and the state's preferences generally become more reflective of the preferences of these favored groups. Similarly, international financial integration has raised the costs associated with pursuing monetary policies that diverge from international trends. The consequent reduction in monetary policy autonomy adversely affects groups that benefit from such policies. By assumption, disadvantaged groups become less powerful.

Using the aforementioned second-image reversed approach, which looks at the interaction between agents and structure—i.e., the influence of international system variables on the policies pursued by individual states, I trace the effect of the transformation of the global financial order on the domestic politics and macroeconomic policy of major industrial states. It is my view that the stability of national macroeconomies during the Bretton Woods period rested on the duality of American politico-economic dominance and the widespread acceptance of national Keynesian economic ideas (which were exported from the United States). This duality allowed the historic compromise between business and social, nationalist and internationalist, interests to take place. By noting the importance of ideas, I am challenging the dominant Neo-Realist paradigm that sees structure as the result of the interaction among units rather than as a generative entity capable to reproducing itself in the actions of units. This ontological issue is the "agent-structure" problem. Structures are not metaphysical, they represent the preferences of agents—not state agents necessarily, but substate agents or non-state actors. By breaking with the state-centric paradigm, we can solve the agent-structure problem by locating the source of structure creation at the substate level—i.e., in the preferences among non-state actors, particularly the domestically-based actors in dominant states who through their transnational connections influence the rules that define how an issue area game is played.

In Chapter II, I will outline the conceptual framework. Building upon the work of Gourevitch's second image reversed, and Keohane's regime analysis, I argue for a structural explanation for the political decision to proceed with financial liberalization. Three structural variables, taken together, explain the global liberalization phenomenon that has been sweeping the advanced industrial states. Central to understanding the political environment that spawned the Bretton Woods regime is that of "embedded liberalism" (Ruggie, 1983), which treats the emergence of the liberal postwar international economic regime as a consequence of an historic shift in the social consensus among, and within, principal industrial states. This consensus accepted the application of free trade policies abroad in return for government intervention at home to protect social interests. Beginning in the late 1970s and becoming dominant in the 1980s was what Cerny calls an "embedded financial orthodoxy," or global neoliberalism. Just as Keynesianism was adopted in response to failures of classical liberalism to address the economic problems of the 1930s, New Classical (and New Keynesian) economic thinking has been adopted to address the changed conditions of the last 25 years.[11] This economic ideology explanation fits nicely with a macroeconomic structural explanation that posits financial liberalization as the result of changed production processes and the rise of non-state actors limiting the autonomy of the state. Finally, these two explanations complement the hegemonic explanation, which posits liberalization as the result of the preferences of a still financially dominant United States. The hegemonic and macroeconomic structural arguments fuse in explaining the dismantling of domestic financial regulatory frameworks in advanced industrial states in the 1970s and 1980s.

In Chapter III, I discuss the historical evolution of the key arrangements, which, together, provide the framework of the postwar regime and shaped the structure of the global macroeconomy. This chapter is in line with much of the literature on global economic relations since the end of the Bretton Woods era in the early 1970s. To outline briefly, the argument is that the post-World War II global economy that lasted from the late 1940s to the early 1970s was one of unprecedented growth and prosperity. The arrangements created at Bretton Woods were crafted in order to avoid the destabilizing conditions that eventually led to the collapse of the world economy in 1929-31. I will first detail the interwar period that, in hindsight, was not the completely anarchic era portrayed by writers in the "hegemonic stability" school. Indeed, central and private bankers worked closely in concert in order to build a new international monetary and financial order. Their failure rested on the inadequate recognition of sociopolitical conditions that rendered a liberal order infeasible.

The Bretton Woods period was also one of stable exchange rates, based nominally on gold, but in practice on the U.S. dollar. The near "dollar standard" could be sustained as long as the United States possessed the strongest and most productive economy in the world. With dollars, and the goods that only they could buy, at a premium, the United States could exact seigniorage that offset the costs of being the consumer of last resort and the world's banker. Fixed exchange rates conditioned the international adjustment process; the American dollar allowed for international liquidity; American leadership provided the international confidence that the regime was sound. But as the supply of dollars moved from under- to oversupply, the strains on the preservation of the Bretton Woods regime became great. The makeshift arrangements to maintain the regime, such as gold-pooling and the creation of Special Drawing Rights (SDRs), failed to address the fundamental deficiencies of the regime. The refusal of the major economic powers to come to terms on a major currency realignment led to a real overvaluation of the U.S. dollar, which undermined its economic competitiveness. As the American government strove to limit the outflow of dollars, the Eurodollar market sprung up as an alternative source of liquidity. And as the American government fell deeper in the quagmire of the Viet Nam War, fissures in the postwar geostrategic structure reduced confidence in American leadership.

Chapter IV analyzes in more detail the evolution of aggregate demand management as a policy tool in the macroeconomic structure. The Great Depression of the 1930s left most governments with greater responsibility for the general welfare of their citizens. As the price for accepting free trade policies abroad, national Keynesian policies, which varied in the amount of government intervention to protect social interests harmed by the vicissitudes of a market economy, were instituted by industrial states. Demand management became a powerful tool in promoting both the new welfare and growth requirements for political economic success in the postwar era. Demand management included, for mid-sized industrial states, the "subsidization" of business interests, who felt threatened in a free trade world. This subsidization created a "moral hazard" condition that later exacerbated the costs of economic restructuring.

If the Great Depression created conditions for the expansion of government's role in the economy, the Great Inflation of the 1970s revealed the limits of government power to affect economic outcomes. No other event signaled the change of raw material supply conditions in the post-Bretton Woods era more than the 400 percent increase in the price of petroleum in 1973-74, and a further 300 percent increase in 1979-80. The twin "oil shocks" revealed the vulnerability of market economies to sources of supply. The increase in manufacturing input prices created a "supply shock" that led to simultaneous inflation and recession. The supply shock further revealed the limits of Keynesian demand management policies.

The failure of government to steer the macroeconomy came as a major blow to national policymakers. The presence of stagflation, supply shortages, and the end of productivity growth, led to a questioning of Keynesian nostrums. When combined with (a) the enhanced power of capital interests (flowing from the newfound mobility of capital), (b) global production (as low value-added manufacturing was "outsourced" to new and lower cost regions of the world), and (c) the breakdown of the Phillips Curve relationship, national Keynesianism came be revised at best (in the form of so-called New Keynesian economics) and scrapped at worse (in favor of Monetarism, Supply-side economics, or the New Classical school of rational expectations). The breakdown in consensus among macroeconomic theorists has left policymakers bereft of any clear strategy to deal with the changed economic environment. New Classicists would argue that government should not have any interventionist power in the economy for it can only distort optimal efficiency. There exists a "crisis of policy" as governments' macroeconomic tools to reduce long-term unemployment and raise real wages have proven largely impotent for the since 1973.

The failure of any one government to solve the riddle of sustained economic growth and current account balance has led many academics and policymakers to call for greater international coordination of policies among industrialized states. The first Group of Seven summit conference was held in response to the oil shock-induced world recession of 1975. Since that time G-7 meetings, with too few exceptions, have been public relations shows for unpopular politicians. The fact is that international coordination, as anyone familiar with the Prisoners' Dilemma or Stag Hunt games knows full well, is difficult to conceive in practice. The temptation to exploit the position of the other, or to withdraw cooperation once one's own goals are realized, is too great—and the other player(s) know that. Coordinative efforts to reduce German and Japanese current-account surpluses through domestic reflation and currency appreciation, with a simultaneous reduction in the American current account deficit through fiscal contraction and currency depreciation, have been failures.

Chapter V continues the theme in Chapter IV by looking at changes in the domestic financial systems of major states. Here I review the changes from "relationship finance" to market-based allocation of credit. Relationship finance refers to the arrangements where large financial institutions hold ownership shares in large industrial enterprises, or where large industrial enterprises have preferential access to credit from the government (usually in the form of subsidized loans). Although financial laws differ among states, most advanced economies underwent dramatic financial regulation in the 1930s. These regulations were set up to insulate finance from market fluctuations that were held to be detrimental to sustained economic growth. Banks and other financial product vendors willingly accepted a "bargain" with the government, whereby they agreed to be regulated in exchange for geographic and market segmentation. As alternative sources of finance emerged in competition with traditional suppliers, and with macroeconomic conditions turning unfavorable to sustained bank profitability, financial vendors demanded a renegotiation of the "bankers' bargain," which was manifested in the deregulatory drive of the 1980s.

As the home states of the leading financial centers reformed their domestic regulations, pressure was placed upon other industrialized states to emulate. That is, as the "pioneers" of regulatory reform reaped the benefits of their adaptation to changed parameters, pressure was placed on the "laggards" to do the same. I borrow from urban politics literature a model that explains tax and regulatory reductions in central cities. Territorial states, like cities, increasingly had to compete for capital as domestic investors took advantage of off-shore opportunities that offered higher rates of return. Governments were forced to either restrict the outflow of capital through controls, or to raise domestic rates of return—which required the partial dismantling of the existing domestic regulatory framework. Relationship finance was replaced by price-driven finance.

Chapter VI shows how financial liberalization should be looked at within the context of states attempting to regain the lost capabilities to affect their economies. With capital mobility—the *bête noire* of international Keynesianism—increasingly impossible to stop with the advance of the transnationals and the Eurocurrency markets, governments sacrificed fixed exchange rates in an attempt to preserve their policymaking autonomy. To maintain closed financial markets in the face of open markets abroad creates incentives for financial market operators to circumvent restrictions and shift funds from national to offshore markets. Given the deeper and more profitable markets abroad, governments will have less borrowing capability in national markets without liberalization. But capital mobility enhances the power of capital to influence government policy. Whereas governments in the past could raise or lower interest rates, or increase or cut back expenditures in order to compel capital-owners to increase or decrease the money supply and aggregate demand, today's governments run the risk of "capital strikes" or "capital flights" in response to certain macroeconomic policies. Finally, with the end of fixed exchange rates, credibility of policy becomes an important criterion in maintaining exchange rate stability. Just as the Great Depression passed on an inflationary bias to macroeconomic policymaking in the Bretton Woods era, the Great Inflation of the 1970s transmitted a disinflationary bias to policy in the 1980s.

I further trace the demand for financial liberalization to the changed international macroeconomic structure. The shift from fixed to flexible exchange rates spawned an era of uncertainty that led to adaptive innovation within the financial community. Financial derivatives, and the markets that trade in them, were established to reduce the new uncertainty. When merged with growing offshore markets, the profit opportunities created by "extra-regulatory financial moves" led to demands for deregulation among long-protected national financial institutions. Governments in mid-sized industrial states, such as France and Italy, were willing to acquiesce to these demands because of the "moral hazard" condition of their national industries. Because national industries came to rely on readily accessible credit from the government, their evaluation of risk became skewed and their budget constraints were soft. However, with the changed global economy, and greater financial integration, governments could no longer guarantee credit access. National financial institutions had to be strengthened, and national markets deepened, in order to maintain a ready supply of funds. However, since capital increasingly moves to where profit opportunities are greatest, governments have less incentive to implement profit-dampening regulation.

Furthermore, I discuss the theoretical implications of existing levels of financial integration for national economic policy autonomy. Following the work of Frieden (1991), I argue that while financial capital is extremely mobile across borders, other types of investment (especially equities and sector-specific capital) are far less mobile. Taking a high level of capital mobility as given, I explore how various interest groups are expected to behave in this environment, and argue that international capital mobility tends to remake political coalitions by way of its impact on the effects of national policies. I examine the policy preferences of various socioeconomic groups toward financial integration, with emphasis on the differential effects of increases in capital mobility. The focus is on questions concerning which actors are better (or worse) off after financial integration than before and how the various actors can be expected to respond politically to this change in economic environment. While, over the long run, international financial integration tends to favor capital over labor, especially in developed countries, in the shorter run—which is more relevant to politics and policies—financial integration favors capitalists with mobile or diversified assets and disfavors those with assets tied to specific locations and activities such as manufacturing.

I conclude in Chapter VII by speculating on these efforts to restore high economic performance in major OECD countries and discuss further capital market integration, national financial market regulatory reform, and international cooperation.

NOTES

1. Government-induced interest-rate ceilings and targeted credit. the aim of these policies is (1) to give disadvantaged contituencies access to affordable credit; (2) to spur investment by keeping credit cheap for industrial users; and (3) to channel savings into certain sectors of the economy deemed "strategic" by the government.

2. Government-mandated restrictions on financial lending to only certain groups of borrowers; e.g., certain financial institutions lend only to industrial borrowers, others only to homeowners, still others are restricted to lending only to finance equity and debt issues.

3. I prefer the term "regulatory reform" over "deregulation" because it better captures the complexity of regulatory change. Regulations are not merely "lifted." Rather, the rules concerning property rights, contracts, currencies, and mechanisms to guard against market failure are changed. See Cerny (1993b: 51).

4. In a system of multiple political sovereignties, financial asset-holders have the ability to move their savings from areas offering relatively poor return on investment to areas promising higher marginal rates of profit or lower production costs. The differential rates of expected return are caused by uneven rates of economic growth, a factor that is important in the military-political competition among states (Gilpin, 1981).

5. The actual "disciplining" capacity of financial openness is a subject of debate. Given that both surplus and deficit states pursued openness indicates that both perceived benefits from a new international financial arrangement. This issue is taken up in Chapter 3.

6. A school of thought in macroeconomic theory that holds that markets clear quickly in absence of government interference. Indeed, it holds that short-term economic volatility is caused by ill-conceived government intervention.

7. According to portfolio theory, asset-holders seek to maximize risk-adjusted returns through portfolio diversification, in which the size of any asset holding is proportional to the size of that asset in the overall market. Internationally, if the American stockmarket represent 40 percent of the world

equities market, American portfolios should have a 40 percent American and a 60 percent foreign share.

8. At the height of American power during the period of Marshall Plan aid, the comparable figure for the United States was only 11.5 percent.

9. This "information asymmetry" argument dovetails nicely with the "rational expectations hypothesis" developed in the early 1970s. This is detailed in Chapter 3.

10. Borrowing from the literatures on innovation (Vernon, 1966) and economic development (Gerschenkron, 1962), I argue that hegemony rests upon first-producer advantages in leading sector (i.e., high value-added) industries. Hegemony exists only to the extent that the leading states possesses a monopoly on leading sector industrial production. International financial integration speeds the process of diffusing first-producer advantages to other states.

11. Most macroeconomists accept the rational expectations hypothesis (REH) in one form or another. The New Classical school accepts the REH but maintains thar markets clear quickly (thus, there is no need for government intervention), while New Keynesians also accept the REH but holds that wages and prices adjust slowly—causing short-term economic fluctuations (thereby justifying the relevance of government intervention).

CHAPTER II

Implications of a New Financial Order

> The transnationalization of the economy involves the globalization of
> production, capital and technology flows, and the growth of world
> trade, often through the operations of transnational corporations and
> international investors. It can also be related to a tendency towards a
> globalization of certain aspects of culture, involving the question of
> which values and ideologies would be most likely to promote the
> spread of transnational firms and capital mobility. Other key
> questions concern the effect on governments and the world economy
> of huge flows of short-term capital; the structural power and
> influence of transnational enterprises and international investors, and
> the consequences of transnationalization on the rise and fall of
> countries in the interstate system. This latter issue is also related to
> the question of hegemony and order in the global political economy,
> seen not only in terms of the dominance of one state in an interstate
> system, but also in terms of the rising power and hegemony of
> internationally-mobile, transnational capital (Gill and Law, 1988:
> xxiv).

The globalization of financial markets has been one of the most
spectacular developments in the world economy in recent years.
Although international financial markets flourished in the late
nineteenth and early twentieth centuries, they were almost completely
absent from the international economy during the three decades that
followed the financial crisis of 1931. Beginning in the late 1950s,
however, private international financial activity increased at a

phenomenal rate. Transnational capital movements have come to swamp international payments in the current account (i.e., trade in goods and services). In 1973 typical daily foreign-exchange trading amounted to only $10 to $20 billion; in 1983 it was still modest at around $60 billion. But by 1992, surveys conducted by a number of central banks put the volume of foreign exchange traded daily in London, the United States, Japan, Singapore, Switzerland, Hong Kong, Germany, and France at over $900 billion (including swaps, forward transactions, futures and options). Figures from the national central banks in 1995 suggest that daily turnover is now close to $1.3 trillion.[1] Against that, the total foreign-exchange reserves of governments in the advanced industrial economies amount to only $640 billion (Woodall, 1995: 10). The ratio of foreign-exchange transactions to world trade jumped from 10:1 in 1983 to over 75:1 in 1995.

The rapid growth of international capital markets since the 1960s has had a dramatic impact on macroeconomic policymaking in the advanced capitalist countries and on patterns of international coordination of macroeconomic policies. International capital market integration has reduced governments' ability to pursue effective macroeconomic policies that diverge from the preferences of financial asset-holders who hold the financial purse-strings, and has greatly increased international macroeconomic volatility. Capital market integration rendered ineffective the strategies of international policy coordination that governments had relied on to insulate national macroeconomic policymaking from international pressures in the 1950s and 1960s, and encouraged governments to experiment with a variety of measures intended to improve their competitive advantage in a relatively open world—the "competition state" (Cerny, 1993).

Several factors stemming from financial transnationalization have altered not only the scope but also the substance of government economic intervention. Growing transnational constraints have undermined Keynesian demand management policies through their effects on capital flows, the exchange rate, and the like. Monetary policy has become the principal instrument of macroeconomic control. Yet at the same time, these "exogenous" constraints have increasingly meant that monetary policy instruments have themselves become blunted. The consequence is that governments, even where they seem to be able to live beyond their means (as in the United States), increasingly measure their performance according to criteria acceptable to the financial markets. They must be seen as "strong" or "sound" if they are to retain the confidence of the transnational financial community. Rather than a system of "embedded liberalism," what we have today is one of "embedded financial orthodoxy" that sets an international "bottom line" for government economic intervention more broadly.

The globalization of finance, however, does not merely constrain the role of the state *per se*. Financial power—and the capacity and will of both state and private-sector actors to use that power—has been at the core of the structure of the international system, especially the issue of international hegemony, since the modern state system emerged in the nineteenth century. If we look at the history of British and American hegemony, however, and at the decline and failure of those hegemonies—including the long interregnum during much of the first half of the twentieth century—what we see is a situation in which the most crucial factor is not so much broad economic power, nor cultural dominance, nor military power—as important as those are—but financial power (Barkin, 1992). The crucial element of financial power is a stable, guaranteed, international payments system. Without such a system, trade decays into mercantilism and protectionism.

The rest of this chapter will examine the role of structure as a determinant of state policy change. This examination will take place within the larger theoretical debate over the competing significance of agents and structures as the source of social change. It is the argument of this study that only an interactive approach, that takes into account (a) state policy choices, (b) the changes those choices wrought on the international system, and (c) the feedback constraints that the system then imposes on the states themselves, will yield answers to questions concerning the rising significance of financial asset-holders posed in the introduction.

STRUCTURALIST EXPLANATIONS OF THE LIBERAL GLOBAL FINANCIAL ORDER

There are two basic ways that one can look at the choice of macroeconomic adjustment policies. One approach stresses the structural change that robs governments of discretion. Governments "have no choice but to bend to the winds of change." If this is so, then it should make little difference what the policy preference of a given government is. In the case of deep depression, even the staunchly non-interventionist government would increase expenditures on public works and transfer payments. In the American political economy, such transfer payments act as "automatic stabilizers," and are triggered without government edict. Likewise, a social-democratic government may cut spending and regulation in face of severe supply-side constraints. A second approach views government action as voluntaristic, and not determined by structural factors. Governments, according to this perspective, are always faced with a list of options. What option is chosen reflects the prerogatives of "national purpose." This brief discussion of the sources of policy choice leads us to a consideration of what has become the agent-structure problem.

The agent-structure problem has its origins in two truisms about social life that underlie most social scientific inquiry: 1) human beings and their organizations are purposeful actors whose actions help to reproduce or transform the society in which they live; and 2) society is made up of social relationships, which structure the interactions between these purposeful actors (Wendt, 1987: 337). Taken together these truisms suggest that human agents and social structures are, in one way or another, theoretically interdependent or mutually implicating entities. Thus, the analysis of action invokes an at least implicit understanding of particular social relationships (or "rules of the game") in which the action is set—just as analyses of social structures invokes some understanding of the actors whose relationships make up the structural context. It is then a plausible step to believe that the properties of agents and those of social structures are both relevant to explanations of social behavior. "The 'agent-structure,' or 'micro-macro,' problem reflects the meta-theoretical need to adopt, for the purpose of explaining social behavior, some conceptualization of the ontological and explanatory relationship between social actors or agents" (Wendt, 1987: 336-337).

Structuralists set out to explain structural outcomes, such as international financial integration, directly in terms of structural causes. There is to be no role for intentional action or for individual goals, preferences, and beliefs. Against this, I argue for the desirability of inserting actions between structural preconditions and structural outcomes. Of course, these actions must be explained in the usual way by the actor's preferences and beliefs. Structuralists have made the point that if these preferences and perceptions are in turn explained by the agent's position in the social structure, then the structures are after all doing the real explanatory work: "the 'actors' are, as it were, mere conduits for these structural causal forces" (Taylor, 1989: 116).

However, the causal origins of beliefs and preferences are not always purely structural. Taylor (1989) argues that changes in preferences and beliefs can be the direct result of intentional actions— of their own bearers or other actors—and sometimes the result may be intended. Not only social structures, but other preferences and beliefs of the agent in question, along with intentional actions must be known in order to explain changes in preferences and beliefs. Actor preferences and beliefs are at least partially explained by the origins of the social structure in which the actor is located. However, the social structure, intended by no one, is often the product of *past* intentional actions and are maintained or transformed by actions. I devote a large section of this thesis to showing how capital controls and Keynesian demand management policies were firmly ensconced and viewed as successful, on the eve of the international financial revolutions of the 1970s and 1980s, as a result of intentional actions.

The "embedded liberal" framework of the Bretton Woods period developed from intentional actions. The international financial revolution would not have occurred, according to Structuralist accounts, if the advanced industrial states had managed to coordinate their macroeconomic policies in order to solve the "dollar overhang" problem of the late 1960s and the stagflation problem of the 1970s. They were unable to do so in large part because they presided over nationally-segmented economies. But this state of affairs was the product of intentional actions, for national policymakers had sought autonomy from external constraints in order to pursue high-growth strategies.

Rational choice scholars have often been berated for taking preferences and beliefs as given and unchanging. As Taylor (1989: 119) points out, while it is true that rational choice scholars have taken little interest in the origins of preferences and beliefs, "recognizing that an intentional explanation is only a part of the explanatory story, and that the explanation of the desires and beliefs that it takes as given need not be intentional, neither obviates the need for intentional explanation nor renders it trivial."

Returning to the onset of international financial integration, it can be argued that the causes of the breakdown of the Bretton Woods

financial control regime rest with certain structural conditions. In terms
of social transformation, there must be a "weakening of the state's
repressive capacity sufficient to provide an opening for . . . revolt"
(Skoçpol, 1985). In terms of capital mobility, the capacity of the states
to control capital movements and maintain "financial repression"
weakened, leading to demands by domestic financial asset-holders for
greater autonomy from state authorities. From a purely structural
perspective, international financial integration is seen as the product of
a political crisis whose causes lie at the state's relations to other states
(i.e., the decline of the systemic stability maintained by the hegemonic
state) and to its own domestic sectoral interests (e.g., financial asset-
holders). When the hegemonic state in the system decides to pursue
more open financial policies, mid-sized and small states encounter
intensified economic pressure to carry out reforms in order to compete.
However, smaller states are reluctant to initiate such efforts in this
direction due to organizational rigidities and sectoral opposition. To
attempt liberalizing reform risks losing the support of many of those on
whom it depends. As a result, the state may attempt to insulate itself
from international change. However, the international conditions that
sustained national economic segmentation have eroded, and domestic
financial asset-holders have taken advantage of the state's weakened
condition (through capital flight and investment strikes) which have
hastened the collapse of capital controls and demand management
policies. Thus, the success of financial asset-holders' "revolt against
state control" is conditioned on certain structural conditions: the
relations between financial asset-holders must be internationally those
of a strong community with considerable autonomy from the state.

Of the structural preconditions for international financial
integration, it was because financial asset-holders sought to reduce the
political risk of state regulatory and macroeconomic (often inflationary)
policies through access to external financial markets that it was
individually rational for them to participate in efforts to overthrow the
financial capital control regime. Supplying this motivational link
between structural conditions and structural outcomes make for a better
explanation. If structural changes (such as the shift toward capital
mobility) are to explained, and if structures are sets of relations that are
fairly stable over relatively long periods of time, then the changes
cannot be explained only by purely structural preconditions. But simply
inserting motivational links between structural preconditions and

structural change still will not do: "if the outcome is the product of actions, each of which is intentionally explained in terms of desires and beliefs (or causally explained by individuals coming to hold these desires and beliefs), and if the preferences and beliefs are causally explained in terms of locations in social structures, then we have changes supposedly being explained solely by unchanging desires and beliefs" (Taylor, 1989: 121).

"Social changes are produced by actions; social changes require new actions. New actions require changed desires and/or beliefs. So either one or more of the explanatory structures must change or, if structures are (relatively) unchanging, as on most definitions they must be, the changes in desires and beliefs must have some other source" (Taylor, 1989: 121).

As a result of their position in the national political economy financial asset-holders, before capital mobility, had certain preferences and beliefs, including preferences for greater portfolio diversification, lower taxes and inflation, and beliefs about the state capacity to control international financial transactions. These preferences and beliefs explain the inaction of financial asset-holders during the heyday of the Bretton Woods period. Then, certain events, such as advances in technology and the opening of offshore markets, caused financial asset-holders to modify some of these preferences and beliefs—particularly their beliefs about the capacity of the state to control cross-border financial transactions and about the state's probable attitudes to greater financial openness. As a result, actions that were not rational before became rational—that is, financial asset-holders took advantage of new opportunities that became available as a result of the state's inability to control cross-border financial transactions and offshore markets. These new opportunities led to action through financial asset-holders' changed beliefs about them.

While the Structural approach decomposes a system into units and the constraints facing them, Structurationist scholars from sociology argue that agents and structure are "mutually constitutive yet ontologically distinct entities. Each is in some sense an effect of the other; they are 'co-determined'" (Wendt, 1987: 360).

Powell (1994) argues that if agents and structures are conceptually inseparable, two consequences would follow. First, we would no longer be able to study the constraining effect of structure by theoretically holding the units and their preferences constant while varying the structure in which they interact. "If units and structure are inseparable so that each is at least partly the effect of the other, then variation in the structure will also change the units" (1994: 321). Second, challenging the separability of units and structure makes the units an object of inquiry and directs our attention to systemic change and transformation. Thinking about units as being endogenous shifts our attention away from a positional model to what Dessler (1989) calls a transformational model. "In a positional model like Waltz's formulation of Neo-Realism, structure is an environment in which action takes place (i.e., structure being the 'setting' or 'context' in which action unfolds). Structure is, in other words, a set of constraints. In a transformational model, structure is a medium of activity that in principle can be altered through activity. Structure shapes action and is shaped by action" (Powell, 1994: 321). The goal of a transformational model is to explain how structure and agent interact. To do this requires that we explore the role of ideology, interests, rules, and beliefs.

One line of research that is predicated on the interaction of units and structure is that of Gourevitch's "second-image reversed" argument. Gourevitch argues that the international structure shapes domestic institutions and states' preferences. This approach is important for it redefines the units in the system. "Rather than treating states as unitary actors, states are decomposed into more basic units. The hope here is that we will be able to separate these more basic units from the constraints facing them" (Powell, 1994: 323). This type of interactive, second-image reversed argument is a major advance over the prevailing third-image explanations from Neo-Realism.

Since the publication of Waltz's *Theory of International Politics* in 1979, Neo-Realism has been the dominant school of thought in world politics. Waltz's *Theory* revitalized the lagging appeal of Realist explanations of interstate behavior by recasting them from a more "scientific" basis. Waltz attempted to analytically disaggregate system-level properties from unit- (i.e., state and societal) level properties in order to build a true "theory" of interstate politics. "By depicting an international-political system as a whole, with structural and unit levels at once distinct and connected, neorealism establishes the autonomy of international politics and thus makes a theory about it possible" (Waltz, 1995: 74). Neo-Realism develops the concept of system structure, which affects the interacting units and the outcomes they produce. "International structure emerges from the interaction of states and then constrains them from taking certain actions while propelling them toward others" (Waltz, 1995: 74).

Waltz's concept of international structure is based on the arrangement and interaction of the states that compose the system. Two elements of international structure are constants: (1) the international system is anarchic rather than hierarchic, and (2) it is characterized by interaction among units with similar functions (Keohane, 1986: 166). It is the third element of structure, the distribution of capabilities across states in the system, that varies over time and leads to system transformation. "In an anarchic realm, structures are defined in terms of their major units. International structures vary with significant changes in the number of great powers. When their number changes consequentially, the calculations and behaviors of states, and the outcomes their interactions produce, vary" (Waltz, 1995: 74).

The question of levels of analysis must arise in any attempt to understand behavior within systems because it defines the layers of the system within which explanations are sought (Buzan, 1993: 33). Singer warns that selection of micro- or macro-level analysis is not a methodologically trivial matter. Macro-level analysis (conforming to Waltz's structural level), while permitting "a comprehensiveness that is lost when our focus is shifted to a lower . . . level, . . . tends to lead the observer into a position which exaggerates the impact of the system upon the national actors and, conversely, discounts the impact of the actors on the system" (Singer [1961], 1994: 88). Micro-level analyses, while permitting the observer a greater detail of state or society-level variables unavailable at the system level, "may . . . lead us into the opposite type of distortion—marked exaggeration of the differences among . . . sub-systemic actors" (Singer [1961], 1994: 90).

Singer notes that an implication of selecting micro-level analysis is that it raises the question of goals, motivation, and purpose in state policy and interest group action. Do state policymakers formulate positions and execute actions of their own choosing or are moved toward those imposed upon them by forces which are primarily beyond their control? Involved in answering this question is whether state goals are consciously intended or are unconsciously impelled.

Related to the question of intent is the question of strategy selection in the pursuit of goals. Structural explanations resolve this question by attributing identical goals to all actors. Under Neo-Realism, the internal attributes of states are given by assumption rather than treated as variables. States are assumed to be unitary rational actors and are undifferentiated in terms of goals. Because states seek to survive in an anarchic system, the policies of successful states are emulated by others. Therefore, strategy choice becomes one of the diffusion of the optimal policy in meeting a challenge. For micro-analysts, the unitary rational actor assumption is relaxed. Because individuals and groups have different goals and interests, and because they differ over the best methods of implementing them, policymaking involves conflict and competition (Cashman, 1993: 91). Political elites struggle among themselves to exert power over the making of policy (Allison, 1971). The occasion for a decision mobilizes a wide variety of political forces (both inside and outside of the government) to join in the political struggle. Furthermore, policy options are linked to institutional interests, with options not likely brought forward without their reflecting some institutional preferences.

The above "bureaucratic politics," or "interest group," model suggests that actor behavior is influenced not so much by the objective realities of their physical and social environments as by the fashion in which these objective realities are perceived and evaluated, however distorted or incomplete such perceptions may be. To be sure, "real" factors will have an impact on state performance even in absence of their recognition. As Singer notes, such "an individual will fall to the ground when he steps out of a tenth-story window regardless of his perception of gravitational forces, but on the other hand such perception is a major factor in whether or not he steps out of the window in the first place" ([1961], 1994: 92). Such interest group "phenomenological" approaches to policymaking are not incompatible with structural explanations. Indeed, it is the perceptual rather than objective basis for preference choices that allows for interest group and structural explanations to be linked. Thus, as Singer acknowledges, "it may be argued that any description of national behavior in a given international situation would be highly incomplete were it to ignore the link between the external forces at work upon the nation and its general foreign policy behavior" ([1961], 1994: 92).

Nau (1990) has commented that if a state fails to consider scarce resource factors, it risks, at some point, economic decline and bankruptcy. Structural constraints not only limit policy, but may themselves be created by policy. By failing to meet performance tests effectively, state policies allow external pressures to accumulate; and these pressures may eventually result in compelling circumstances or crises. In this sense, state policies create crises rather than just react to them.

Structural models of world politics tend to focus on only selective "system sectors" or "issue areas" in the field. Even within the Neo-Realist camp, Thompson (1988: 36) notes a polarization in the group's topical interests, with "one set of analysts . . . interested primarily in international political economy questions . . . [while] the other set of analysts largely ignores international political economy questions and concentrates instead on the classical war and peace *problématique*." One notable exception to this divergence of interests among Neo-Realist scholars is Gilpin (1981), whose analysis of system stability and hegemonic war offers a link between IPE and security interests. Gilpin's work is further significant in that he uses a version of the hegemonic stability thesis—an argument developed by Neo-Liberal scholars—and, inadvertently, despite his Neo-Realist credentials, he places the source of structural change at the state/society level.

According to Gilpin, ". . . actors enter social relations and create social structures in order to advance particular sets of political, economic, or other types of interests. Because the interests of some of the actors may conflict with those of other actors, the particular interests that are most favored by those social arrangements tend to reflect the relative powers of the actors involved. . . . Over time, however, the interests of individual actors and the balance of power among the actors do change as a result of economic, technological, and other developments. As a consequence, those actors who benefit most from a change in the social system and who gain the power to effect such change will seek to alter the system in ways that reflect . . . the interests of its new dominant members" (1981: 9). For Gilpin, it is differential rates of economic growth among states that leads to changes in the hierarchical arrangement of the interstate system. Because relative high levels of economic growth allow for some states to enhance their capabilities above the level of prestige that the interstate system allows those states to possess, feelings of relative deprivation may turn these states into revisionists, who will then seek to change the interstate structure through hegemonic war. Such hegemonic wars are violent equilibrating processes that bring the hierarchy of system prestige back in line with the hierarchy of system capabilities.

As the most efficient and technologically advanced economic power, the hegemonic state has the most to gain from participation in the world market economy. It also has the most to gain from a smoothly functioning international economic system. However, the question remains as to what constitutes "hegemony"? Cox (1987) defines hegemony as "economic dominance or preponderance at the core of the world system with a corollary implication that other types of dominance (e.g., military, cultural, and so forth) are likely to be aligned with the spatio-temporal concentration of economic power" (Thompson, 1988: 114). Neo-Liberal Keohane (1984) stresses the preponderant economy's need to possess a productive edge in high-value added goods. Wallerstein, in agreement with Cox in the Neo-Marxist World-Systems school, stresses the importance of the hegemonic power's "rule-making" authority.

The importance of rules, i.e., governing structures, takes us appreciably away from the Neo-Realist assumption of system anarchy. It is in this area that Neo-Realist, Hegemonic, and Regime analyses converge. Whereas Neo-Realist approaches focus primarily on material capabilities and balance-of-power relationships, Liberal Interdependence approaches focus principally on interactions and processes within a given structure of power. Cooper (1968) noted nearly three decades ago a "strong trend toward economic interdependence among industrial states, [that] makes the successful pursuit of national economic objectives much more difficult." Webb (1994) noted that international financial integration "rendered ineffective" the strategies of international policy coordination that governments had relied in to insulate national macroeconomic policymaking from international pressures. Globalization of production has transformed separate states into competing national economies (Laux, 1989). Governments no longer have a monopoly over the decision-making domain, as firms and individual investors foster "the rapid movement of capital and technical knowledge across national frontiers" (Cooper [1968], 1991: 111). Cooper presaged developments in the 1980s when he wrote, "as financial markets become more closely integrated, relatively small differences in yields on securities will induce large flows of funds between countries" and ". . . flows should respond more quickly to policy measures designed to influence them" ([1968], 1991: 111-112). For Cooper, developments at the structural level influence the behavior of states as they respond to the new structural conditions.

Keohane and Nye (1977) likewise note the effects of technological change on increases in capital flows, which reveal the "sensitivity" of national economies to international developments and limit their strategies. In *Power and Interdependence,* the two authors explored the question of what constitutes world politics under conditions of extensive interdependence. They noted that relationships of interdependence "often occur within, and may be affected by, networks of rules, norms, and procedures that regularize behavior and control its effects" ([1977], 1991: 131). Referred to as international regimes, Keohane and Nye blazed a trail that other scholars in the Liberal school of thought were to follow (Krasner, 1983). International regimes are defined as social institutions around which actor expectations converge in a given area of international relations. Regimes arise because actors forego independent decision-making in order to deal with the dilemmas of common interests and common aversions (Stein, 1990: 39). They do so in their own self-interest, for in both cases jointly accessible outcomes are preferable to those that are or might be reached independently. Whereas most Liberal Interdependence scholars define mutual dependence as the reciprocal dependence among states, I would expand the definition to include the dependence of states on non-state transnational actors. That is, all states share mutually their dependence on actors who, because of their lack of sovereignty, have the ability to focus their efforts exclusively on influencing the choice of policy alternatives of governments (thus, constituting a structural force in the world economy).[2]

Structural power has two dimensions. First, it is the ability to shape and determine the rules of engagement of the global political economy within which states, their political institutions, their economic enterprises, and professional people have to operate. Second, structural power means more than the ability to set the agenda of discussion or to design the international regimes of rules and customs that govern international economic relations. Structural power, in this sense, confers the ability to decide how things shall be done, the power to shape frameworks within which states relate to each other, relate to society, or relate to corporate enterprises. In the next section, I will examine how states have attempted to temper the structural power of non-state actors through regimes. Unfortunately, regime models that have been used by IPE scholars to date are based upon maintenance of an open trading system. One contribution this study makes is that those interstate efforts dealing with finance are quite different.

DILEMMAS OF COMMON AVERSIONS

Regimes established to deal with the dilemma of common interests differ from those created to solve the dilemma of common aversions. The dilemma of common interests occurs when the Pareto-optimal outcome that the involved states mutually desire (e.g., free trade) is not an equilibrium outcome (Stein, 1990: 39). To solve such dilemmas and guarantee the Pareto-optimal outcome, the parties must collaborate, and all regimes intended to deal with dilemmas of common interest must specify strict patterns of behavior (e.g., the transparency and reciprocity guidelines in the various GATT rounds) and ensure that no one cheats. Because each state requires assurances that the other will also eschew its rational choice, such collaboration requires a degree of formalization.

Regimes intended to deal with the dilemma of common aversions, by contrast, need only facilitate coordination. Such situations have multiple equilibria, and these regimes do not guarantee a particular outcome or compliance with any specific course of action, for they are created only to ensure that particular outcomes be avoided (Stein, 1990: 41-42). Nevertheless, such coordination is difficult to achieve when states disagree in the choice of preferred equilibrium. The greater this conflict of interest, the harder it is for them to coordinate their actions. Yet once established, the regime that makes expectations converge and allows states to coordinate their actions is self-enforcing, for any state that departs from it "hurts only itself." Thus, there is no problem of policing and compliance. Defections do not represent cheating for immediate self-aggrandizement, but are expressions of relative dissatisfaction with the coordinative outcome. Departures from regime-specified behavior, thus, represent a fundamentally different problem in coordination regimes than in collaborative regimes. In the next chapter, I will review the creation of the Bretton Woods international financial regime, which was a coordination regime. The advanced industrial states after World War II had a common interest in averting a return of financial capital mobility, which was held at the time to be the cause of the great economic downturn of the 1930s. The capital control regime lasted until some states (notably Britain) allowed themselves to become havens for uncontrolled financial transactions to gain advantages in attracting financial capital, and the United States—in an effort to solve its current-account imbalances—first encouraged American transnational corporations to take part in the new offshore markets and later dismantled the financial control regime altogether.

The conception of regime that is being presented here is interest-based. As Stein points out, the same forces of autonomously calculated self-interest that lie at the root of the anarchic international system of the Neo-Realists also provide the foundation for Neo-Liberal international regimes as a form of international order. The same forces that lead states to bind themselves together in collective security arrangements to escape the Hobbesian state of nature also lead states to coordinate their exchange-rate policies in order to maintain economic stability. National policymakers wish to preserve their autonomy in choosing preferred policy alternatives. International financial integration constrains such autonomy. Therefore, states have an incentive to create coordinative regimes to restrict financial asset-holders from shifting their capital from one state to another. As a result, international financial regimes attempt to solve the dilemma of common aversions. Thus, because state behavior is best explained as the intermediation of preferences,[3] that are in turn rooted in other (structural) factors, regimes are maintained as long as the patterns of interest that gave rise to them remain. When these patterns of interest shift, the character of the regime may change, or even collapse. International economic regimes provide a permissive environment for the emergence of specific kinds of international transaction flows that actors take to be complementary to the particular fusion of power and purpose that is embodied within those regimes. The emergence of several specific developments in transnational economic activities, such as free capital movements, can be accounted for, at least in part, by the contribution of international monetary regimes, which provide part of the context that shapes transnationalization.

Hegemonic models of international economic relations postulate only one source of regime change, the rise or decline of dominant or hegemonic power, with two directions of regime change—greater openness or closure. I believe that regimes change due to non-power reasons located at the substate level. These include changes in the national macroeconomic structure, reflecting the activities of financial asset-holders and other economic agents, and in economic doctrine, reflecting problem-definition and the range of choice available to address the central economic problem of the day. I will discuss the hegemonic and non-state actor approaches in the next two sections.

HEGEMONIC STABILITY ARGUMENTS OF THE INTERNATIONAL FINANCIAL REGIME

It was Charles Kindleberger (1973) who first argued that a liberal international economic order requires a "hegemon," or dominant state, at its center to function in an orderly and productive way. He also defined the basic requirements of such a hegemonial system. An international monetary regime refers to the principles, norms, rules, procedures, instruments, facilities, and organizations that govern financial relations between countries. International monetary regimes can be classified according to: (1) the way in which exchange rates are determined; (2) the form that international reserve assets take; and (3) the degree of government control over international capital flows. Under the exchange rate classification, we can have a fixed exchange rate regime with a narrow band of fluctuation around a par value, a fixed exchange rate regime with a wide band of fluctuation, an adjustable peg regime, a managed floating exchange rate regime, or a freely floating exchange rate regime. Under the international reserve classification, we can have a gold standard (with gold as the only international reserve asset), a purely fiduciary standard (such as a pure dollar or exchange standard without any connection to gold), or a gold-exchange standard (a combination of the other two). And, under the capital control classification, we can have restrictions on international capital flows through exchange controls, official intervention in forward markets, and multiple exchange rates.

A well-functioning and stable international monetary regime is one that maximizes the flow of international trade and investments and leads to an "equitable" distribution of the "gains from trade" among states. An international monetary regime can be evaluated in terms of how it resolves problems of adjustment, liquidity, and confidence. *Adjustment* refers to the process by which balance-of-payments disequilibria are corrected. Adjustment measures can be either internal (e.g., domestic "austerity" programs) or external (e.g., changes in exchange rates). A stable international monetary regime is one that minimizes the costs of, and the time required for, adjustment. *Liquidity* refers to the amount of international reserve assets in circulation to settle temporary balance-of-payments disequilibria. A stable international monetary regime is one that provides adequate international reserves so that countries can correct balance-of-payments deficits without deflating their own economies or being inflationary for the world as a whole. *Confidence* refers to the attitudes of holders of liquid financial resources toward currencies. A stable international monetary regime is one that maintains the knowledge that the adjustment mechanism is working adequately and that international reserves will retain their absolute and relative values.

A capitalist or market system is apt, as experience has shown, to suffer from cyclical booms and slumps, and to fail periodically to match demand and supply. The hegemon thus has to function in three ways in order to preserve order in the system: 1) whenever necessary it must offer an outlet for surplus production by absorbing foreign goods into its domestic market; 2) it must act as a "lender of last resort" to maintain monetary liquidity through use of its currency as an international medium of exchange; and 3) it must generate an outflow of capital or credit to keep the system expanding, thereby promoting investment and economic growth consonant with fundamental liberalizing ambitions. Kindleberger (1973) argued that Britain played this role more or less successfully in the three to four decades before World War I, and the United States played it in the two decades following World War II. Between the wars, however, Britain was unable and the United was unwilling to do so. The result was that the world suffered from the worst depression in its history.

Hegemonic stability arguments predict economic policy coordination when a dominant or "hegemonic" power exists that has a large stake in the international system and is willing to assume the costs of supporting a liberal economic order, including opening its market to foreign imports, providing capital for investment in other countries, and allowing its currency to serve as the reserve monetary unit of the system. The modern transnational capitalist market system of the nineteenth and twentieth centuries was constructed and maintained predominantly under the aegis of one power, first Britain and later the United States. In both cases, moreover, the limitations of that same hegemony were manifest in the system itself—embodied in the profound tension between specific national interests, on the one hand,

and the imperatives of the international marketplace, on the other. In particular, growing conflicts between the national interests of the hegemonic state, on the one hand, and the conditions necessary for international economic stability and economic efficiency, on the other—conflicts intensified by the hegemon's relative economic decline—undermined the financial stability and economic efficiency of the international marketplace.

According to this explanation, the United States created and led an open world economic order after World War II as long as its international power was disproportionate. As competitors emerged, however, the U.S. became less willing to absorb the costs and less able to extract the benefits of liberal policies (Keohane, 1980).

NON-STATE ACTOR APPROACHES TO FINANCIAL REGIME CHANGE

Locating the source of change at the substate level is difficult to measure directly, for it is based upon changes in how individuals view their environment. As the discussion of the agent-structure issue revealed, agents are often bound to act in certain ways—often under the direction of higher authority—because they accept as legitimate the purview of that authority. However, in times of technological change, with the scope of knowledge expanded dramatically, agents begin to question the legitimacy of authorities and the doctrines that they espouse. This challenging of state authority becomes pronounced when the basis of state authority is performance, which is found lacking. The enhanced capability that communication and information technologies give to financial asset-holders would be of little use unless those asset-holders felt they could and needed to offset the political risk of state policymaking autonomy.

Information technology becomes a transformative force that makes international financial integration a structural variable in world politics. If money can be characterized as "information on the move," then technology is the ultimate multiplier. Technology has expanded the capacity of financial asset-holders to generate and manipulate information and knowledge. Financial asset-holders, whose capabilities for independent action have been enhanced, develop new products and services in order to break the hold of state authorities and hedge the risk of political actions. New networks of like-minded individuals emerge, not as organized "interests" in the traditional sense, but as independent actors whose individual actions collectively become a constraining parameter on state autonomy. Indeed, the fact that financial asset-holders do not view themselves as an "interest group" may increase their capacity for independent action. Because they take advantage of the political fragmentation of the international system, financial asset-holders can and do shift capital to areas offering the most favorable investment climate—thereby increasing the competitive pressure on states to implement regulatory reform and liberalize financial flows.

It is through the macroeconomic structure that changes in the activities of financial asset-holders have been the most acutely felt. Macroeconomic structure refers to the systemic layout of the national economy, including the interrelations among economic variables. More directly, it is the set of mechanisms for managing the overall level of economic performance—output, employment, and growth (Marglin, 1990: 6). Fluctuations in national economic activity are based upon the behavior of consumers, the organization of labor markets and industry, the workings of financial markets, and the machinations of governments. The incentives that lead to economic fluctuations are configured through macroeconomic structural mechanisms.

To be successful, macroeconomic management must meet two requirements. On the one hand, the level of aggregate demand must be set at a level adequate to utilize fully the available productive resources, both capital and labor. On the other hand, the share of output devoted to capital formation must be sufficient to achieve a high rate of growth of the capital stock, and over time the demand for investment and supply of saving must grow in balance with each other. Investment demand is an essential element of the macroeconomic structure. Since the 1930s, governments have intervened in the price mechanism in order to influence investment demand.[4] While such policies did speed industrial growth after the Second World War, this is not to say that governments know the precise relationship between credit allocation and investment demand at all times. Indeed, periodic inflationary and recessionary cycles reveal the limits of government knowledge of macroeconomic phenomena. Suffice it to say that governments pursue certain aggregate demand policies based upon certain *a priori* assumptions about economic incentives. To the extent that these assumptions coincide with the "real world" economy, economic performance is judged satisfactory as the key objectives of non-inflationary growth and full employment are reached. To the extent that these assumptions are in error, the macroeconomy will underperform long-run growth patterns,[5] setting the conditions for economic "hard times" (Gourevitch, 1986).

A major cost of such government intervention and the provision of subsidized credit has been the creation of an "overdraft economy" (Loriaux, 1991), where there exists an incentive for business to become indebted, over-manned, and less adaptive to a changing environment (i.e., "moral hazard"). Implicit government subsidies create soft budget constraints that lead to maladaptive behavior among industries. When taken to an extreme, a macroeconomic structure akin to that of the former socialist economies of eastern and central Europe can develop. Though no Western country suffered from the fate that befell the former socialist economies, soft budget constraints induced by non-market credit allocation left many an industry unprepared for the major upheavals of the 1970s. The rapid increase in major industrial input prices put tremendous pressure on profit margins during that decade. Government efforts to stimulate demand only exacerbated the taut supply situation. Furthermore, subsidized government credit softened the blow of tighter profit margins for many industries, which led to less than optimal resource reallocation. As profit margins continued to shrink, industries laid off workers. This combination of events led to reduced revenues and greater expenditures for governments. In an era of segmented national financial markets, holders of capital within a political domain may be unwilling to invest when real rates of return are negative—which is the case in a highly inflationary environment. Opening up financial markets may serve as a mechanism to increase the total availability of credit for a mid-sized economy. The downside is that the government loses control of the credit allocative process.

As explained in Chapter IV governments accepted this tradeoff, largely believing that a flexible exchange rate regime offered policymakers the freedom to pursue nationally-tailored macroeconomic policies. With the exchange rate floating, in order to equalize cross-national rates of return, policymakers believed that they had tapped into a vast new source of credit from which to continue the "overdraft economy." However, increased marketization led to demands for positive real rates of return on investment. The increased competition for capital, now on a global scale, imposed a new discipline on governments, that force them to reorient their macroeconomic policies to respond to market pressures.

Policymakers may prefer to proceed on the basis of clear-cut, quantitative evidence, but they cannot afford to refrain from acting in its absence. Policy elites and counter-elites need to have some notion of how much support each of them can bring to bear on behalf of a given policy; otherwise they run the risk of being unable to back up demands or ward off threats, or being defeated in the contest over resources and influence. Economic doctrine provides the blueprint that governments use in determining economic policy. Doctrine answers the questions about the relationship among economic variables and provides the assumptions about incentives to induce preferred macroeconomic outcomes. Peter Hall's (1989) analysis of the power of economic ideas brilliantly demonstrates how doctrine, at a point of academic and policy receptiveness to new ideas, can have a dramatic effect. In Kuhnian fashion, the adoption of a set of ideas as doctrine lends a sense of credibility to that set that is not easily dislodged. Quite often, a doctrine is clung to in spite of a growing mass of evidence of its obsolescence. It takes a major breakdown of the putative relationship among explanatory and outcome variables in order for academic to reject the prevailing doctrine. It takes a new set of ideas that explains both the phenomena that the previous doctrine had, as well as new phenomena that the previous doctrine was incapable of explaining.[6]

Hall (1989), in his analysis of the impact of Keynesianism on politics, listed three analytic perspectives of economic doctrine: economist-centered, state-centered, and coalition-centered. The economic-centered perspective focused upon the paradigmatic struggle within academia over the acceptance of Keynesian economic ideas. Here, Hall is implying an epistemic community (Haas, 1992) argument, in that economists are held up in society as experts. The state-centered perspective, borrowing from the work of Weir and Skoçpol (1985), focuses on the reaction to new economic ideas by state institutions: "In the sphere of policy formulation, the relative openness of policymaking institutions to advice from . . . economists [will] affect the speed with which developments in economic theory can be incorporated into policy . . ." (Hall: 11). The coalition-centered perspective places change in the economic policy squarely in the political arena. As Hall points out: ". . . a nation's readiness to implement Keynesian policies may be said to turn on the ability of its politicians to forge a coalition of social groups that is large enough to sustain them in office and inclined to regard Keynesian measures as something that is in their interest" (Hall 1989: 12).

By contrast, in the late 1970s and 1980s, at the heart of neoliberal (here to mean neo-Classical economic) doctrine were the beliefs that private property and accumulation were sacrosanct, and that without the private sector, growth would be endangered (Gill and Law, 1988: 93). An example of the force of such beliefs is the way in which neoliberal ideas about the need to control inflation have become widely accepted, and embodied in disinflationary policies, in the advanced industrial states since the early 1980s. Moreover, a central aspect of neoliberal ideology is the belief that economic conditions cannot be properly controlled by governments (a centerpiece of the previous Keynesian consensus), and that somehow, economic outcomes are the product of "natural" market forces. In this construct, the best that governments can hope to do is to aid the workings of the market, and consequently to promote economic efficiency in the private sector. In so far as this framework of thought has come to be accepted by a large and growing number of people, as well as those in politically significant positions within the state, it implies a redefinition of the "limits of the possible," as well as a realignment of politics in advanced industrial states towards the Right. This ideology argument has tremendous explanatory power, for political coalitions embracing new economic doctrines that appear to alleviate the principal socioeconomic concern of the day (depression in the 1930s or stagflation in the 1970s) can attract additional support, supplant an existing regime, and implement their preferred policy. What is important to take out of this section is that while large powerful states may "create" regimes, they do so largely because their macroeconomic structure is conducive to the promotion of a more liberal international order.

My argument is that international financial integration is a structural phenomenon that has constrained the ability of national policymakers to conduct their preferred policy alternatives.[7] Unlike Neo-Realist explanations, I argue that the sources of structural change are found not only at the level of interaction among states, but at the level of structure itself. However, I do not view structure as a mere meta-physical veneer. Rather, structure reflects the interests of important substate groups and non-group collectivities who, through their positions of influence, impose their preferences upon policymakers. That is, states are not unitary rational actors, but are institutions for the intermediation of interest groups. And as intermediators, in the marketplace of economic ideas, the "embedded liberal" ideas of the 1940s have been replaced by the "embedded orthodoxy" of the 1980s.

EMBEDDED FINANCIAL ORTHODOXY?

Most explanations of the globalization of financial markets discount the role played by states. According to this view, unstoppable technological and market forces, rather than state behavior and political choices, were the prime movers behind the phenomenon. In recent years, a growing number of scholars in the field of international political economy (Hawley, 1987; Banuri and Schor, 1992; Goodman and Pauly, 1993; Helleiner, 1993, 1994; Cerny, 1993) have challenged this historical account. While not ignoring technological and market developments, they emphasize the importance of states in the process of globalization.

Macroeconomic adjustment policies have changed since the 1960s in response to changing economic structures and corresponding patterns of interdependence in the global economy, and in particular to the growth of international capital mobility. Hegemonic stability arguments about international policy coordination usually identify the abandonment of fixed exchange rates in the early 1970s as the key turning point in postwar international monetary cooperation, with the preceding period of fixed exchange rates characterized by extensive international policy coordination and international economic stability, and the subsequent period of fluctuating exchange rates characterized by a breakdown of policy coordination and increased economic instability. The key factor, from this perspective, was the change from a system of fixed exchange rates to a system of flexible exchange rates. Furthermore, the so-called breakdown of the Bretton Woods system is often explained as a consequence of declining American hegemony.

But an analysis of the record of international coordination of international macroeconomic adjustment policies suggests that coordination was at least as extensive in the late 1970s and 1980s as it was in the late 1950s and 1960s (Webb, 1991; 1994). What changed were the types of policy subject to coordination and the level of intrusiveness of international policy coordination with respect to domestic policymaking. International coordination in the 1960s focused on balance-of-payments financing and exchange rate coordination—

"external" adjustment policies that are inherently international. Low capital mobility and limited trade flows (in contrast to the 1980s) meant that fixed exchange rates could be maintained without seriously constraining national macroeconomic policymaking autonomy. The fixed exchange rate system was abandoned in the early 1970s, when increasing capital mobility made it impossible for governments to stabilize exchange rates without subordinating monetary policy to that end. By the late 1970s, coordination efforts focused on monetary and fiscal policies—policies that had traditionally been considered "internal." This is a much more intrusive type of policy coordination, since it demanded that governments alter macroeconomic policies central to their domestic political programs.

Although international economic instability was much greater in the 1980s than in the 1960s, this was less a consequence of the posited erosion of American hegemony than it was of the increasing international integration of capital markets. As capital became more mobile, international economic policy coordination had to become more extensive simply to maintain the level of stability achieved in the 1960s. The instability of the late 1970s and 1980s reflected the obstacles to making international policy coordination more extensive than it had been in the 1960s, not a breakdown of coordination.

Arguments about declining American hegemony are therefore inconsistent with the observed overall pattern of international policy coordination (with increasing coordination of policies closer to the core of national autonomy, i.e., monetary and fiscal policies), nor do they explain why the types of policies subject to coordination have changed. An economic-structural argument, focusing on how changes in the structure of the international economy—especially the policy strategies—provide a better explanation for these important shifts in patterns of policy coordination.

The historical analysis presented in this study develops three lines of argument that help to explain patterns of international coordination. Those arguments are based on: (1) the economic-structural constraints that capital mobility and the transnationalization of production have placed upon governments; (2) the hegemonic interest of a liberal state in setting the conditions for deregulation that other states are forced to follow (i.e., deregulatory arbitrage) in order to maintain domestic economic growth; and (3) the emergence of a common neoliberal normative framework among macroeconomic policymakers. In addition to demonstrating the limits of hegemonic stability, this study also reveals the limits of the economic-structural argument by showing that states with differential power resources reacted variably to global neoliberalism and that domestic politics of macroeconomic policies (especially fiscal policy) consistently affect how states react to international market pressures on macroeconomic policies.

The emphasis on how changes in the structure of the international economy influence the possibilities for domestic macroeconomic policy choices should not obscure the fact that those structural changes themselves were the product of policy choices. Changes in technology of international finance did not mean that capital mobility was inevitable—yet technological changes did lead to closer integration of national capital markets than policymakers had intended or expected when the crucial decisions and non-decisions were taken. Thus, the constraints on macroeconomic policymaking autonomy imposed by international capital mobility are best understood as an unintended consequence of earlier choices to liberalize trade and investment. Furthermore, given the character of the international economic interdependence that has emerged in the wake of trade and investment liberalization, it now would be extremely difficult (short of autarky) for any government to escape these constraints on macroeconomic policymaking autonomy.

Most histories of the globalization of finance stress the influence of technological changes and market developments. The growth of global telecommunications networks is shown to have dramatically reduced the costs and difficulties of transferring funds around the world. At least six market developments are said to have been significant (Helleiner 1994). The first was the restoration of market confidence in the safety of international financial transactions in the late 1950s. This confidence had been shaken by the 1931 crisis and subsequent economic and political upheavals. The second was the rapid increase in the demand for international financial services that accompanied the growth of international trade and transnational corporate activity in the 1960s. Third, private banks responded quickly to the global financial imbalances caused by the 1973 oil price rise, encouraging enormous deposits by oil-producing states and the borrowing of those funds by deficit countries. Fourth, the adoption of flexible exchange rates in the early 1970s encouraged market operators to diversify their assets internationally in the new volatile currency markets. Fifth, the disintegration of domestically focused postwar financial cartels throughout the advanced industrial world in the 1970s and 1980s forced financial institutions to enter the international financial arena to supplement their declining domestic profits; such a move also enabled them to evade remaining domestic regulatory constraints. Finally, the market innovations that were created in this increasingly competitive atmosphere, such as currency and interest rate futures, options, and swaps, also reduced the effective risks and costs of international financial operations.

According to this interpretation, states have played only a minor role in the globalization process. In particular, states are said to have been unable to stop the trend because of the impossibility of controlling international capital movements, which in turn is said to have stemmed from two characteristics of money: its mobility and its fungibility.

International financial markets were able to develop only within a broader institutional structure delineated by the power and policies of states. Helleiner, in examining the transition from the capital restrictiveness of the Bretton Woods era to the capital mobility of the past quarter century, asks two questions: How were the actions and decisions of states important to the globalization process? Why did states increasingly embrace an open liberal international financial order after having opposed its creation in the early postwar years? He argues that advanced industrial states made three types of policy decisions after the late 1950s that were important to the globalization process: (1) to grant more freedom to market operators through liberalization initiatives; (2) to refrain from imposing more effective controls on capital movements; and (3) to prevent major international financial crises.[8]

The policy decision to allow market operators a greater degree of freedom through liberalization moves was first in evidence in the 1960s when Britain and the United States strongly supported growth of the Euromarket in London. This market served as an offshore regulation-free environment in which to trade financial assets denominated in foreign currencies, predominately U.S. dollars. In a world of extensive capital controls, it was a kind of "adventure playground" for private international bankers, marking a significant break from the restrictive financial relations that had characterized the early postwar period. Although the market has sometimes been described as "stateless," it could not have survived without the backing of Britain and the United

States. Britain's support for the Eurodollar market was crucial because locating the market in London meant that it could operate free of regulation. The support of the United States was equally important because of the dominant presence of American transnational banks and corporations in the market. Although it had the power to do so, the United States did not prevent the TNBs and TNCs from operating in the Eurodollar market.

States also granted financial asset-holders an extra degree of freedom after the mid-1970s when they began to abolish their postwar capital controls. Once again, the United States initiated this liberalization by removing the various capital controls it had introduced briefly in the mid-1960s. Britain followed in 1979, eliminating its forty-year-old capital controls. The American and British actions were copied by other advanced industrial states in the 1980s.

The second type of policy decision of states was to refrain from imposing more effective capital controls. Although it is true that states find it difficult to control capital movements, the authors of conventional histories of the globalization process have generally overlooked the fact that the Bretton Woods architects discussed these difficulties and outlined two specific mechanisms for overcoming them (I will discuss these mechanisms in the next chapter). First, they argued that capital controls could be made to work through cooperative initiatives in which controls were enforced at both ends, that is, both in the country that sent the capital and in the country that received it.[9] Second, they concluded that evasion of capital controls could be prevented through the use of comprehensive exchange controls in which all transactions—capital account and current account—were monitored for illegal capital flows.

The importance of the third type of policy decision—to attempt to prevent major international financial crises—is rarely acknowledged by those who point to the inevitability of the globalization trend in the face of market and technological pressures.[10] The danger posed by these crises is that, if uncontained, they would likely encourage market operators to retreat to their domestic markets and prompt states to introduce tight capital controls. It was concerns to prevent such crises that prompted policymakers in the 1930s and 1940s to construct the capital control regime in the first place.

NOTES

1. Figures in 1995 constant dollars.

2. Rosenau (1990) notes that states yield partial jurisdiction to non-state actors when governments are paralyzed by prior commitments and non-state actors may be able to break the stalemate. The rise of the Eurocurrency markets may be looked upon as an example of this phenomenon. The American government was bound by its commitment to defend the value of the currency through maintenance of its current account balance. However, the American government also derived strategic benefits from the overseas "imperial" investments (i.e., U.S. military bases and transnational investment). The development of the Eurocurrency markets set up a sovereign-free source of capital to finance American overseas investment without deteriorating the American current account position.

3. Just as financial intermediation is the process through which banks accept savings and lend to borrowers, governments "accept" the articulated interest demands of social groups and through a bargaining process present policy for constituents, that is a mix of their policy preferences.

4. The provision of government-subsidized capital for national industry in order to accelerate the modernization in a number of mid-sized capitalist states in the postwar period is a prime example.

5. I would argue that policy errors are examples of financial asset-holder dissatisfaction with economic management, given that inflationary periods lead to higher premiums on bond yields and recessionary periods to discounts. The simple yield curve offers much information concerning market expectations. To the extent that financial asset-holders have access to more reliable information, their expectations become a leading indicator of economic performance.

6. This was the case in the 1930s. Classical liberal economics—which included both Say's Law, which states that supply creates its own demand, and the principle that the economy tends toward long-run full employment—proved inadequate in addressing the problem of high long-term unemployment. Keynes' *General Theory* was revelatory for opening up new options for policymakers.

7. The assumption here is that while policymakers may differ over the alternatives to achieve certain economic outcomes, they are largely in agreement in terms of what the outcomes should be. Structural constraints close off certain avenues to the achievement those outcomes.

8. While I challenge Helleiner on the point that states could control financial transactions to the degree that had prior to the 1970s, I agree that the

states largely abandoned efforts at enforcing controls beginning in the mid-1970s. The principal disagreement between Helleiner's analysis and my own is that Helleiner discounts the technologically-enhanced ability to financial asset-holders to circumvent controls *and their willingness to use those capabilities.* Just as Helleiner argues that states are no longer willing to exercise powers that were willing to exercise at an earlier period, I argue that financial asset-holders are now willing to exercise their capabilities. In both cases, actors' views of the possible (and probably successful) have changed.

9. I would argue that Helleiner's characterization of the game is misspecified. Rather than a cooperative game to achieve a common interest in exchange rate stability, the Bretton Woods regime was a coordinative game to avoid the common aversion of financially-induced economic instability. The specification of the game says much about its long-term prospects for success.

10. Kapstein's 1989 study of the Basle Accord is an exception.

CHAPTER III

The Historical Evolution of the Key Arrangements

> Freedom of capital movements is an essential part of the old *laissez faire* system and assumes that it is right and desirable to have an equalization of interest rates in all parts of the world . . . In my view the whole management of the domestic economy depends upon being free to have the appropriate rate of interest without reference to the rates prevailing elsewhere in the world. Capital control is a corollary to this (Keynes [1980], in Helleiner, 1993: 26-27).

The post-World War II global economy of the Bretton Woods era (1945-73) was one of unprecedented growth and prosperity. This Great Expansion was brought about by the confluence of three events. First, World War II ended with Europe shattered and the United States the dominant political and economic actor on the world stage. The liberal free market ideology of the United States was exported to much of the world. Second, again as a consequence of the decline of Europe, the great empires, which undergirded mercantilist trading practices, passed into history. Freer trade again became the dominant mode of international commerce. With the United States as the dominant economic actor, it took upon itself the task of providing the international collective goods of a free trade regime and international security, while allowing weaker states to "free ride" on that regime and security. Therefore, while overall American trade barriers came down dramatically, those of Europe and Japan fell more slowly. In the case of Western Europe the United States promoted the creation of a trading bloc that, though American goods imports remained disadvantaged, stimulated intra-European trade. At the same time, the tariff barrier of the European Community stimulated the growth of American transnational corporations, as they "jumped the tariff wall" and established subsidiaries in Western Europe. The impact that transnationals were to have on global production was not appreciated until the 1970s.

Third, while the Bretton Woods era promoted freer trading relations, it actively discouraged capital mobility (Helleiner, 1993; 1994a, 1994b). The endorsement of capital controls at Bretton Woods represented a dramatic departure from traditional liberal financial practices. The departure was the result of the socio-ideological "breaking with orthodoxy" that took place within industrial countries in the aftermath of the financial crisis of 1929-1931 and the economic downturn of the subsequent Great Depression: "Largely discredited by the crises, the private and central bankers who had dominated financial politics in the 1920s were increasingly replaced in positions of financial power by Keynesian-minded economists, industrialists, and labor leaders" (Helleiner, 1994b: 164).

The Bretton Woods era was to become "the golden age" (Marglin and Schor, 1990) of Keynesian economics, which is based on a national model of economic policymaking. No longer would governments allow the vagaries of the business cycle to wreak havoc on the real economy. Demand management, pump priming, and fiscal and monetary stimulus became the new tools of the postwar governing elite. Indeed, the entire notion of "macroeconomics" as a separate field of the economics discipline was born out of this period. But national policymaking autonomy, i.e., the ability of governments to stimulate demand during recessionary periods and contract demand during inflationary episodes, was based on the assumption of the immobility of capital. As long as capital remained domiciled within the state, a government could access it through changes in the domestic interest rate. Therefore, in a recessionary economy, national policymakers could lower the cost of national capital through reductions in the national interest rate. Interest rate reductions lower the cost of borrowing and increase the opportunity cost of holding interest-bearing assets (i.e., bonds). Therefore, bondholders sell and more cash is put into the economy. If one were to take the same recessionary conditions occurring in a world of capital mobility, a government that lowers interest rates (i.e., the rate of return on bond investments) runs the risk that national bondholders may send their money abroad—seeking higher interest-bearing assets rather than keeping cash in the domestic economy. Therefore, in a world of international capital mobility, national policymakers are stripped of much of their discretion in setting macroeconomic policy.

In this chapter, I will review the key arrangements that undergirded the postwar economic system. As outlined in the last chapter, my analysis will emphasize the international systemic, the domestic macroeconomic structural, and the economic doctrinal elements of policy change. As background to how these institutions functioned during the Great Expansion, the historical record of Depression and World War II is essential. The first legacy of the Depression was the commitment to the welfare state. The trauma of unemployment on a mass scale changed the way people throughout Europe and North America would think about the role of government. Equally significant, the Depression marked a "structural break" in financial affairs (Helleiner, 1993: 22). The collapse of the gold-exchange standard and the rise of currency blocs severed the interconnectedness that had bound the world economy together since the late nineteenth century. Capital controls became accepted as a means of containing destabilizing flows and allow for internal macroeconomic stabilization. Given the wide divergence in policy approaches in the 1930s, such controls became a necessary part of policy.

As Gourevitch (1986) describes, no country, whatever its domestic politics and policies, could escape the grip of collapsing trade, skyrocketing unemployment, and escalating value of real debt. As the Depression rippled around the world, most countries responded with the same economic policy—deflation, the response prescribed by liberal, or orthodox, analysis of the market economy. It did not work. After some two to four years of failure most countries abandoned deflation and broke with orthodoxy. Initially, most of them turned to familiar deviations from classical rules: tariffs, devaluation of the currency, leaving the gold standard, and some corporatist regulation of domestic markets. Some countries broke more drastically to try more unusual departures from standard views. They experimented with demand stimulus through deficit spending (known after the war as Keynesianism), social welfare systems, extensive regulation of and subsidies for markets, and some degree of public ownership of production.

During the 1930s these departures from economic liberalism were experimental and uneven both within and across countries. In that decade the divergence in economic policy mirrored divergence in political form—from constitutional government in Britain, Sweden, and the United States to authoritarian corporatism in Italy and Germany and communism, which did not even recognize private property rights in the USSR. With policy consensus already shattered by the Depression, the transforming impact of World War II pushed change even further. The war created new opportunities to resume a debate begun in the 1930s over how to accommodate new changes in the international division of labor and the international business cycles that are part of that division.

In the industrialized countries, the postwar years saw the construction of an accommodation. It was not automatic. It required action to structure both the economy and politics. The role of the United States in shaping the context of the new liberal order was indispensable. The United States came to use its influence abroad in the immediate postwar years (e.g., through the Marshall Plan, the Occupation Authorities in Germany and Japan, and its access to transnational labor organizations) to directly shape outcomes, by seeking to moderate the structure and political direction of labor movements, to encourage the exclusion of Communist parties from participation in governments, and generally to discourage collectivist arrangements where possible or at least contain them within acceptable Center-Left bounds. By 1950, in policy terms, the innovations of the 1930s had become the established and institutionalized norms for the democratic market economy. The Western economies functioned not through free-market orthodoxy but through regulation and intervention aimed at ensuring market stabilization and political peace both within and between countries.

A COMMON VISION DESTROYED

An international economy emerged for the first time during the century of comparative peace lasting from the Congress of Vienna to the outbreak of the First World War. It was international in the sense that trade, capital, and people moved with relative ease between countries, especially between the industrializing states of Western Europe and the peripheral suppliers of raw materials and foodstuffs. According to

Rogowski: "Between 1840 and 1895, world trade roughly sextupled in nominal terms; from then to 1913, it more than quintupled" (1988: 21). During the century global exports, in constant dollars, multiplied from $550 million to $19.8 billion (Eckes, 1975: 2). Using data compiled by Woytinsky and Woytinsky (1955), Eckes estimates that in the fifty years before the First World War the value of world trade rose an average of 34 percent per decade and the volume of trade climbed 36-37 percent each decade. The flow of international investments contributed to the rapid growth of trade. British foreign investment alone grew from $4.9 billion in 1870 to $19.5 billion in 1914 (Woodruff, 1966: 150). Total foreign investment at the start of the First World War was close to $40 billion—nearly half of which going to the British dominions, the United States, and Argentina (Schwartz, 1994: 151). The result was a new pattern of economic interdependence that linked states together through trade and finance at a time when nationalism was strengthening states politically.

This first international economy was comparatively unstructured, emerging as the result of private, not government, initiatives. About 40 percent of all nineteenth-century British investment, for instance, went directly into railroads, and a further 30 percent went indirectly, through government borrowing, to railroads and other social overhead capital (Schwartz, 1993: 155). From 1870 to 1914, the fact that the gold standard worked owed more to a large and growing supply of credit instruments, including stocks and bonds, than to any expansion in the supply of metallic money. According to Triffin (1964), increased credit money accounted for 90 percent of the expansion of the global supply of bank reserves from 1816 to 1914. Schwartz (1993: 167) points out that the gold standard worked during the 1870 to 1914 period because it reflected the contemporary flow of investment and goods in the real economy.

A number of factors, some unique to the nineteenth century, contributed to the evolution of this international economic system. The absence of major power war and the widespread belief that governments had few responsibilities for economic management or social welfare allowed private activity to expand with few impediments. Also, the rapid pace of European industrialization and new technological developments—especially the railroad, which allowed for transport of bulk commodities over land—encouraged and made the possible Ricardian economic development strategies of comparative advantage in trade (Rogowski, 1988; Schwartz, 1993). The nineteenth century economy was, however, unstable and subject to periods of booms and busts. Capital movements were largely free of government interference—and government protection. Thus, vast flows of capital—mostly from London—waxed and waned according to private speculation. Great fortunes were both made and lost. The spread of industrial capacity from Britain and northwest Europe to central Europe and the United States after 1865—along with the development of new agricultural zones in the Americas and Oceania—contributed to a worldwide depression in 1873-96. However, in this period, British foreign direct investments created the conditions for a new industrial revolution at the turn of the century.

When World War I broke out in 1914, the "classical" gold standard as it had functioned during the previous decades came to an end. The old pillar of stability and cohesion was gone. It has often been stated that World War I was a watershed in economic as well as political history. It was clear that the closely knit fabric of the prewar world economy had been torn apart. Four years of armed conflict involving all major industrial states hastened underlying forces that were altering the foundation of the prewar system even before the outbreak of war. The war provided the occasion for an expansion of governmental activities, not merely over trade and payments, but over all aspects of economic activity. The war weakened the nineteenth-century political and economic elite consensus that had managed to prevail until 1914. After 1918, statesmen, politicians, business leaders and intellectuals had less faith in the principles of classical liberalism, and new precedents were established for government involvement in domestic economic and social regulation.

Suspension of the gold standard and currency convertibility during the war removed the outside discipline that had previously harmonized the price structures of independent countries. Freed from gold-standard discipline, governments printed inconvertible paper money to mobilize domestic resources, and inevitably inflation advanced unevenly, distorting the relative values of national currencies. By 1919, for example, wholesale prices had increased approximately 200 percent over 1913 levels in the United States, 300 percent in Britain, and 430 percent in France (Eckes, 1975: 7). This rate of inflation imperiled a quick return to the gold standard, partly because it stretched existing gold reserves and threatened to drain Europe of gold, precipitating a serious bout of deflation.

In addition, the war concluded with the world's stock of monetary gold inadequate and unevenly distributed. While other prices jumped, according to Eckes, the value of gold fixed by monetary authorities did not, and, as a consequence, the world output of gold actually declined about one-third between 1915 and 1922. What gold there was in official reserves was redistributed, and the United States emerged with 34 percent of all monetary gold, compared to 27 percent before the war (Eckes, 1975: 7). With inadequate gold reserves countries could not accept the obligations of fixed parities, unless outside assistance was available.

Perhaps the most significant economic consequence of the war was the decline of Britain as the dominant trade and financial center and the rise of the United States as a global economic power. World War I turned the United States from a debtor to a creditor, and, as the leading source of long-term capital in the 1920s, the United States had to adjust its economic policies to the new role. As Frieden (1988) points out, the foreign economic policy of the United States in the interwar period was closely tied to domestic political struggle between domestic economic actors with conflicting interests in the international economy, and thus different foreign economic policy preferences. After World War I, there was a dramatic expansion in American overseas investment, especially overseas lending. By 1929 American overseas private assets were $21 billion—equivalent to one-fifth of the country's gross national product, a level that reached again only in 1981 (Frieden, 1988: 63). Many U.S. banks and corporations in technologically-advanced and extractive industries saw great opportunities for overseas expansion, and fought for U.S. foreign economic policy to be assertively "internationalist." Other U.S. corporations, mostly in traditional labor-intensive industries that served principally the domestic market, saw the world economy primarily as a competitive threat and fought for protection and "isolation." Through the 1920s and early 1930s, the two broad coalitions battled to dominate foreign economic policy. The result was an uneasy standoff, in which the two camps entrenched themselves in different portions of the state apparatus, so that policy often ran on two tracks and was sometimes internally contradictory.

Though it is often asserted that the United States in the interwar years "failed to accept the mantle of 'hegemonic leadership'" that had passed from Britain, the contribution by Americans to the stabilization of the world economy after World War I was in fact substantial. While the United States government remained outwardly aloof, an informal coalition of central and private bankers took charge of monetary reconstruction and proceeded to stabilize European economies (Eckes, 1975; Helleiner, 1993). With the encouragement of central bankers—especially Benjamin Strong of the New York Federal Reserve Bank and Montagu Norman of the Bank of England—a consortium of American banks quietly cooperated to work out in 1924 the Dawes loan to Germany, and took steps to stabilize both the dollar and the pound. Though the U.S. government itself was unwilling to commit itself to Europe's recovery in a direct way, it was willing to see private American capital play a key role in this process (Walter, 1991: 124). During the 1920s, the United States lent about $10 billion overseas—equal, in real terms, to one-quarter of all nineteenth-century lending by all creditor countries and rivaling the post-World War II Marshall Plan (Schwartz, 1994: 192).

On the other side of the Atlantic, British authorities, determined to maintain London's position as the world's banking center and to restore the pound's prestige, embarked on a controversial austerity program designed to wring out wartime inflation and appreciate sterling. Austerity at home, combined with a $200 million gold credit from the New York Federal Reserve Bank, set the stage for Britain's decision to restore sterling convertibility at the prewar gold parity in April 1925 (Eckes, 1975: 12). Unfortunately, British policymakers underestimated the difficulties. For, at the old par value, sterling was overvalued, perhaps between ten and eleven percent, and, as a result, British manufactures, already becoming technologically obsolete, experienced added difficulty competing in world markets. Unemployment mounted and public pressures grew as the authorities doggedly pursued stringent domestic policies so as to reduce wages, prices, and profits in order to maintain gold convertibility.

Britain's experience with stabilization is a classic demonstration of what became known as the Mundell-Fleming condition: the difficulty of achieving simultaneously a stable exchange rate, unrestricted capital mobility, and domestic policy discretion. No longer, it appeared, would domestic opinion tolerate sharp, unpleasant internal adjustments to support exchange-rate stabilization. Moreover, the interwar British experience revealed that economic structures in industrial states were less flexible than previously. Trade union resistance to wage cuts, government social welfare policies, and business reluctance to reduce prices all impeded domestic and income adjustments.

After Britain anchored sterling to gold, France stabilized the franc—at an undervalued level—and more than thirty other governments made similar decisions. European countries had suffered a major economic setback. One way to reflate moribund economies is through export promotion. Maintaining an undervalued currency makes domestically-produced goods relatively cheaper on the international market and makes foreign-produced goods relatively expensive on the domestic market. Thereby, an undervalued currency can both boost net exports and protect domestic producers of import-competing goods.

The "free riding" of France and other continental states on the British-backed gold-exchange system undermined the international monetary stability. As Kenneth Oye (1985) reveals in his study of interwar monetary diplomacy, the increasing misalignment of exchange rates eroded confidence in sterling as growth in official sterling reserve balances by other European states increased possible one-time losses from a devaluation of the British currency.

During the late 1920s the central bank monetary powers, led by America's Strong and Britain's Norman, supervised and aided the piecemeal stabilization process. First, they fixed the value of major currencies in terms of gold. "In a time of prosperity, these conservative governments [the United States and Britain] acted on the orthodox belief that the defense of parities, through intervention on exchange markets if possible and through domestic deflation if necessary, was essential to the preservation of business confidence, the pursuit of financial preeminence, and the promotion of economic growth" (Oye, 1985: 177). Second, to facilitate internal economic adjustments, in moves that foreshadowed those of the post-World War II International Monetary Fund, they often provided gold credits to the local central banks in return for government assurance to pursue orthodox economic policies (i.e., maintain a balanced budget, follow non-inflationary monetary policy, and preserve central bank independence). These conditions established, the central bankers provided credit references enabling local governments to borrow additional sums from private bankers to undertake specific internal reconstruction programs.

From 1925 to 1929 the world economy regained its prewar momentum. Between the return of Britain to the gold standard, now a "gold-exchange" standard, in 1925, and the French stabilization in 1928, most of the other principal countries of the world had returned to the gold standard. The U.S. Federal Reserve was able to announce in August 1928 "the practical completion of the world's monetary reconstruction" (Dam, 1982: 45). Once more, currencies became relatively stable and convertible. Despite distortions of protective tariffs, commerce flourished, and by 1927 the volume of world trade was approximately 20 percent higher than in 1913. Stable and convertible currencies enabled trading states to balance their earnings from one region with payments to other areas, thus lubricating the way for an effective international division of labor (Eckes, 1975: 14).

Currency stabilization established a favorable climate for capital movements. The flow of long-term capital rose steadily from 1919 to 1929, especially after 1925. Whereas London supplied the bulk of investment capital before World War I, New York emerged as the principal capital exporter in the 1920s. American capital exports helped to provide the stabilizing countries with the requisite liquidity. In 1928, for instance, the United States invested $1,099 million abroad; Britain, $569 million; and France, $237 million. During the decade before the 1929 collapse, the United States supplied about $7 billion of the approximately $10 billion invested overseas (Eckes, 1975: 14).

While United States did supply the critical margin of liquidity required to sustain a high level of international transactions and to facilitate repayment of war debts and reparations for most of the 1920s, the capital flows slowed down abruptly in 1928 as funds were diverted into short-term financing of the New York Stock Exchange boom. These so-called "hot money" flows, and the speculative "bubbles" they create were a major source of financial market instability. As mentioned in the introduction of this work, a successful international monetary and financial order must meet three criteria: liquidity, adjustment, and confidence. On the adjustment front, the cost of austerity increasingly became onerous for Britain, and the commitment of American business to internationalism was shaky at best. Just as the New York financial community sought out new opportunities to lend, domestic import-competing corporations demanded the continuation of protection. As Eckes points out, the United States tried to lend abroad and protect a balance of trade surplus simultaneously. This is possible as long as capital flowed abroad in sufficient volume to cover debt repayments and to provide the dollars other countries needed to continue buying American exports.

In October 1929, the third criterion, confidence, became an important factor. The central bank officials who devised the currency stabilization and convertibility programs, in their haste to reconstruct a gold-exchange standard, gave inadequate attention to the market value of currencies or differences in national price levels. As a result, stabilization was piecemeal and uncoordinated. Britain's overvalued parity exposed her domestic market to more intense import competition, reducing her export competitiveness, and compelling monetary authorities to maintain artificially high interest rates to protect that country's gold reserve. France, on the other hand, selected an undervalued rate. This permitted France to gain an export surplus and accumulate gold. French gold reserves increased from $954 million in 1927 to $1,633 million in late 1932, and the flow of gold to Paris placed added strain on London and other monetary centers (Eckes, 1975: 16).

The dynamics of these currency moves should not be lost upon scholars of power politics. Britain adherence to the prewar parity was as much, if not more, a reflection of British elites' desire for London to remain the world financial capital. After all, financial prowess bestows influence to those who possesses it. London as a financial center was intimately tied to London as an imperial capital. It can be said that the British government maintained overvaluation in a misguided attempt to portray strength (Walter, 1991: 123). The steadfast refusal to devalue is part of a strategy to convey stability of the currency. Stable currencies are the ones in which internationally-traded commodities are priced. Therefore, the key currency country does have, to some extent, market power over those prices. Furthermore, given that the key currency in a gold-exchange standard also serves as a reserve asset, maintenance of stability is crucial in order to preserve its "store of value" function.

The drop in American capital flows, coupled with the growth of French reserves and their conversion into gold, put strong pressure on the pound. British gold reserves were probably even less ample than before World War I and now Britain suffered from an overvalued currency. When the 1931 Macmillan report showed, in an attempt to reassure the foreign exchange markets, that Britain's net short-term liabilities were only £254 million, the market found the news anything but reassuring in view of the fact that the Bank of England's total holdings of gold were only about £150 million and most of that was required as domestic backing for the pound (Dam, 1982: 46). In July 1931 alone, the Bank of England lost nearly £32 million of gold. Despite foreign credits, withdrawal of foreign balances beginning in mid-July reached £200 million by mid-September. On September 21, 1931, the British government suspended sterling convertibility into gold, effectively leaving the gold standard.

The international monetary and financial system, established on the ashes of the classical gold standard, had no adequate adjustment and corrective mechanism and functioned poorly. Besides, international cooperation and coordination were severely lacking which made the system crisis prone, particularly when occasional crises of confidence precipitated mass transfers of gold and currencies from monetary center to another. That the gold-exchange standard was less stable than the old gold standard became known in the 1920s when political unrest, uncoordinated currency alignments, and divergent interest rates in major money centers encouraged periodic movements of speculative capital from country to the next. To control these disruptive capital movements required a greater degree of monetary and financial coordination than the central bankers had developed. In brief, institutions and procedures had not evolved quickly enough to cope with the expectations and scope of operations of the new exchange system. Given that the interwar parities reflected prewar conditions, the stress on governments to maintain them in the face of transforming social expectations proved too great. As Eckes commented, "in the unbalanced world of the 1920s, then, countries sought the best of two systems—they wanted the benefits of fixed currency rates and open markets, but they also wanted the advantages of economic self-determination. This conflict, a basic one between the requirements of international and internal stability, became critical when the world plunged into the Great Depression" (Eckes, 1975: 17).

BREAKING WITH ORTHODOXY

The Great Depression of the 1930s was the greatest economic catastrophe since the industrial economy's beginnings in the mid-eighteenth century, marking a turning point in global economic history as deflation shattered fragile international economic ties and forced governments to sacrifice the advantages of interdependence in order to shelter domestic economies from the uncertainties of the world economy. Statistics compiled by the League of Nations measure the Depression's crippling impact on world and national economies (Eckes, 1975: 19): between 1929 and 1932 world prices dropped 47.5 percent, and the value of world trade declined over 60 percent; the volume of world trade fell about 25 percent; an estimated 25 million industrial lost their jobs; in twenty-four countries for which statistics were available, the total income lost reached $60 billion in 1932, a figure approximately equal to the total income of all these countries, exclusive of the United States and Britain in 1929. In the United States, between August 1929 and March 1933, the real output of goods and services declined by one-third, industrial production plummeted by one-half, one-fourth of the labor force became unemployed, the banking system was closed, and the values of financial assets and real properties were destroyed (Jones, 1990).

In disaster, the international division of labor[1], already becoming more intense in the crisis of the late nineteenth century, deepened dramatically. The expansion of the years before the First World War had spread productive capacity into new areas, deepened it in older ones, and brought into being a new generation of products and a new round of production techniques. The failure of the major economic powers to resurrect a stable liberal international economic order from the ashes of the Great War set up the conditions of the liquidity crunch and crisis of confidence that precipitated the crash of 1929.

In 1931 the Depression entered a second phase with the great contraction brought on by the global currency crisis. After Britain abandoned the gold-exchange standard, the world monetary system disintegrated into rival blocs and autarkic units. The effect of suspension of gold payments by London was a sharp depreciation of sterling against all gold-exchange standard currencies. Fifteen countries followed Britain off gold in 1931, and another nine did so in 1932. Most of these countries, chiefly those in the British Commonwealth and including some others that held reserves primarily in sterling, elected to allow their currencies to depreciate with the pound.

The rise of currency blocs and imperial preference zones severed the interconnectedness of the world economy. The end of the fixed exchange rate system created uncertainty in the currency markets. Large fluctuations in currency values hindered trade and stimulated large moves of speculative capital. This period witnessed the extensive use of capital controls as a policy tool as well as a shift in the locus of policymaking authority. Largely discredited by the Depression and currency crisis, the private and central bankers who had dominated financial politics before the 1930s were increasingly replaced at the levers of financial power by professional economists, industrialists, and labor groups working through their respective finance ministries or treasuries (Helleiner, 1993: 22). Where the bankers had advocated a laissez-faire approach to domestic financial issues, and the following of automatic "rules of the game" in the international financial sphere, these new groups favored a more interventionist approach that would make domestic and international finance serve broader political and economic goals.

During the 1930s economic policymakers grappled with seemingly unsolvable problems. The ideal liberal international economy consisted of relatively stable exchange rates and relatively unrestricted movements of goods and capital. No longer, however, could realistic policymakers single-mindedly promote these foreign economic objectives without regard to the internal implications of external stability in a liberal world. Their problem was one of reconciling the advantages of specialization and efficiency in a liberal world with the requirements of internal stability of prices and employment.

Like the departure from the gold standard, the increasing use of capital controls represented an important part of the structural break from liberal traditions in financial affairs (Helleiner, 1993: 22). While the pre-1931 period was not entirely free of capital controls, their use was limited to achieving short-term security goals—such as denying to enemy states access to one's own capital markets. After 1931 capital controls became a permanent feature of new macroeconomic strategies.

After leaving the gold-exchange standard, British authorities decided in 1932 to create an Exchange Equalization Account, which permitted intervention in the foreign exchange markets while insulating the domestic money supply from the otherwise direct influence of those transactions (Dam, 1982: 47). Japan and Germany went further in both their use of capital controls and in the setting up of bilateral trading systems that allowed Tokyo and Berlin to manipulate its trade for maximum mercantilist advantage.

In the United States the incoming Roosevelt Administration, supported by a coalition of farmers, labor groups and "progressive" business leaders, had to choose whether to push for international accords to stabilize currencies and revive trade and investments or concentrate on domestic recovery. It, not surprisingly, opted for the latter through a depreciation of the dollar in the foreign exchange markets. The goal was to reflate domestic prices of internationally-traded commodities. In choice of policy, the Roosevelt Administration was opposed by the banking community which generally favored governmental initiatives to strengthen currencies, reduce the debt burden, and liberalize trade and investment flows.

The administration signaled its intention to manage the foreign exchange value of the dollar by imposing exchange controls and a gold export embargo, thereby taking the dollar off the gold-exchange standard and creating a state monopoly over the supply of domestic gold. In the summer of 1933, Roosevelt delivered his "bombshell message" (Eckes, 1975: 22), shattering the World Economic Conference that was meeting in London to negotiate a stabilization arrangement among the United States, Britain, and the gold-exchange countries.

The Depression, as mentioned earlier, was a realigning event that upset the existing order of macroeconomic policymaking. The election of the Roosevelt Administration was a triumph of a coalition that placed domestic recovery above of international stability. The Depression had already reduced the volume and value of trade and investment, thereby reducing the resources available to the New York financial community. The arrival in Washington of a new generation of "policy managers" —particularly in the Treasury Department of Henry Morgenthau—created an adversarial coexistence between government and finance akin to that between management and workers in industrial relations. While in the latter relationship, management needs workers for the enterprise to prosper, it battles with workers over wages and working conditions. Banning non-factory unions and Taylorization of labor are ways to reduce worker power and make them a more pliant resource. Likewise, by weakening finance's ties abroad and introducing regulations separating investment and commercial banking for instance, government was attempting to rein in its most powerful yet unwieldy resource. A series of important initiatives was launched in an effort to bring financial and monetary policy under greater control from Washington. These new regulations (detailed in Chapter 5) were introduced to moderate competition, increase investor protection, and reduce the power of the New York financial community.

The Roosevelt Administration's international financial policy of dollar devaluation (the gold value of the dollar declined from a pre-1933 parity of $20.67 per ounce to $35 in January 1934, when it was pegged at that level by the Gold Reserve Act) met only limited success as other states countered with devaluations of their own. The cumulative effect of these competitive devaluations was further instability in international monetary and financial relations. A brief attempt at regional monetary coordination, the so-called "gold bloc" of Western and Central European states, came under pressure with the American devaluation. Gold bloc member Belgium devalued its currency by 28 percent in March 1935 (Salvatore, 1990: 626). In September 1936 the French government withdrew from the bloc. Fear of a new round of competitive devaluations abounded when the French, British, and American governments agreed to the Tripartite Agreement, one of the first moves toward multilateralism in monetary affairs.

Under the Tripartite Agreement, each government committed itself to convert any balances of its own currencies acquired by the other governments at an announced price, which was subject to change at any time, so long as the conversion was made within twenty-four hours; the conversion would be at the price in effect at the time of the currency's acquisition, not at the time of conversion (Dam, 1982: 49). The Tripartite Agreement represented a cease-fire by the governments of the three major money centers to rein in competitive and speculative pressures. Clearly, the cost of further instability was greater for all parties than any gains that could be achieved through devaluation. In effect, the game of monetary relations had changed from Prisoner's Dilemma to one of Chicken.

The Tripartite Agreement marked a transition point. First, the United States had emerged as the dominant player on the international financial stage (between 1928 and 1938 American gold reserves increased from 37 to 56 percent of the world's supply) (Eckes, 1975: 24). Second, governments, operating through their finance ministers, displayed unprecedented determination to collaborate and intervene in private currency markets so as to stabilize currency values. One important manifestation of this was the proliferation of exchange stabilization funds. Third, the agreement signaled the subordination of central banks to national treasuries. The decline of central banks in favor of treasuries in international monetary and financial relations had a direct impact on the negotiation of the Bretton Woods agreement. It was assumed from the very beginning that the structure of the postwar international monetary and financial system was an issue for governments, and specifically for treasuries, and that central banks would play a strictly subordinate role (Dam, 1982: 54). In the words of John Maynard Keynes, the chief British negotiator:

> Not merely as a feature of the transition but as a permanent arrangement, the plan accords every member government the explicit right to control all capital movements. What used to be heresy is now endorsed as orthodoxy (quoted in Helleiner, 1995: 164).

PRESENT AT THE CREATION: THE BRETTON WOODS CONFERENCE

Recalling how economic nationalism had turned prewar neighbors into enemies, and ultimately brought ruin to all, American Secretary of the Treasury Henry Morgenthau opened proceedings on the creation of new international monetary and financial order in Bretton Woods, New Hampshire, in July 1944. During the interwar years the gold-exchange standard remained a collection of informal arrangements among private and central bankers. By the time of its ultimate collapse, with the devaluation of the gold bloc currencies in 1936, both the national and international rules of the monetary and financial game had changed. The coming of war and the initiation of planning for the postwar order had the effect of encouraging a decisive shift away from liberal financial traditions. Morgenthau explained the rationale for this experiment in world monetary organization by saying, "We have come to recognize that the wisest and most effective way to protect our national interests is through international cooperation" (Eckes, 1975: x). Morgenthau and other officials recognized the historic significance of their deliberations. For the first time in peace preparations, governments had acted on the assumption that finance must serve as the handmaiden for world politics if victors were to overcome the dislocations of war and establish a durable framework for lasting peace.

The dominant role of the United States and Britain in postwar economic planning affected the Bretton Woods regime in important ways. The anticipated economic position of the two countries at war's end established the parameters of possible arrangements. Given that American influence was greater than that of the British, the final draft of the accords more reflected the positions of the American executive branch at that time.

The Bretton Woods accords culminated a dramatic shift in economic power, underway since the late nineteenth century, from Britain to the United States. American industrial predominance was already an accomplished fact even before the First World War. American financial predominance became unquestioned during the interwar years. The material capacity of American political and economic elites to exercise the management of world order had existed since 1920. However the United States was a country with a small international sector (i.e., the proportion of total output derived from the export of goods of services). American industry was domestically-focused. Financial interests, though powerful and led by the big New York City banks, were limited in size and direct influence on the larger "real" economy.

The Depression had shattered old notions of the government's role in the economy. The "management revolution" and planning techniques implemented in mass industry were gradually being adopted by governments, who sought to control aggregate demand conditions in much the same manner as corporate managers controlled inventories. The freedom of financial capital interests was circumscribed as the breakdown of international transactions shifted political influence to relatively immobile industrial capital and labor: "By 1936, the New Deal had vastly expanded organized labor's membership and power through such measures as the Wagner Act; had sealed a new alliance between workers and the Democratic party; had laid the foundations of the welfare state in the United States" (Rogowski, 1989: 71). This period, which included wartime controls, also witnessed the greatest intervention by government into the operation of the American economy. In chapter 3 I will detail further the acceptance demand management policies in the United States, their subsequent export to the rest of the industrialized world—under American aegis, and their eventual downfall in the stagflation years of the 1970s.

The Bretton Woods Conference deliberants had before them three fundamentally different solutions to the monetary and financial instability that had brought their states to ruin in the 1930s: (a) fixed rates under a gold standard; (b) flexible fiduciary currencies; and (c) controls. Each of these solutions provided a different answer to the question of how can states with divergent macroeconomic structures and currency systems maintain external equilibrium and obtain the benefits of open trade and investment in a world economy. Basically, adherence to the gold standard required sacrificing domestic stability for maximum gains from trade, capital, and currency movements. Both flexible rates and controls tended to subordinate international gains to the need for expansionary domestic economic policy. Flexible rates subjected the burden of adjustment to the market—permitting currencies to adjust imbalances—and involved minimum government intervention and interference with movements of goods and capital. Controls, by contrast, were dependent on extensive official management of international economic contacts to prevent (assuming effective government management) destabilizing fluctuations of currencies and domestic economies. While it provided greater security, it reduced the gains from economic efficiency and seemed to disrupt multilateral trade and investment patterns.

While debate continued in academic circles, officials reached a consensus centered on a return to fixed, but adjustable, currency values anchored to gold; continued restrictions on short-term capital movements; and more vigorous, and coordinated, government management of domestic economies through continuous application of monetary and fiscal tools. The new emphasis was on coordinated national management to even out business cycles, regulate capital movements, and adjust currency values; but this management, it was understood, would have to take place, at least in the short-run, without formal infringement on the sovereignty of each state to regulate its own destiny.

While the Bretton Woods negotiations are often portrayed as a battle of wills between Britain's John Maynard Keynes and America's Harry Dexter White (Eckes, 1975; Dam, 1982; Nau, 1990) over the design of the postwar international economy, they were in agreement on the issue of international movements of private finance. Both Keynes and White outlined early on in the negotiations two central reasons why capital controls would be necessary in the postwar world (Helleiner, 1993: 26). First, international financial movements could not be allowed to disrupt the policy autonomy of the new interventionist welfare state. Their key concern was protecting the new national macroeconomic planning techniques that had emerged in the 1930s. Drawing on the experience of the 1930s, Keynes and White both reasoned that capital controls would be a necessity in order to prevent speculative capital flows that could undermine national policymaking. Second, such speculative flight capital could place an undue balance-of-payments constraint on the domestic macroeconomic objectives of debtor states, by denying such states the liquidity needed for successful adjustment.

Keynes went even further in noting that not only "speculative" financial flows, but even "normal" flows which responded to interest rate differentials between countries could disrupt national macroeconomic planning. Detailing what became the "global monetarist" view of the 1970s and 1980s, Keynes noted that a country with a current account deficit that attempted to maintain lower interest rates than the prevailing international norm would find itself subject to severe "disequilibrating" outflows of such movements. Similarly, a country with a current account surplus wanting to raise rates above the those existing elsewhere (i.e., the "world rate of interest") would attract "disequilibrating" capital inflows. If interest rates were to be determined by domestic macroeconomic priorities and not by considerations of external balance, such financial movements would need to be controlled in order to avoid external constraint on such policy.

Keynes and White noted that the policy autonomy of the new welfare state was threatened by financial movements in two other ways. First, the new domestic financial regulatory structures that had been created for the purpose of facilitating industrial and macroeconomic planning would be undermined if savers and borrowers had access to external financial markets. Second, the welfare state also had to be protected from capital flight induced by "political reasons" or a desire to evade "burdens of social legislation." In Chapter V, I go into greater detail on how capital's "exit" option limits policy autonomy and perforce a change in the budget allocation of governments to one that better benefits capital interests.

In addition to wanting to protect the policy autonomy of the new welfare state, Keynes and White also favored capital controls in order to preserve a stable international exchange system and liberal trading order. Noting that speculative financial movements were "one of the chief causes of foreign exchange disturbances," such capital flows would need to be controlled if a stable set of exchange rates was to be maintained. Furthermore, capital controls, by stabilizing exchange rates, would facilitate free trade by smoothing the adjustment process, thereby dampening protectionist sentiment.

Although Keynes and White noted that capital movements from states with a surplus on their current account to those with a deficit were to be favored—in that they would help maintain an equilibrium in the international monetary system—the two policymakers made it clear that the overriding "norm" in their plans was that of controlling capital (Helleiner, 1993: 28). The disruptive nature of "speculative" and "disequilibrating" movements of capital flows was so severe that states had to be given the right to use capital controls. The priority given to capital controls reflected the importance they attached to the goal of defending the policy autonomy of the new welfare state. The particularly disruptive nature of financial movements made a liberal financial order less easy to reconcile with desires for policy autonomy than a liberal trading order.

The priority given to controlling finance also reflected the "secondary" status of a liberal financial system in their vision of a liberal international economic order. Faced with the prospect of a liberal financial system disrupting a stable international exchange rate system and liberal trading order, there was consensus at Bretton Woods that the former should be sacrificed in order to preserve the latter. The skepticism towards the benefits of a liberal financial system partly reflected the way in which the international lending of the 1920s had ended in the financial disaster of the early 1930s. It was also a product of the fact that "free finance" had not achieved the same sacred status as "the gold standard" or "free trade" in liberal thinking. Indeed, when the virtues of international capital movements had been discussed in the pre-1931 period, it had usually been in terms of their contribution to the gold standard and a liberal trading system. Among those who had initiated academic discussion in the interwar period of the absolute benefits of a liberal financial system, there was a widespread feeling that the classical case in favor of free trade was less relevant to the financial sector. "Embedded Liberalism"—the desire to create an open international economy that would not interfere with the policy autonomy of the new welfare state—was thus pushed in the "embedded" direction in the financial sector (Helleiner, 1993: 29).

The Bretton Woods arrangements did not set the stage for the international financial integration of recent years. As Helleiner (1993, 1994) points out, they built a multilateral order in which capital controls and financial interventionism were strengthened. The failure of the central bankers to stabilize exchange rates after the First World War, followed by the depression, shifted power to Keynesian "embedded liberals," who wanted to defend the policy autonomy of the new welfare state from international financial market pressures. At the same time, the alliance between bankers in New York and London, which had dominated politics in the 1920s, was weakened. Keynesian policies of nationally-segmented finance with state macroeconomic intervention (and in some cases, state direction of credit allocation) become the norm in Western industrialized states.

Just as the Bretton Woods order was reaching its height, with the convertibility of European currencies in 1958, the seeds of its eventual breakdown were being sowed. The alliance between bankers in New York and London was reconstructed, this time in the guise of transnational banks—which provided funding for the growing American transnational corporate presence in Europe. This alliance was instrumental in creating the external currency markets in the 1960s, and encouraging financial integration in the 1970s and 1980s. What is intriguing about this development was that it occurred in the shadow of American predominance in the postwar international economic order.

"SMITH ABROAD, KEYNES AT HOME": THE BRETTON WOODS REGIME

American politico-economic dominance and embedded liberalism combined after the Second World War to foster an international regime of "Smith abroad and Keynes at home." That is, while international economic coordination was promoted on exchange rate management and the lowering of trade barriers, there was a period of significant policy autonomy, in which national financial markets were relatively self-contained and governments had an enhanced degree of policy latitude. According to Gourevitch (1986), the Depression of the 1930s contributed to World War II by shaping the coalitions that took power in dealing with it. The war then reopened issues of political economy by shaking loose the political settlements of the 1930s. In postwar years the policy debate resumed, augmented by the titanic consequences of the war itself. This time the countries of Western Europe and North America converged in their approaches to policies and economic policy, building in effect a compromise to end the battles of the thirties. They built accommodations, *de facto* or *de jure*, among societal actors.

Labor accepted capitalist management of an economy run on the basis of market incentives (even for nationalized industries) in exchange for a welfare system, high wages, employment-oriented macroeconomic policy, and constitutional protection of organizing rights. Agriculture kept the extensive system of market stabilization in exchange for its support of broad programs for labor and business. Business accepted these policy shifts in exchange for maintenance of many of the regulatory mechanisms that stabilized markets and controls over investment and management. Under American leadership the compromise was attained in the context of an open world economy.

Although policy mixes vary substantially among Western governments, the character of state activism in economic management from 1945 onward diverges strongly from both the classical and protectionist policy patterns that predominated in earlier decades. The system produced by this compromise sustained prodigious economic growth, and successes strengthened the accommodation. Keynesian policies of demand management, which achieved prominence in American academic and policy circles during the war, were exported to the rest of the industrialized world during the reconstruction period after the war (Hall, 1989). Keynesianism assumes a relatively closed market with limited capital mobility, which gave governments enhanced power and legitimacy to intervene in the economy with countercyclical fiscal and monetary policies. The shift in domestic political forces and attitudes occurred in most major countries after the war and was reflected in a significantly greater contribution of government expenditure to GDP in the following years. According to Walter (1991), government expenditures as a percentage of GDP in France rose from 29 percent in 1938 to 39 percent in 1960 and 50 percent in 1985. Figures for the same years for Germany were 37 percent, 32 percent, and 49 percent; in Britain, 29 percent, 35 percent, and 46 percent; and in the United States 22 percent, 28 percent, and 38 percent.

The pursuance of Keynesianism nationally was underwritten by U.S. monetary and economic leadership internationally, with the issue of capital controls being at the center of alternatives under consideration in creating a new international monetary regime. The U.S. government, reflecting the evolution of attitudes among both the policy and the business communities against protectionism, held a bias against controls. Because the United States was dominant in the production of high value-added goods, it stood to gain most from an unrestricted trading system (Epstein and Schor, 1992: 138). The State Department, since the late 1930s, had been pushing for non-discrimination, free trade, protection of overseas investment, and multilateralism. American financiers were looking forward to an era where dollar-based financing would dominate the financial landscape with free movement of capital.

The postwar international economic order was born on the efforts of the United States to shore up Western European governments against what American policymakers perceived as a threat of growing Soviet and Communist influence. That policy prompted the United States to shelve its liberal reformist ambitions, as embodied above all in the Bretton Woods agreements, and to assign priority to European political and economic integration (Loriaux, 1991). The final policy position agreed to in the International Monetary Fund's Articles took the view that controls on capital should be removed as soon as possible. However, in view of the economic difficulties facing member countries, the timetable for the elimination of controls was extended. The Bretton Woods agreements acknowledged the legitimacy of capital controls, and instructed member states to aid in the enforcing those controls (Hawley, 1987: 7). The agreements did not foresee, and were not intended, to facilitate the free movement of capital, nor did they officially recognize the dollar as an internationally acceptable reserve and transaction currency. Still, only the dollar represented a national economy that was able to support a key currency. A fixed relationship was established between gold and the dollar ($35 per ounce of gold) and a commitment by the U.S. government to exchange gold for dollars at any time made the American currency the universally accepted "currency against which every other country sold or redeemed its own national currency in the exchange markets" (Triffin, 1978-1979). The postwar reconstruction of Europe and Japan through the Marshall and Dodge Plans, respectively, and the rearmament of Europe, further ensured the dollar's status as the reserve and transaction currency.

The willingness of foreign central banks to hold dollars as a reserve and of individuals and firms to transact their business in dollars ensured that the United States could run a continual payments deficit with little threat to the dollar's status or stability prior to 1958. These *de facto* loans by foreign governments, individuals, and firms transformed the United States into a *de facto* central bank able to create global liquidity, promote trade expansion, and simultaneously run long-term payments deficits. This method of financing under the Bretton Woods system was nearly automatic. It also bestowed upon the United States a special financial privilege (Triffin, 1960). When Europe was devastated and in need of reconstruction aid, the inflow of American dollars was a welcome source of liquidity and alleviated possible disinflationary adjustment measures from taking place. In the 1950s, continued U.S. military and economic aid, heavy American private investment, and the growing American appetite for imports and tourism all helped stimulate and stabilize world prosperity and development (Calleo, 1987: 84).

After 1960, the American outflow of dollars began to seem excessive. Triffin (1960), writing at the time, focused attention on the U.S. liquidity ratio—the declining ratio of U.S. gold reserves to outstanding dollar liabilities. In 1958-59, the United States lost $3.4 billion in gold reserves, compared to $1.7 billion in the previous eight years (Walter, 1991: 166). As the international public and private role of the dollar steadily grew over the 1950s and 1960s, the desire of the rest of the world to accumulate reserves and to maintain their gold composition was gradually eroding the U.S. gold stock and ultimately the gold convertibility of the dollar (Walter, 1991: 167). The costs of extensive U.S. military activities, foreign economic and military aid, and massive private investments produced increasing payments deficits. Given these circumstances, the possibility that the United States might devalue the dollar led to a loss of confidence by others and to their unwillingness to continue to hold dollars as reserve currency (Kegley and Wittkopf, 1995; Calleo, 1987; Nau, 1990).

Beginning in the mid-1960s, the situation of the dollar glut became a major source of grievance between the United States and Europe, particularly France: "the accumulating dollar balances in the central banks of Europe and Japan were seen as little better than forced loans, sometimes to finance activities that many Europeans opposed" (Calleo, 1987: 85). De Gaulle in particular viewed American "exorbitant privilege" in world currency markets as part of the overall American politico-economic dominance of Europe. For De Gaulle, and for an increasing number of American analysts as well, the U.S. payments deficit reflected the expenses of *Pax Americana*. "The hegemon's overseas costs were not being met by its overseas income" (Calleo,

1987: 86). As Gilpin (1981) points out, one way to bring costs and resources into balance is to reduce foreign-policy commitments. The most direct method of retrenchment is unilateral abandonment of certain of a state's economic, political, or military commitments. The Nixon Administration's closing of the gold window on August 15, 1971 can thus be viewed as part of an overall strategy of retrenchment, which included the Nixon Doctrine, Vietnamization, and an emphasis on "burden-sharing" with the allies.

The liquidity-confidence trade-off that underlies the payments deficits explanation of the collapse of the Bretton Woods order does not stand unchallenged. According to monetarist economists, the demise of the Bretton Woods order emanates from the very Keynesian practices that the regime had protected. For most Western governments, the outcome of the American provision of global liquidity and maintenance of international stability was a world economic order that enhanced and prolonged the viability of their postwar interventionist and demand-management policy orientation. It was that policy orientation, in turn, that ultimately generated conditions of "moral hazard" in the political economy of industrial states. Government intervention in the domestic economy to promote growth created the belief among both businesses and individuals that government had "solved" the business cycle. When economic downturns did occur, businesses looked to the government for fiscal and monetary stimulus in order to continue growth. When a state had more expansive monetary conditions than the norm in the international system, its excess money tended to flow out as a payments deficit. The increasing monetary interdependence of the industrial economies led to massive transnational movements of capital. It was these capital movements, precipitated by financial market operators, that disrupted the regulated Bretton Woods regime. Speculative capital movements, according to monetarists, "had nothing directly to do with the American basic [payments position], but were movements of short-term capital . . . responding to international monetary conditions" (Calleo, 1987: 86). The shift toward "full employment surplus" macroeconomic growth policies in the U.S. led to both expansionary fiscal and monetary policies in the mid-1960s.

Meanwhile, in Europe, the effects of the Keynesian welfare were taking hold in the form of an increasingly regulated microeconomy. According to Loriaux (1991), American financial hegemony created opportunities for state interventionist strategies in mid-sized industrial economies. Among these opportunities was the creation of credit-based financial systems, which provided plentiful credit at often negative real interest rates. Credit-based financial systems, however, are inherently inflationary because of a built-in bias toward easy monetary policy. As long as the American-centered, fixed exchange-rate system remained in effect, domestic inflation would not affect international competitiveness, because the national currency could be devalued. While Keynesian policies were well-suited and effective in an environment of robust global economic growth and steadily growing international trade that prevailed in the 1950s and 1960s, they did not prove themselves well adapted to a world of slow growth and changing patterns of international trade that emerged by the 1970s. Credit-based financial systems are especially fragile under conditions of slow growth, for firms that borrowed heavily at subsidized credit rates are forced to retrench in order to meet the fixed financial costs. An 1977 OECD study, cited by Nau (1990: 171), concluded that domestic policy errors in the 1960s contributed significantly to the developments after 1973: "the massive increase in monetary aggregates . . . contributed significantly to . . . the buildup of inflationary pressures . . . ." The same study also went on to note that the marked rise in government microeconomic intervention (i.e., market regulation) during the 1960s and early 1970s—with public expenditures increasing its share of OECD member-state GDP by four percentage points in 1964-74.

Although this expansion of the public sector enjoyed political support, it significantly raised economic costs. In France, where planning was already an important element in French economic policy, the government came to rely more heavily on public sector controls and instruments to consolidate French industry and develop national champions in key industry sectors (Nau, 1990: 172). As Hall (1989: 187) notes, "if the state actually intervened . . . more in the economy and society, that was not simply because its action was considered more desirable or more legitimate than in the past[; rather] the liberalism/interventionism issue was . . . transformed in this period by a new perception of the economic world as a system of [policy] action." Growth, employment, and purchasing power were no longer understood as results and balances; they became policy objectives. Keynesianism appeared within this context as the policy prescription best suited to this new situation.

The collapse of the international financial regime of fixed exchange rates and capital immobility, along with the diminishing effectiveness of national Keynesian policies, ushered in a decade of global crisis in the 1970s. With interventionism meeting with fewer and fewer successes, and the inadequacies of national Keynesian policies becoming increasing apparent, in the late 1970s and 1980s, industrial states embarked on financial liberalism.

Financial market liberalization was not a dramatic event, but rather an evolutionary process, as Western governments sought to cope with the changed international political economy. Indeed, deregulation of the financial sector is as much a response as a catalyst for liberalization. I will attempt to demonstrate that the change from fixed to flexible exchange rates altered the macroeconomic policy mix for governments. Liberalization can therefore be looked upon as an attempt by those governments to rebuild lost capability and to enhance the credibility of their policy options. No area of financial market liberalization reveals the changed position of government relative to financial market operators more than the rise of the Eurocurrency markets. Individual states (principally, the United States and Britain) initially supported these external currency markets as a means of unilaterally offering financial traders a location in which to operate without regulation (Helleiner, 1994: 12). These markets proved to be more successful than ever imagined, eventually undermining the power of governments themselves to manage financial flows. The competitive pressures to attract capital eventually undermined the capital control regime so carefully crafted at Bretton Woods.

PROMETHEUS UNBOUND: THE RISE OF THE EUROCURRENCY MARKETS

One of the more remarkable developments in the world political economy since the early 1960s has been the globalization of financial markets. As mentioned in the introduction, private international financial activity has grown at a phenomenal rate. But if the above discussion proved anything, it is that the Bretton Woods arrangements were crafted with the intent of controlling "flights of hot money."

But just how did international finance break out of the jail imposed upon it by states? The most popular explanation points to technological and market pressures (Helleiner, 1995). On the technological side, the creation of increasingly sophisticated telecommunications technologies has dramatically reduced the costs and difficulties involved in transferring money around the world. On the market side, five developments are said to have been significant. The first was the restoration of market confidence in the safety of international financial transactions in the late 1950s, a confidence that had been shaken by the crises and economic upheavals of the 1930s. The second was the rapid expansion in market demand for international financial services that accompanied the growth of trade and transnational corporate activity in the 1960s. The third was the depositing of enormous surplus funds in international banking markets by OPEC states after the 1973 oil price increase. The fourth was the move to flexible exchange rates in the 1970s, which encouraged market actors to diversify their assets internationally in the new volatile currency markets. Finally, the unravelling of inward-looking domestic financial compartmentalization across the advanced industrial world in the 1970s and 1980s pushed financial market operators into the international financial arena as a means of coping with increased domestic competitive pressures.

The growth and development of the external currency market—popularly known as the Eurocurrency market or the offshore market—are two of the more significant developments in world financial markets of the last three decades. From a small almost accidental beginning, the external currency market has evolved to a complete network of financial centers spanning the globe and providing much of the innovation in international banking and finance for the world.

The folklore associated with the development of the Eurocurrency market has it that the market started as a response of the Soviet government to political risk in the 1950s (Agmon, 1985: 24). At the time the Soviet government needed to transact in U.S. dollars, but in the days of the Cold War it was felt that there existed a real risk in placing these funds under the jurisdiction of the U.S. government. The solution was to transact in U.S. dollars in London. By doing that, the transactions were located outside the jurisdiction of both the American and British governments. Neither the U.S. government, nor its monetary authorities, has jurisdiction over U.S. dollar transactions outside the United States. The British government and the Bank of England have no jurisdiction over transactions in foreign currencies as long as the parties involved are not British nationals (individuals or corporations). What began as a solution to a specific and rather marginal problem of one country has grown to become one of the main features of the capital markets of the world today. The growth of what is basically a regulation-free market in the face of ever-growing government intervention laid the foundation for the collapse of the international capital control regime.

The largely unanswered and seldom-asked question is why these markets were allowed to operate. Agmon (1985) phases the same issue in a more traditional way by posing the following two related questions: (1) What is being "sold" by the external currency market to both business firms and individuals? and (2) What is the comparative advantage of the external currency market compared to the domestic capital markets in the major national economies of the world?

The external currency markets of the world supply services of financial intermediation. In doing so, they provide the same services as any other financial market, whether in New York, London, or Tokyo. The main difference is that due to their special position, and with the tacit approval of the governments of the world's leading national economies, they are free of government regulations and control. The absence of government control allows the external currency market to provide one explicit and two implicit special services to the business and investment communities: lower costs on both loans and deposit (the explicit advantage) and immediate and complimentary response to liquidity needs and a reduction in political risk due to future changes in existing regulations (the implicit advantages).

Johnston (1982) documented the efficiency of the external currency market in providing relatively high return to depositors and low cost to borrowers. The release from reserve requirements and cumbersome reporting requirements, and the ability to refuse service where it is not profitable makes the external currency markets more cost-efficient in providing services of financial intermediation than their domestic counterparts. In addition, the two implicit advantages of external currency markets make them a world-class political risk shelter.

Variable and uncertain inflation is often both the by-product of the struggle among rent-seeking groups as well as the triggering of a constant continuation of such a struggle. It follows that changes in monetary policy can be initiated to serve needs other than pure economics and finance: for example, the common belief in the United States that an election year brings about relatively "easy-money" policy. In some other times, tight monetary policy or credit control may be imposed in an attempt to accomplish a certain political goal. The existence of a fully developed capital market where monetary policy cannot control credit expansion or contraction allows firms and individual investors to avoid some of the risks arising from unpredicted changes in monetary policy. The mere fact that deposits and loans in a certain currency are traded in the external currency market makes this currency less susceptible to monetary policy risks. Thus this currency becomes internationally more acceptable. The ability of the external currency market to counteract changes in monetary policy that are inconsistent with the demand for a certain money by firms and investors is due to the way by which credit is expanded and contracted in these markets.

An example of how governments and external currency markets interact are in the initiation, development, and growth of the external currency markets in London. These currency markets have many dimensions. London benefited from government-initiated activity that has made these markets international financial service centers (Helleiner, 1993: 83-84). For the growing community of transnational corporations with investment and trade interest in Western Europe, a conveniently located financial center "near the scene of action" was an attraction. For depositors the London market serves as a location where they can avoid current and future government control. This section reviews the complex and sometimes paradoxical role of governments in the establishment and character of external currency markets.

In the 1950s, the British government, more than other Western European governments, hoped that the move to dollar convertibility of European currencies (achieved in 1958) would bring freedom for capital movements, in order that London's international activities could be bolstered. However, the hopes of British financial authorities were frustrated when, with currency convertibility having been achieved, a series of balance-of-payments crises forced them to impose increasingly tighter restrictions on the international use of sterling in capital transactions (Helleiner, 1994: 83). These crises were triggered by capital flight in response to loss of confidence in British macroeconomic policy. These restrictions suggested to London bankers that the British government's commitment to the Keynesian welfare state, in the face of substantial balance-of-payments difficulties, would mean that they would not be able to operate freely at the international level after restoration of convertibility.

During the 1957 sterling crisis, the bankers stumbled upon the Eurodollar market as a solution to their problems:

> The catalyst for the market's development was the restrictions on British banks' use of sterling to finance trade between countries outside the sterling area. Customers whose trade had been financed by sterling acceptance credits continued to demand from London financiers a new mechanism for financing such trade. The London bankers found that they could satisfy this demand by offering dollar loans against their dollar deposits of overseas residents. This business proved so attractive that when the restrictions were removed in early 1959, the bankers continued their new Eurodollar activity. By shifting their business to a dollar basis, the London operators had found a way to preserve their international business without being encumbered by British capital controls (Helleiner, 1993: 84).

The Eurodollar market created by the private operators was actively encouraged by British financial authorities. To them, it represented a solution to the problem of how to reconcile the goal of restoring London's international position with the Keynesian welfare state and Britain's deteriorating economic position. The Bank of England was an active proponent of the Eurodollar market. It not only refrained from imposing regulations on market activity, but took several important measures, such as the 1962 decision to allow the issue of foreign securities denominated in foreign currencies in London, thereby permitting the growth of a Eurobond market. The move was particularly well timed to enable London to replace New York as the leading international capital market after the United States instituted a capital controls program in 1965.

Hawley (1987), in his study of American attempts to restrict capital flows in the 1960s and 1970s, writes that it was not coincidental that it was at the height of American economic dominance in the early 1960s that the issue of capital controls arose—and with it, growing U.S. government apprehension of the activities of American transnational corporations. Transnational corporate investment, until that time, was an important source of global liquidity that the United States provided to the rest of the world. However, these dollar outflows were undermining the country's payments position, leading to persistent deficits in the capital account from the late 1950s onward. The capital controls, according to Hawley, signaled the emergence of the politics of American hegemonic decline in the international system. The controls had dual strategic purposes: to place protection of the U.S. world power position ahead of private sector expansion abroad, and to maintain domestic political coalitions constructed around the Keynesian welfare state.

Hawley points out that capital interests were at cross-purposes. Given that maintenance of an open international economic order rested on American leadership, massive transnational capital flows from the United States would undermine that very leadership. The division between state and transnational capital was played out in the context of the politics of international monetary regime crisis mentioned in the previous section. The fallout over the implementation of mandatory capital controls revealed a the division of capital interests between those tied to the domestic economy—and thereby defended government macroeconomic discretion—and those tied to international business.

The mandatory capital control program strengthened state intervention in markets, especially financial markets. One result was to stimulate financial innovation through the "Eurodollar escape valve" (Hawley, 1987: 106). It was partly the purpose of U.S. government policy to use the Eurodollar market to finance a significant portion of American transnational corporate investment, which otherwise would have been financed directly from American capital markets and from the domestic resources of American transnational corporations. This Eurodollar escape valve was to have a high cost. By contributing to the growth of the innovative Eurocurrency system, U.S. government policy promoted the internationalization of commercial and investment banks. As Hawley (1987: 106) points out: "As transnational banks and corporations became more dependent on new financial markets, their interests were transformed. Increasingly they had a direct stake in the internationalization of finance—this was, ironically, in reaction to restrictive policies by the United States and other states to protect their 'national interest.'" American capital controls, instituted to protect the credibility of the dollar, promoted a large foreign dollar overhang through the growth of the Eurodollar market. This financial innovation was to allow for more effective speculation against the dollar in foreign exchange markets.

Hawley concludes that while the controls were "a tactical success, permitting alternative sources of financing and muting political opposition [to restrictions on the outflow of dollars from the United States], . . .they were a strategic failure: this was evident in the speculative currency crises of 1967, 1969, and 1970, and in the ultimate collapse of the Bretton Woods system in 1971. By promoting the use of the Eurocurrency escape valve, U.S. state intervention buttressed financial innovation which in the long run contributed to the collapse of the dollar-gold exchange standard."

BRETTON WOODS REASSESSED

The movement of capital across national borders has long raised sensitive political questions. Whatever the benefits, international capital mobility complicates national economic management. Short-term capital flows are highly sensitive to interest rate differentials and exchange rate expectations. Indeed, the mere announcement of a change in economic policy can trigger massive capital inflows or outflows, undermining the anticipated benefits of the new policy. For this reason, most governments regularly resorted to various types of controls on short-term capital movements in the decades following World War II (Helleiner 1993, 1994).

In recent years, however, the world has witnessed a remarkable shift away from the use of capital controls. In country after country, governments have abolished controls and dismantled the bureaucratic machinery used to administer them (Goodman and Pauly, 1993). The United States ended restrictions on capital outflows in 1976, Britain in 1979, and the most members of the European Community throughout the 1980s. In the rare instances where governments have re-imposed controls, such as during the 1992-93 exchange crisis in the Europe, their temporary nature has usually been emphasized. This general trend toward liberalization has stimulated a growing body of research on the political and economic consequences of capital mobility. In this study, a principal aim is to address two prior puzzles: First, why did policies of capital liberalization converge across a rising number of industrial states between the late 1970s and the early 1990s? Second, why did some states move to eliminate controls more rapidly than others? Goodman and Pauly (1993) argue that the movement away from controls on short-term capital flows did not result, as regime or epistemic community explanations might predict, from the emergence of a common normative framework or widespread belief in the benefits of unfettered capital mobility. Nor has it simply reflected the overarching power of a liberal state. Instead, they contend that it was driven by fundamental changes in the structures of international production and financial intermediation, which made it easier and more urgent for private firms—specifically, corporations and financial institutions whose aspirations had become increasingly global—effectively to pursue strategies of evasion and exit. For governments, the utility of controls declined as their perceived cost thereby increased.

Three explanations can be given for the widespread use of capital controls and the wariness of states throughout the advanced industrial world to accept a liberal international financial order in the early postwar period. First, the use of capital controls was prompted in part by the need to protect the macroeconomic planning mechanisms developed in the 1930s. Although they acknowledged the validity of the liberal case that some capital movements were beneficial, national Keynesians argued that capital controls were necessary to prevent the policy autonomy of the new interventionist welfare state from being undermined by speculative and disequilibrating international capital flows (Helleiner, 1993). The embedded liberal normative framework in finance was strongly backed by a new alliance of Keynesian-minded state officials, industrialists, and labor leaders who had increasingly replaced private and central bankers in positions of financial power in the advanced industrial world during the 1930s and World War II. Whereas the bankers continued to support a liberal ideology in finance, members of this new alliance favored more interventionist policies that would make finance the "servant" rather than the "master" in economic and political matters.

The second explanation of the support for the restrictive Bretton Woods financial order was the widespread belief in the early postwar period that a liberal international financial order would not be compatible, at least in the short run, with a stable system of exchange rates and a liberal international trading order. This belief stemmed from the experience of the interwar period, when speculative capital movements had severely disrupted exchange rates and trade relations. It also reflected early recognition of a point that has increasingly been emphasized in recent years by Gilpin (1987) and others: that different elements of a liberal international economic order are not necessarily compatible. Faced with a choice between creating a liberal order in finance and building a system of stable exchange rates and liberal trade, policymakers in the early postwar period generally agreed that free finance should be sacrificed.

The third explanation concerns the sympathetic attitude adopted by the United States toward the use of capital controls in Western Europe and Japan. Although this stance in part reflected the first two factors, it also stemmed from American strategic goals in the Cold War after 1947. On one hand, American strategic thinkers were reluctant to alienate their Western European and Japanese allies by pressing for unpopular liberalization moves. On the other, as Loriaux (1991) points out, American strategic thinkers actively supported financial interventionism abroad as part of a larger effort to promote economic growth in Western Europe and Japan. Indeed, American officials were often more enthusiastic advocates of embedded liberal financial policies abroad than were the policymakers in these countries for this reason. The Cold War thus prompted the United States to assume an accommodating or "benevolent" form of hegemony over Western Europe and Japan (Keohane and Nye, 1977). After 1947, it both yielded to their preference for capital controls and actively supported measures that might foster their prosperity.

Why did states increasingly embrace an open, liberal international financial order in these ways beginning in the late 1950s, after supporting the restrictive Bretton Woods order in the early postwar years? There are three explanations for this change in attitude.

First, attempts to preserve the Bretton Woods order met with several inherent political difficulties. The creation of the Eurocurrency markets showed the ease with which individual states (the United States and Britain) could significantly undermine the order unilaterally by offering mobile financial traders a location in which to operate without regulation. Equally important, individual states—once again the United States and Britain—could unleash competitive pressures that indirectly encouraged liberalization and deregulation throughout the system. When these two states supported growth of the Eurocurrency markets in the 1960s and then liberalized and deregulated their financial markets in the 1970s and 1980s, foreign financial centers increasingly witnessed their business and capital migrating to these more attractive markets. To compete effectively for this mobile financial business and capital, they were forced to follow the lead of Britain and the United

States by liberalizing and deregulating their own financial systems. This "competitive deregulation" in finance was a central reason for the flurry of liberalization activity throughout the advanced industrial world in the 1980s.

Political difficulties also hindered the implementing of more effective capital controls. The introduction of cooperative controls could easily be vetoed by a major state or group of states. The use of comprehensive exchange controls would impose large economic and political costs, especially in the increasingly interdependent world economy of the 1970s and 1980s, as policymakers in Britain and France in 1976 and 1982-83 were forced to recognize. Thus, although it may have been technically possible to control capital movements more effectively, it was politically difficult to implement in practice.

The second explanation for the unraveling of the Bretton Woods financial order relates to the strong interest of the United States and Britain after the late 1950s in promoting a more open international financial order. The United States abandoned its early postwar support for the restrictive Bretton Woods order in large part because of its changing global position. In the early postwar years, the economic strength of the United States and its strategic interests in the Cold War encouraged it to assume a "benevolent" hegemonic position in the Western alliance. Many analysts (Gilpin, 1987; Calleo, 1982, 1987; Strange, 1988) have suggested that beginning in the 1960s, the United States gradually adopted a more self-centered or "predatory" foreign economic policy because of growing current account and budget deficits. In particular, the United States began to seek foreign help in financing and adjusting to these deficits in order to maintain its policy autonomy. This more aggressive foreign policy strategy relied largely on what Strange (1988) calls the unique "structural power" of the United States within the emerging open global financial order. Its hegemonic position in trade may have been declining, but the United States retained a dominant position in this financial order well into the 1980s because of the relative attractiveness of U.S. financial markets, the preeminence of the American financial institutions and the dollar in global markets, and the relative size of the U.S. economy. This hegemonic position in the emerging open global financial order provided the United States with a fundamental reason for promoting the globalization process from the 1960s through the 1980s.

In addition to the inherent political difficulties associated with maintaining the Bretton Woods financial order and the unique "hegemonic" interests of the United States, the third explanation for states' growing enthusiasm for the globalization process was the increasing rejection of the embedded liberal framework of thought in favor of a neoliberal framework in the 1970s and 1980s (Pauly, 1988; Schor, 1992). Neoliberal advocates favored a liberal international financial order on the grounds that it would enhance personal freedom and promote a more efficient allocation of capital both internationally and domestically. Neoliberals also rejected the two reasons outlined at Bretton Woods for justifying capital controls. First, they disregarded the postwar concern that speculative capital flows would disrupt the Bretton Woods exchange rate system by arguing strongly in favor of flexible exchange rates. Second, they did not seek to preserve the policy autonomy of the interventionist welfare state but rather supported freer domestic markets and more orthodox fiscal and monetary policies. Indeed, neoliberal advocates praised international financial markets for prompting states to adopt these policies.

Although the ideological shift to neoliberalism took place at varying rates of speed and degrees of intensity in different countries, several factors explain its prevalence throughout the advanced industrial world. Many policymakers began to embrace neoliberal ideas for the practical reason that they found it increasingly difficult to continue to support embedded liberal policies in the increasingly open financial environment of the 1970s and 1980s. The shift was also encouraged by important thinkers such as Milton Friedman who developed neoliberal ideas and helped to build intellectual networks, often transnational in scope, in order to promote them, as had Keynes and his supporters in the 1930s and 1940s (Hall, 1989). The neoliberal movement gained strength from the economic slowdown in the 1970s and early 1980s, which, like that of the 1930s, eroded support for existing economic paradigms and created an intellectual climate in which neoliberal ideas were more easily embraced. Finally, neoliberal ideas were also supported by a coalition of social groups throughout the advanced industrial world in the 1970s and 1980s that differed considerably from the that which had supported embedded liberal ideas in the early postwar period. This coalition included representatives of transnational corporations, who increasingly favored a liberal international financial order as their operations became more internationalized, and officials of private financial institutions, who had, for the most part, supported financial liberalization throughout the postwar period but whose enthusiasm was strengthened by the competitive financial environment of the 1970s and 1980s. The neoliberal financial message also found strong support among officials of central banks, finance ministers, and international financial institutions, who had often been wary of the interventionist financial practices of the early postwar years.

As this section detailed, financial liberalization efforts can be explained by looking at changes in the macroeconomic conditions in the advanced industrial states beginning in the late 1960s, changes in the policy positions taken by the United States—the leading state in the international political economy, and changes in the ideological framework, as policy failure reopened the debate on the relative roles of governments and markets in enhancing societal economic welfare.

Whatever its institutional manifestations, political authority represents a fusion of power with legitimate social purpose. The relationship between states and various non-state actors is a parameter that encompasses the authority structures through which citizens are linked to their governments. The prevailing interpretation of international authority focuses on power only. "Historically these authority structures have been founded on traditional criteria of legitimacy derived from constitutional and legal sources; individuals were habituated to comply with the directives issued by higher authorities. People did what they were told to do because that was what one did" (Rosenau, 1995: 195). Such an interpretation ignores the dimension of social purpose or unifying ideology, which provides a normative framework for economic policy choice. With the expansion of analytic skills of citizens, including their recognition and increased articulation of interests at variance with those of the state, the traditional authority structure parameter has eroded. "Throughout the world today . . . the sources of authority have shifted from traditional to performance criteria of legitimacy. Where the structures of authority were once in place . . . they are now in crisis, with the readiness of individuals to comply with governing directives very much a function of their assessment of the performances of the authorities" (Rosenau, 1995: 195).

NOTE

1. The global distribution of capital, in order to take advantage of low-cost production sites in developing countries. An international division of labor reflects the emergence of global economy, and the rationalizaton of production on a global scale. Such a rationalization occurred in the late 19th century with the incorporation of the "areas of European settlement" (i.e., North America, Argentina, Australia, and New Zealand) into the world agricultural markets. These low-cost producers greatly increased world foodstuffs supplies, leading to price declines and a global agricultural depression. Likewise, the United States, Germany, and Russia became new low-cost producers of steel, which again led to price declines.

CHAPTER IV

National Economic Policymaking in an Era of Global Finance

Governments and regulators will certainly not let up in their efforts to work together and to pool resources against the marauding vandals. Governments still have immense powers, including the power to surprise markets with policy moves. And, from time to time, the vandals may suffer severe losses because of their own self-confidence, causing them to reconsider their actions and their own vulnerabilities. But when the financial authorities themselves start to show surprise at how the markets react to their moves, one begins to wonder who, if anyone, is in charge (O'Brien, 1995: 151).

Up to the early 1970s Keynesian economics exercised a major influence over policymakers in most OECD countries. Originally with monetary, and then fiscal policy, the governments of the advanced industrial economies attempted to achieve the levels of investment, employment, and technological capability required to generate the revenues—both private and public—sufficient to guarantee nationally defined norms of social welfare, and thus electoral survival (Laux, 1989: 353). This chapter analyzes the efforts made by the governments of the advanced countries to respond to shifting economic conditions in the years since the Second World War. It focuses on the capacities of the different governments to intervene selectively to shape industrial outcomes. More specifically, the chapter begins with the notion that an examination of national financial structures can illuminate the economic strategies of these governments and the political conflicts that

accompany industrial adjustment. The particular arrangements of
national financial systems limit both the marketplace options of firms
and the administrative choices of government. That is, financial
markets in each country are one element that delimits the ways in
which business and the state can interact. The structure of the markets
at once influences a government's capacity to exert industrial
leadership and the nature of the political conflicts that arise from its
economic objectives. Very simply, in market economies where freely
moving prices allocate goods and services, money is not only a medium
of exchange but also a means of political and social control: it is one
way of deciding who gets what. Therefore, by following the money
flows in the market economy and dissecting the institutions that
structure that flow, we can learn a great deal about the uses to which the
society's resources are put, by whom, and how control is obtained and
exerted.

Active demand management policy attempts to use monetary and
fiscal policy to reduce the variability of output growth around its
medium-term trend path, while at the same time controlling the rate of
inflation (Massey, 1995: 59). Fiscal policy seeks to alter the levels of
aggregate demand through decisions about the level of government
revenue and expenditure. Monetary policy can be used to influence
demand through control of the money supply, the availability of credit
and the rate of interest. There is no general agreement about how
unstable the economy would be if left to its own devices. The Classical
economic view is that market economies tend to operate in the region
of full employment of both labor and capital. Apart from relatively
short periods, as the result of an exogenous shock, there may be
transitory unemployment. However, there are stabilizing mechanisms
that tend to return the economy to full employment fairly quickly.
Keynesians argue that advanced economies are inherently unstable and
may depart from full employment for long periods of time in the face of
adverse shocks, or at least can take quite a long time to return to full
employment, due to rigidities in goods and labor markets. The
Keynesian view tends to be that these problems can be mitigated by
appropriate management of the government's contribution to aggregate
demand.

By the early 1970s, however, the then prevailing Keynesian
viewpoint began to encounter serious problems. In the first place it
seemed unable to explain the simultaneous increases in inflation and

unemployment being experienced in most developed countries. The frequent resort to fiscal stimuli, and the failure of repeated expansionary budgets to stem the inexorable rise in unemployment, generated widespread loss of faith in the ability of government to stimulate economic activity by means of discretionary fiscal policy measures. This resulted in a critical reappraisal of policy by officials in OECD countries during the 1980s.

CENTRAL BANK INDEPENDENCE AND CREDIBILITY

The Group of Six (G-6) states differed in their conduct of macroeconomic policy. In the continental European states and Japan, policy was aimed at maximizing the rate of growth. Monetary and discretionary fiscal policy was therefore systematically expansionary, notwithstanding the absence of an intellectual commitment to Keynesianism in these countries. In the United States and Britain, policy was markedly less expansionary.

Epstein and Schor (1990) argue that this difference can be explained by structural differences among the states. Most important are the degree of independence of the central bank, the nature of relations between financial and industrial capital interests, the specifics of the wage-setting process, and, finally, the position of the country in the world economy. In the view of the two authors, the expansionism of France, Italy, Germany, and Japan, and the relatively more restrictive stance of the United States and the United Kingdom, during the 1945-73 period, can be explained by reference to these factors. In the previous chapter, it was showed that central bank authorities were regarded as the instruments of financial asset-holders, who were more concerned with exchange-rate and domestic price stability than with employment prospects and growth. During the 1930s an 1940s central bankers became administratively subordinate to national treasuries, which were responsible for carrying out government macroeconomic policies. The central banks became agents of the governments, which increased the money supply in order to facilitate expansionary policies.

Since 1973, in all countries, the benefits from expansionary policy were reduced by structural changes in the international monetary regime and increasing inflation. These changes, in the view of Epstein and Schor, eroded the distinctions between France, Germany, Italy, and Japan (Group A), on the one hand, and the United States and the United

Kingdom (Group B) on the other. Although some countries attempted
to pursue expansionary policies throughout the 1970s, the difficulties of
doing so eventually prevailed. Inflation rose dramatically during the
decade as supply conditions tightened and profits were squeezed. The
breakdown of the Phillips Curve relationship between price inflation
and unemployment meant a decade of stagflation as real economic
growth among the G-6 states declined from the 6.0 percent per annum
during the 1947-67 period to only 2.3 percent during 1974-80 (Nau,
1990: 378, 386). Annual inflation rose from 4.1 percent per annum
during 1947-67 to 9.6 percent per annum during 1974-80 (Nau, 1990:
378, 386). Governments responded to stagflation with a general shift to
restraint, which was quite dramatic after 1980. The economic
environment in which policy is formulated was dramatically altered in
the 1980s in order to combat inflation. The shift from interest rate to
monetary aggregate targeting by national central banks in the early
1980s led to historically high interest rates—5.3 percent among G-6
members in 1983 compared to 2.8 percent average in 1963-72 (BIS,
1983: 67)—and the highest unemployment levels in the postwar era—
7.8 percent average in 1981-87 compared to 2.5 percent average in
1947-67 (Nau, 1990: 378, 386).

Proponents of state "non-intervention" polices, whether of fiscal
consolidation or simple monetary aggregate rules, have emphasized that
such policies may yield positive effects through greater inflation-
fighting credibility with international financial markets. When financial
asset-holders are convinced that governments will not (and in some
cases, legally cannot) institute inflation surprises that can reduce
expected rates of return, political risk premiums imposed on
government debt will decrease. Credibility effects dominated
macroeconomic discussion in the 1980s: "they are the logical and
indeed plausible implication of smart forward-looking expectations"
(Fitoussi, et al., 1993). Credibility effects were also present in the some
of the more dramatic policy changes in the OECD economies in the
1980s, such as in fiscal consolidation in New Zealand (Massey, 1995)
and the shift toward the strong-currency option in France (Louriaux,
1991). New Zealand offers an example of institutional reform to resolve
credibility problems, through the formation of a central bank
independent from the government.

To put the credibility problem in a quantitative perspective,
Frantianni and Salvatore (1993: 3), presented data on the differences in

inflation rates and inflation volatility (measured in terms of standard deviation) among the G-6 states.

Table 1: Rates of Inflation and Central Bank Independence in Six Industrialized States

	1971-80				1981-90		
Germany	5.0	(1.4)	4.00	Japan	1.7	(1.3)	2.50
United States	7.3	(2.3)	3.50	Germany	2.6	(1.9)	4.00
Japan	8.7	(5.0)	2.50	United States	4.6	(1.9)	3.50
France	9.9	(2.9)	2.00	Britain	5.8	(2.3)	2.00
Britain	12.6	(6.5)	2.00	France	6.2	(4.0)	2.00
Italy	14.7	(5.4)	1.75	Italy	9.8	(5.2)	1.75

Notes: The first numbers are annual percentage changes in the consumption deflator, while the numbers in the parentheses refer to the sample standard deviation. The third number is the Alesina and Summers (1993) score for central bank independence, with higher scores (on a 1-4 scale) indicating greater independence.

Source: Fratianni and Salvatore (1993: 3) and Alesina and Summers (1993)

The data show a wide dispersion of outcomes, suggesting that the six central banks had different abilities or inclination to affect inflation. There is also an apparent positive correlation between institutional and personal independence and inflation performance. The central banks in Italy, France, and Britain are institutions closely bound to the government, whereas the German, American, and Japanese central banks enjoy high degree of independence.

THE BALANCE OF PAYMENTS AND MACROECONOMIC POLICYMAKING

Since the early 1970s, exchange rates have become more volatile. The real effective exchange rate of the U.S. dollar, which measures the value of the American currency against a trade-weighted basket of foreign currencies, fell 25 percent between 1973 and 1980, before rising 45 percent between 1980 and 1985, and then reversing some 40 percent through 1992. The volume of foreign-exchange transactions has grown much faster than the volume of world trade and faster than even the much larger flows of investment capital. The risks associated with all kinds of foreign exchange trading have increased significantly, but so has the awareness of them, the knowledge to deal with them, and the instruments to cover them. In this section I will examine both traditional and modern approaches to exchange rate determination. Each of these is based upon different assumptions and, therefore, offers different reasons for the occurrence of balance-of-payment disequilibria, and different prescriptions for adjustment. Traditional approaches to exchange rate determination, based on trade flows and purchasing power parity, are more important in explaining exchange rate movements in the long-run. Modern approaches focus instead on the importance of capital markets and international capital flows, and seek to explain short-run volatility of exchange rates and their tendency to overshoot the long-run equilibrium.

One of the central questions to answer in attempting to analyze the scope of financial transformation is to measure the extent of capital flows. The traditional, and most familiar, way to do this is to start from national balance-of-payments statistics.

The balance of payments is a summary statement of all international transactions of the residents of a country with the rest of the world during a year's time. The balance of payments is divided into three components: the current account, the capital account, and official reserves account. The current account records all sales and purchases of currently produced goods and services and unilateral transfers (i.e., gifts or grants extended to or received from abroad), and thus provides the link between the country's international transactions and its national income. The capital account records the change in foreign assets held by the country's residents and the change in domestic assets held foreigners, other than official reserve assets. The official reserves account records the change in the country's official reserve assets (e.g., gold and currencies used as international reserves) and the change in foreign official assets in the country.

International transactions are classified as credits or debits. Credit transactions are those that involve the receipt of payments from foreigners (i.e., domestic currency inpayments). Debit transactions are those that involve the making of payments to foreigners (i.e., domestic currency outpayments). For current account transactions, the export of goods and services, interest earned on domestic resident-owned assets abroad, gifts from foreigners, remittances from domestic residents working (earning money) abroad are all entered as credits because they involve the receipt of payments from foreigners and lead to domestic currency inpayments. The import of goods and services, interest paid to foreigners on foreign-owned domestic assets, gifts and grants to foreigners, and foreign worker remittances back to their home countries are all entered as debits because they involve payments to foreigners and lead to domestic currency outpayments.

Capital account transactions involve capital inflows and outflows. Capital inflows can take either of two forms: an increase in foreign ownership of domestic assets (e.g., domestic factories, hotels, stocks, and bonds), or a decrease in domestic ownership of the same types of foreign assets. Capital inflows are entered into the capital account as credits for they involve domestic currency inpayments—as when foreigners purchase domestic assets. Capital outflows, likewise, can take either of two forms: a decrease of foreign ownership of domestic assets, or an increase in domestic ownership of foreign assets (i.e., foreign investment). Capital outflows are entered into the capital account as debits for they involve domestic currency outpayments—as when domestic residents purchase foreign assets.

All transactions in the current and capital accounts are called autonomous transactions because they take place for business or profit motives (except for unilateral transfers) and independently of balance-of-payments considerations. On the other hand, transactions in official reserve assets are called accommodating transactions because they result from and are needed to balance international transactions, under an international monetary regime of less than freely floating exchange rates. The accommodating transaction items form the official reserve account, and the balance on the official reserve account is called the official settlements balance.

If total debits exceed total credits in the current and capital accounts, the net debit balance measures the deficit in the country's balance of payments. Under a fixed exchange rate regime, the deficit must then be settled in the official settlements balance as an equal net credit in the official reserve account. In this case, the country's stock of official reserves (gold and foreign currency) will decrease by the amount to cover the deficit. Under a flexible exchange rate regime, the deficit is closed by the depreciation of the deficit country's currency.

This trade-based, or elasticities, approach emphasizes trade or the flow of goods and services in the determination of exchange rates. The equilibrium exchange rate is the one that balances the value of a country's imports and exports. If the country faced a trade deficit, then the domestic currency will depreciate under a flexible exchange rate regime. This makes the country's exports cheaper to foreigners and imports more expensive to domestic residents. The result is that the country's exports rise and its imports fall until trade is balanced. International capital flows are important only as passive responses for temporary trade imbalances.

The speed of adjustment depends on how elastic imports and exports are to price (i.e., exchange rate) changes. If the country is at or near full employment, a larger depreciation of the country's currency is required to shift domestic resources to the production of more exports and import substitutes than if the country has unemployed resources. Alternatively, domestic policies may be required to reduce domestic expenditures to release domestic resources to produce more exports and import substitutes, and thus allow the elasticities approach to operate.

The trade-based approach, though crucial in the long-run determination of exchange rates, however, cannot explain either the large volatility of exchange rates during the 1970s or the sharp appreciation of the dollar from 1980 to 1985—in the face of rising American trade deficits. It also cannot explain the failure of American trade deficits to decline when the dollar depreciated sharply from 1985 to 1988.

Another traditional approach to exchange rate determination that is more relevant in the long run than in the short run is that of purchasing-power parity (PPP). The absolute version of the PPP approach postulates that the exchange rate between two currencies is simply the ratio of the two countries' general price levels. That is, according to the law of one price, the same commodity should have the same price in both countries when expressed in terms of the same currency. If the price of the commodity in terms of the same currency is higher in one country than in another, firms will purchase the commodity in the country where the price was low and resell it in the country where the price was high at a profit. This commodity arbitrage would continue until the prices were equal in both countries.

The PPP approach, however, is based on the implicit assumption that there are no transportation costs, tariffs, or other obstructions to the free flow of trade, that all commodities are traded internationally, and that no structural changes take place in either country (Salvatore, 1990:

400). Since trade and commodity arbitrage respond sluggishly, purchasing-power parity is more closely approximated in the long run than in the short run.

In contrast to the trade-based and the purchasing-power parity approaches, in which the exchange rate is determined by the flow of funds in the foreign exchange market, asset allocation approaches postulate that exchange rates are determined in the process of equilibrating or balancing the stock, or total demand and supply, of financial assets in each country. The simplest, the monetary approach, concentrates attention on the domestic demand for and supply of money.

The money supply in each country is assumed to be set exogenously by the country's central bank. The demand for money, however, depends on the level of real income, the general price level, and the interest rate. The higher are real income and prices, the greater is the demand for money balances that individuals and businesses demand for their day-to-day transactions. On the other hand, the higher the interest rate, the greater is the opportunity cost of holding money (i.e., cash or non-interest-earning demand deposits) instead of interest-bearing assets (i.e., bonds). Thus, the demand for money is inversely related to the rate of interest. The higher the interest rate, the smaller is the quantity of money demanded.

When the quantity supplied of domestic money exceeds the quantity demanded by the country's residents, there will be an outflow of domestic money (i.e., a deficit in the country's balance of payments) under a fixed exchange rate regime, or a depreciation of the country's currency under flexible exchange rates. On the other hand, when the quantity demanded of domestic money by home residents exceeds the quantity supplied, there will be a capital inflow (a balance-of-payments surplus) under fixed exchange rates, or an appreciation of the domestic currency under flexible rates.

The more advanced portfolio-balance approach (Salvatore, 1990) postulates that domestic money is only one among a spectrum of financial assets that the residents of a country may want to hold. Individuals and firms hold their financial wealth in some combination of domestic money (currency or non-interest earning demand deposits), domestic interest-bearing assets (e.g., domestic bonds), and foreign currency-denominated assets (e.g., foreign bonds). The incentive to hold bonds (domestic or foreign) stems from the yield, or interest payments, that they provide. They also carry, however, the risk of default and the risk arising from the variability of their market value over time. Foreign bonds are imperfect substitutes for domestic bonds, for the former carries the additional risk that the foreign currency may depreciate, thereby imposing a capital loss in terms of the holder's domestic currency. Holding domestic money, by contrast, is risk-less but also provides no interest.

The opportunity cost of holding domestic money is the interest yield that is forgone on holding bonds. The higher the yield on bonds, the smaller is the quantity of money that individuals and firms will want to hold. While individuals and firms will want to hold some of their wealth in the form of money for transactions purposes, the higher the yield on bonds the smaller the amount of money that they will want to hold.

A change in the investor's preferences, his or her wealth, domestic and foreign interest rates, and expectations will lead investors to reallocate financial assets in their portfolios. For example, an increase in the foreign interest rate raises the demand for the foreign bond but reduces the demand for money and the domestic bond. The reallocation involves a change in the stock of various financial assets in the portfolio. Having been accumulated over a long period of time, the total stock of financial assets in investor's portfolios in the economy is very large relative to yearly flows (additions to the stock) through usual savings and investments. Changes in interest rates and investor expectations that affect the benefits and costs of holding various financial assets are likely to lead to an immediate or very rapid change in their stock, as investors seek to reestablish balance in their portfolios.

The implications of asset allocation approaches to exchange rate determination are profoundly different from traditional long term trade-based approaches. An increase in the foreign interest rates has immediate effects on the foreign exchange market, for investors will reduce their holding of domestic currency and domestic currency-denominated assets and increase their holdings of foreign currency and foreign currency-denominated assets. This portfolio reallocation can move huge sums almost instantaneously. This is contrasted with the change in the flow of merchandise trade that results from, for instance, a depreciation of the country's currency, and which takes place only gradually and over a longer period of time.

The increase in foreign interest rates is likely to lead to a large and quick increase in the demand for the foreign currency in order to increase investors' stocks of foreign currency-denominated assets. This will lead to an immediate and large depreciation of the domestic currency, which is likely to swamp the smaller and more gradual changes that take place through the real goods market, such as changes in trade flows. Of course, the opposite occurs if the home country's interest rate rises relative to foreign interest rates. Because exchange rates are likely to reflect changes in expectations and in financial asset markets, which are not synchronized with changes in trade patterns, exchange rate overshooting often occurs. This happens because a larger depreciation is needed to equilibrate the short term financial asset markets than what the long term real goods market allows. In the long run, as the depreciated currency leads to a change in trade patterns, the exchange rate will adjust to the long term equilibrium position. However, given the huge sums involved when portfolios in the financial asset market are reallocated, currency values are in a constant state of flux. Therefore, currency values can deviate from long term equilibrium even in the long run. This misalignment of currencies often requires major macroeconomic adjustment on the part of domestic policymakers.

Thus, the financial transformation of the 1980s can be viewed as a phase of the structural adjustment initiative launched after the shock of 1979-80. This emphasis on structural adjustment reflected concern about the structural dislocation of the shock, layered on the declining productivity and high inflation of the 1970s. To complement the new "price stability" macroeconomic policies, a range of microeconomic policies designed to improve the adaptability of markets was advocated and, to an extent varying among different countries, adopted (Ostry, 1990: 54). The thrust of the new policy framework was toward enhancing market forces by deregulation and reducing government intervention. In discussing changes in the domestic financial systems, a transition occurred away from fixed and toward flexible asset prices.

As the results of the 1970s and 1980s revealed, the hoped-for national policymaking autonomy proved to be a chimera. While the shift from fixed to flexible rates did relieve the official reserves constraint on governments, the new era of capital mobility imposed a new market discipline on state actions. Whereas under fixed rates, governments could not pursue expansionary policies (and incur payments deficits) beyond the level of official reserves available to prop up a declining currency, under the new flexible-rate system with capital mobility, governments were constrained by the level of confidence that international capital markets held in their policies. While governments could pursue deficit financing of expenditures with foreign capital inflows, these inflows were heavily influenced by market confidence considerations. These considerations, Keynes' "animal spirits," provided the catalyst for the short-term "hot money" flows that had been deemed to be destabilizing for global financial health. As states became increasingly dependent on deficit financing, they became increasingly dependent on the private market operators who control the capital.

THE RISING POWER OF FINANCIAL ASSET-HOLDERS

As late as the mid-1970s governments had precise policy instruments in order to achieve national economic goals. The most important economic goals of governments are (1) full employment with price stability, (2) equilibrium in the balance of payments, (3) a reasonable rate of growth, and (4) an equitable distribution of income (Salvatore, 1990: 523). At the disposal of governments was an impressive array of expenditure-changing, or demand, policies, expenditure-switching policies, and direct controls. Expenditure-changing policies include both fiscal and monetary policies. Fiscal policy refers to changes in government expenditures, taxes, or both. Monetary policy involves a change in the state's money supply and affects domestic interest rates. Expenditure-switching policies refer to changes in the exchange rate, such as a devaluation or revaluation. Direct controls consist of restrictions of capital movements, credit controls, and direct subsidization of industry.

Governments could stimulate economic activity through either expansionary fiscal policy or easy monetary policy. Expansionary fiscal policy involves increasing government expenditures and/or reducing taxes. These actions lead to an expansion of domestic production and income. Easy monetary policy involves increasing the money supply, resulting in a reduction of interest rates. Low interest induces an increase in the level of investment and income.

The effectiveness of these policy instruments has been blunted in recent years by regulatory reform in domestic financial markets, the liberalization of international capital flows, financial innovation, and the investment activities of non-state actors in purchasing and selling financial assets. These changes have yielded tremendous power to financial asset-holders (also called financial market operators). Since 1980, the total stock of financial assets has increased two-and-a-half times faster than the GDP of OECD-member economies, and the volume of trading in currencies, bonds, and equities faster still (Woodall, 1995: 4). As global capital markets continue to grow, so will the economic—and political—power of financial asset-holders. National economic sovereignty, according to a growing number of financial commentators, is being eroded by massive international capital flows. The political implication of this development is that governments may be rendered powerless to defend their state's economic interests.

Since Louis XIV, leaders of governments have harnessed wealth-generation for state interests. Jean Baptiste Colbert, chief minister to the French king, used subsidies and tariff protection to encourage industry, while restricting the outflow of capital from the country. His twentieth-century *dirigiste* successors used state ties to large financial intermediaries to channel credit to favored borrowers, while keeping tight both credit and capital controls (i.e., financial compression).

International financial integration has changed the credit allocation process. With capital mobility, reduced domestic interest rates lead to an outflow of capital in search of higher interest rates abroad, and savings are directed to the most productive investments. Increased competition for capital has created a more efficient financial system, offering better opportunities for savers as well as lower costs for borrowers (Woodall, 1995: 4). New financial instruments, such as derivatives, assist firms in managing financial risk more effectively. The long-term result of greater mobility of financial instruments should be higher levels of investment and growth worldwide.

According to Frieden (1991), international capital mobility has increased the ability of foreign producers to respond to trade protection by locating in protected markets, stimulated the movement of financial assets from capital-rich to capital-poor states, and widened the menu of investments open to asset-holders. These benefits have come at a price. At the time that governments debated the merits of domestic regulatory reform and liberalization of financial flows, few realized the dramatic shift in political influence that was taking place. The past fifteen years in particular have seen a secular shift in the response to increased capital mobility, in which governments the world over have been forced to provide more attractive conditions for financial asset-holders. Such conditions include everything from lower wealth and capital gains taxes to relaxed regulation on financial activities and labor relations (Frieden, 1991: 434). The shift in power from policymakers to financial market operators has triggered four popular worries (Woodall, 1995: 4).

First, it is argued, that the sheer magnitude of foreign-exchange and bond market movements have come to overwhelm monetary and fiscal policies, leaving governments powerless to influence interest rates and exchange rates. As a result, the integration of financial markets has significant effects on the effectiveness and the differential distributional impact of national macroeconomic policies. A trade-off between national macroeconomic policy autonomy and exchange rate stability has developed, with financial market operators more willing to give up autonomy for stability. Furthermore, these financial market operators, who are interested in purchasing interest-rate sensitive assets, favor policies that are disinflationary and maintain the value of the currency.

Second, central banks and governments are accused of sacrificing long-term social and economic objectives in favor of accommodating financial market operators. In the case of monetary policy, the relation between the central bank and the government is an important determinant of policy. The degree of central bank independence varies considerably across space and time among OECD member-states. Independent central banks are found to pursue more restrictive policies (Epstein and Schor, 1990; Alesina and Summers, 1993). In part, this is because independent banks are not statutorily required to finance budget deficits, as many non-independent banks are. But even controlling for budget deficits, independent central banks are less expansionary. To some extent this is due to a traditional, and often statutory, function of the central bank to protect the value of the currency. But it is also because more independent banks are often closely aligned with the financial sector (e.g., in the United Kingdom, the United States, and Switzerland). Alesina and Summers (1993) note that by "delegating monetary policy to an agent whose preferences are more inflation-averse than are society's preferences serves as a commitment device that permits sustaining a lower rate of inflation than would otherwise be possible. By contrast, less independent banks are more closely associated with society's preference for expansionary policies, as expansion helps to fulfill traditional objectives of full employment and high social expenditures. Both econometric research (Epstein and Schor, 1985), as well as two case studies of central bank movements toward independence (the Federal Reserve in 1951, and the *Banca d'Italia* in 1981), strongly support the view that independent central banks are more restrictive.

Third, international financial integration, along with the creation of new financial instruments, is said to have blunted the effectiveness of monetary and fiscal tools, so that changes in interest rates or government borrowing have a smaller impact on the economy. Even within the field of macroeconomic theory, new approaches were developed that argued that state intervention in the economy was irrelevant, if not counterproductive. The new theoretical models drew heavily on rational-expectations hypothesis. Models based on rational expectations implied that, once individuals became aware of the authorities' determination to reduce inflation, they would incorporate this information into their expectations and adjust their behavior accordingly. "New Classical" theorists argued that inflation could therefore be reduced with little or no effect on output and employment, provided economic agents accepted the authorities' commitment to reduce inflation and adjusted their price-setting behavior. Credibility, therefore, was seen as to play a crucial role in reducing the cost of a disinflation program.

Fourth, liberalization and innovation have made financial markets much more volatile as well as much more vulnerable to financial meltdown. The strengthening of bank credit standards, promoted by the Bank for International Settlements (BIS) in the late 1980s, as well as its construction of new set of norms, rules, and procedures to deal with financial crisis, reflect central banker concerns over the operations of fully liberal, deregulated international financial order.

The successful handling of financial crises, as well as the consolidation of the BIS-centered regime, is related to the "hegemonic" interests of the United States in the financial sector (Helleiner, 1994: 19). In assuming a leadership role in promoting financial openness the United States retained its dominant position in the global economy as the largest capital market.

Neoliberal advocates in the financial sector have greater influence in the United States and Britain, than in other industrial states. The U.S.

position in the global political economy adds to the international power of financial market operators. In sharp contrast to the Bretton Woods order of constrained financial power and government control, today financial market operators have come to impose parameters on the ability of government to set macroeconomic policy. As Gourevitch (1978) pointed out in discussing the "reversed second image," the international system may be looked upon as a cause, rather than as a consequence, of domestic politics. The international system, in turn, is made up of two principle components: the distribution of power among states, or the international state system; and the distribution of economic activity and wealth, or the international economy (Gourevitch, 1978: 882-883). Domestic politics are influenced by security and finance. Just as breakdowns of security regimes have led to war and renewed efforts at cooperative behavior at war's end, so have breakdowns of financial regimes led to recessions and renewed efforts at controlling unbridled financial flows, as the Bretton Woods arrangements exemplified.

The collapse of the financial control regime has caused no less concern in the economic policy community than has the end of the Cold War regime in the security community (e.g., Mearsheimer, 1990). Limitations on state autonomy, particularly on the ability of governments to pursue Keynesian demand management policies, have caused great concern among scholars of both statist (Gilpin, 1987; Hawley, 1987) and Structuralist (Chase-Dunn, 1981; Cerny, 1994) perspectives. Liberals (Woodall, 1995), by contrast, take a far more sanguine view of the limitations on state autonomy. According to statists, the state organizes and implements its own international and domestic economic agenda according to its position in the international system. "State sovereignty in the economic realm, especially in times of either prolonged or sharp economic crisis, may well yield policies which differ from [the policy prescriptions of financial asset-holders]" (Hawley, 1987: 146). The constraints placed on the state by the market have increased both the direct and indirect political influence exerted by financial asset-holders.

Structuralists note that enhanced financial power leads to the deformation of productive investment decisions. When economic conditions are prosperous and stable, financial capital flows help support and even foster productive investment. But when the economy has become stagnant and unstable, investors tend to move their capital out of productive investments—because of increasingly uncertain longer-term prospects—and into short-term financial investments. The investment climate becomes increasingly speculative. "The new and increasingly efficient international [financial] system has helped to foster an accelerating circulation of liquid capital, bouncing from one moment of arbitrage to another" (Gordon, 1988: 59).

While a number of financial analysts warn of the increased power of financial asset-holders (Millman, 1995), others note that the markets "provide a healthy discipline which in the long term will encourage better economic policies and performance. If the global capital markets punish profligate governments by demanding higher interest rates, those governments may become more inclined to pursue sound policies" (Woodall, 1995: 4). A new debate has emerged between pro-market and statist analysts over who controls the world economy. Evidence cited in favor of financial market operators includes the inexorable rise in the volume of currency trading and cross-border flows, the proliferation of derivative instruments, which increase the speculators' leverage, and events such as the collapse of the European exchange rate mechanism. "But the evidence of recent years is that governments "lose" to the currency markets only when they attempt to defend positions that are indefensible" (Calverley, 1995: 146).

Pro-market analysts characterize the newfound power of financial asset-holders as akin to "free market vandals sweeping over the established order." Such a characterization is not too far from the one used by Rosenau to describe the breakdown of state-centric paradigms in world politics ("conceptual jailbreaks"). According to Millman (1995), this "vandalism" has rendered governments "powerless empires," controlled by economic policymakers and regulators. "Like the vandals who conquered Rome, the currency traders sweep away economic empires that have lost their power to resist. Time after time, in country after country, when governments can't cope with the new financial realities, traders are the agents of creative destruction."

BARBARIANS AT THE GATES

In Chapter II, I discussed the changes that have occurred in global finance over the past two-and-a-half decades. The globalization of production and the emergence of new international division of labor unleashed led the rapid movement of capital and technical knowledge across national frontiers. According to O'Brien (1992), geographical location no longer matters in finance and financial market regulators no longer hold full sway over their regulatory territory. The disjuncture of sovereignty-bound regulators and sovereignty-free financial market operators reveals itself with governments waging a losing war to gain control over their citizens' private and corporate taxable earnings.

Financial market integration has accelerated due to the growing concentration of market power in the hands of large institutions, such as pension and mutual funds. As populations in advanced industrial countries age, and government budgets are tight, the aging "baby-boomers" are relying less on the state to provide for retirement security and more on private investments. With the end of the Cold War the chief rival to market capitalism has been eliminated. The past seven years has witnessed a dramatic increase in the demand for capital, as formerly closed economies open up to foreign investment. Pension and mutual funds have become powerful players, with fund managers now routinely consulted by emerging market finance ministers. These fund managers now hold the ability to make or break government stabilization programs.

Another factor that has enhanced financial integration, and the ability of financial market operators to evade control by sovereignty-bound regulators, is financial innovation. The advent of flexible exchange rates was a critical factor in creating international financial integration, and meant three things: (1) the growth of the foreign-exchange market; (2) a dramatic increase in transnational capital flows following the liberalization of capital controls after the demise of the fixed rate, controlled system; and (3) the end of dollar hegemony and the emergence of new international economic and currency relationships. "As a result of these changes we now have an international financial system which is often seen as being run by the global investor, where global portfolio preferences determine the fate of currencies rather than some safer world where somehow exchange rates are determined by observable flows of trade in goods and services" (O'Brien, 1992: 33-34).

The foreign-exchange market was the first to globalize in the mid-1970s as controls were lifted and new technology created new opportunities for arbitrage (i.e., exploit price differences between different financial markets). O'Brien points out that offshore financial markets presented a challenge to state authorities. The pools of offshore money threatened national monetary policies and posed a source of inflation. Because the Eurocurrency markets offered cheaper funds from banks not restricted by reserve requirements, and a flexibility unhampered by exchange controls or interest-rate ceilings, there has emerged a two-tier market for currency: Eurocurrency rates and domestic currency rates.

If the 1970s saw the advent of the Eurocurrency markets, the 1980s was the decade of the global securities market boom, driven both by the trend towards securitization of finance and by increased activity by securities firms—as non-state actors—across a larger number of markets worldwide. Securitization means the making of an open market in financial assets; globalization is encouraged by that openness. "Open markets provide for much wider and deeper sets of relationships between buyer and seller, between borrower and investor, than do closed systems based on borrower and depositor relations with individual institutions" (O'Brien, 1992: 40). The role of the securities intermediary becomes one of trading financial instruments rather than taking the full credit risk, by placing the assets with the market rather than on the securities firm's own balance sheet. This greater openness allows more players to be involved in the deals and encourages more open competition outside traditional financial cartels and institutions.

Globalization and innovation were spurred by the new assertiveness of financial market operators. "For the investor, securitization and globalization offer more opportunities, deeper markets, more choice of borrower, more market liquidity" (O'Brien, 1993: 42). Particularly important since the mid-1980s has been the greater attention given to international risk diversification as a key factor in determining the portfolio preference of investors. Diversification has been encouraged both by regulations that have allowed a wider range of risks to be taken on, and by regulations that have actively sought to encourage diversification. However, although exchange controls have been lifted, many governments still require investment institutions (e.g., pension funds and insurance companies) to hedge the bulk of their long-term liabilities by currency, effectively meaning that the funds have to keep a majority of their assets in local currency investments to match their largely local currency liabilities. Despite the restrictions, risk diversification increases the demand for a wider range of financial instruments and opportunities, such as a wider group of currencies, companies, and countries in the portfolio, more markets, and more innovative instruments to manage risk. For example, in the early 1980s currency and interest-rate derivatives barely existed. Yet, by 1994, the total stock of derivatives traded on exchanges or sold over the counter had risen to more than $20 trillion (Woodall, 1995: 9).

THE LIMITS OF POLICY AUTONOMY UNDER COMPETING REGIMES

In this section I will outline briefly the differences that competing international financial regimes can make in the pursuit of macroeconomic policy. Under fixed exchange rates with limited capital mobility, as, for example, under the Bretton Woods international monetary regime, economists and policymakers had a relatively clear idea of the limits of policy autonomy. A government trying to expand unilaterally would soon deplete its foreign exchange reserves and would be forced to adjust through a reversal of the original expansion and possibly by a politically damaging devaluation. "Stop-go" cycles of expansion and devaluation occurred in Britain and France in the 1950s and 1960s.

The situation in the 1970s and 1980s differed dramatically from the conventional version of the limits of policy autonomy that have to do with foreign exchange reserves in a regime of fixed exchange rates. The commitment to defend the exchange rate has been looser in the last two decades. On the other hand, private capital flows have been far more important and free than in the 1950s and 1960s, and the development of offshore markets allowed many countries to borrow much more easily and on good terms to finance current account deficits. Yet, despite these developments, policymakers in major industrial countries still felt constrained by external considerations, and there were many policy reversals following sharp deteriorations in the current account. Britain and Italy in the 1970s, and Germany and France in the early 1980s are major examples.

The implication of this is that there are limits to policy autonomy in addition to those that operate through foreign exchange reserves in a regime of fixed exchange rates. Even in regimes of flexible exchange rates with high capital mobility, the currency depreciation that will accompany any attempt at unilateral monetary expansion may overshoot the medium-run equilibrium exchange rate. This will produce a higher rise in inflation than in a closed economy, as rises in import prices affect domestic wage-setting and seep into the prices of domestic goods. Thus, in an open economy with high capital mobility, flexible exchange rates alter the trade-off between inflation and unemployment. Governments may therefore be less willing to use monetary policy to counteract shocks that increase unemployment. This could partially explain the decreasing returns and eventual abandonment of national Keynesian policies and the rise of monetarist policies—and of the conservative governments that instituted such policies—in the late 1970s. However, governments could, alternatively, resort to expansionary fiscal policies, which, with no monetary accommodation, would lead to an exchange rate appreciation. That improves the trade-off between inflation and unemployment relative to a closed economy, although it worsens possible trade-offs between unemployment and the current account. Reagan administration policies in the 1980s proved to be a natural experiment in this regard, as the fiscal expansion with no monetary accommodation led to both lower inflation and unemployment, while the current account deteriorated markedly. Therefore, under flexible exchange rates and high capital mobility, there is a different conception of the limits of policy autonomy and efficacy. In a relatively open economy, an aggregate demand expansion may create either a worse inflation problem or a worse current account problem, depending on the policy mix, in comparison with a relatively closed economy.

Policy autonomy is further limited, in the long run, through the intertemporal budget constraint. In a world of high capital mobility, macroeconomic policies are eventually constrained by the solvency requirement that the value of external debt should not exceed the present discounted value of the future current account surpluses, net of interest payments (Alogoskoufis, Papademos, and Portes, 1991: 2-3). This means that, ultimately, real external debt must rise at a rate lower than the real interest rate, or that debt as a proportion of GDP must be rising at a rate lower than the difference between the real interest rate and the growth rate of GDP. A stronger version of this "solvency requirement" is that the ratio of net foreign debt to GDP must eventually be stabilized. In other words, an economy must ultimately be in a position to service its external debt, without borrowing at a rate different from the growth rate of GDP. This "sustainability," or "solvency," requirement is a third conception of policy autonomy limitation.

Thus, one can speak of three types of external constraints on macroeconomic policy. The first is the traditional liquidity constraint operating in fixed exchange rate regimes with low capital mobility. The second is the different trade-off between unemployment and inflation and unemployment and the current account in relatively open, compared to relatively closed, economies. This applies under flexible exchange rates with high capital mobility. Finally, there is the sustainability or solvency constraint that the value of external debt should not, ultimately exceed the present discounted value of future current account surpluses, net of interest payments.

POLICYMAKING UNDER CONSTRAINTS

The central question that international financial integration poses for political scientists is whether such integration has reduced the effectiveness of government policies. Because macroeconomic policies in the post-World War II period were used to set certain national societal objectives, the effectiveness of government policies is of major political and sectoral import. Andrews (1994), citing Cooper (1968), maintains that the degree of international financial integration is a third-image attribute of the international system, since a high degree of capital mobility systematically circumscribes the sustainability of national economic policies. Andrews notes two rival explanations of financial integration as a structural variable. The first, and the position taken here, is that the degree of international financial integration "constrains state behavior by rewarding some actions while punishing others" (1994: 197). The alternative explanation is that the degree of financial integration among states is a "consequence of national policy decisions to liberalize national financial markets—and the consequences associated with these decisions are fully reversible." While acknowledging that political factors (e.g., the hegemonic interests of the United States, the emergence of new domestic coalitions in support of liberalization, and shifts in economic ideology) encouraged the process of financial liberalization, as Andrews points out, none of these factors precludes a structural interpretation of the consequences of financial liberalization once undertaken.[1] Bryant (1987: 69) attacks the policy-driven explanations for financial integration by arguing that "technological nonpolicy factors were so powerful . . . that they would have caused a progressive internationalization of financial activity even without changes in government separation fences and the inducement of differing regulatory, tax, and supervisory systems." Andrews notes that even government policy changes were themselves induced by systemic factors. He writes that "the widespread abandonment of capital controls by the advanced industrial states since the late 1970s and the movement toward competitive reform of domestic market regulations were rational responses to similar competitive difficulties" (1994: 200). Perhaps the most interesting evidence in support of structural explanations comes from the cases of governments led by left-of-center political parties (e.g., France and New Zealand) which nonetheless proceeded with substantial financial liberalization efforts.

But what effect does financial liberalization have on the national macroeconomic policymaking? Woodall (1995) points out the popular belief that global financial integration and innovation have blunted the effectiveness of monetary policy by reducing the ability of central banks to set interest rates. As mentioned in the previous section, the rise of the offshore Eurocurrency markets created an alternative source of capital for businesses that were not under the control of national regulators. For monetary policy to be effective, governments must be able to control the money supply and there must a stable relationship between money supply and money demand in the economy. These two criteria for effective monetary policy were seriously undermined by financial innovation and the expansion of global finance.

Prior to the 1980s, governments controlled the money supply through a combination of interest-rate changes and regulation (Crook, 1992: 29). The narrow definition of money (M1) was the sum of all coins and paper currency in circulation, plus certain checkable deposit balances at banks and savings institutions. Checkable deposits, by law, were prohibited from paying interest. By driving up interest rates the central bank could make bonds more attractive to purchase. Instead of holding money to finance transactions, individuals and firms will opt to hold more of their wealth in the form of interest-bearing bonds. With prohibitions on interest-bearing checking accounts, and limited foreign competition, monetary policy was relatively straightforward.

During the 1980s monetary policy became more difficult to pursue. Financial market deregulation lifted the ban on interest-bearing checking accounts. A broader definition of money (M2) now included, in addition to M1, all types of checking account balances, plus new forms of savings account balances (e.g., money market deposit accounts), plus shares in money market mutual funds. The degree of financial innovation spurred some economists to adopt still broader definitions of money (M3 and so on) which included more types of bank deposits and other closely related assets. "The problem with this approach is that there is no obvious place to stop, no clear line of demarcation between those assets that are money and those that are merely close substitutes for money—so called near moneys" (Baumol and Blinder, 1988: 255).

As regulatory reform continued, interest rates were increasingly being set by the market. Governments could still influence short-term interest rates, through central bank purchases and sales of government securities through transactions in the open market (i.e., open market operations), but they could no longer easily alter the interest-rate differentials among different assets. Financial liberalization has changed the interest-rate relationship between the quantity of money supplied and demanded. As people shift their holdings of wealth between different financial assets, different measures of money send out different policy signals. Woodall (1995: 11) points out that in 1993 the 11.6 percent growth in M1 in the United States indicated substantial inflationary pressures, while the modest 1.5 percent increase in M2 signaled an economic slowdown. The collapse of the stable relationship between money supply and money demand means that the job of central bankers has become more difficult, for the choice of following pre-set monetary or interest rate rules are no longer available.

The proliferation of assets included in the money supply would hardly matter if all measures of money moved together. However, changes in interest rates, financial innovation and expectations can influence the various monies in relation to each other. That is why, throughout the 1980s, governments found that attempts to control their chosen money supply measure often failed (Crook, 1992: 30). Even when the "money supply" changed as it was supposed to, demand did not change in a reliable way.

This observation proved the notion that policymakers change the way in which the economy operates when they try to act upon it. That is, economic agents will alter their behavior when they incorporate information about the government's "policy rule." An historical example of a government policy rule is the belief that there is a long-term trade-off between inflation and unemployment, and that monetary policy can be used (at the cost of a slight higher rate of inflation) to make the economy grow faster and so reduce unemployment. In the late 1950s British economist A. W. Phillips plotted data on unemployment and the rate of change of wages for several extended periods of British history over scatter diagrams, and sketched a curve that seemed to fit the data. This "Phillips Curve" showed that wage inflation normally is high when unemployment is low and is low when unemployment is high. During the 1960s and 1970s, economists often thought of the Phillips curve as a "menu" of the choices available to policymakers. In this view, policymakers could "fine tune" the economy—calibrating the optimal mix of high employment and stable prices. In the 1970s the economy suddenly behaved far worse than the Phillips Curve relationship predicted. According to an increasingly vocal group of economists, the failed Phillips Curve relationship rested on the erroneous belief in adaptive expectations. On this view, economic agents guess at inflation in the coming year by implicitly putting weights on inflation rates in previous years; last year's rate would be given a large weight, inflation in earlier years smaller weights (Lucas, 1973; Sargent and Wallace, 1975). The problem with this method of forecasting future inflation is that it is backward-looking. Apply this method to an economy with accelerating inflation and the result would be that expected inflation trails behind actual inflation, with the forecasting errors being persistently negative and increasing. The crucial insight from the literature on Rational Expectations is that individuals and firms learn from their mistakes. If errors follow a pattern, they hold information that can be used to make a more accurate forecast. Rational expectations, therefore, cannot err systematically. If expectations are rational, forecasting errors will be random.

The Rational Expectations argument is important in discussing the influence of financial market operators on macroeconomic policymaking. The increase in computerization and other communications technology has led to a dramatic increase in the amount of financial information available to economic agents. Governments no longer hold a monopoly on economic data. The diffusion of information increases the optimal allocation of financial resources. That is, the government can influence output only by making unexpected changes in aggregate demand. But this is not easy to do when expectations are rational, because people understand what the policymakers are up to. According to Rational Expectations economists, if the monetary and fiscal authorities typically react to high unemployment by increasing aggregate demand, economic agents will soon come to anticipate this reaction—and improved communications technology reducing the time-lag for the anticipation to take place. An easy monetary policy can stimulate growth only for a short period; in the long term it will feed through into accelerating inflation.

The same rational expectations arguments that declare the impotence of central bank discretion also offer the hope of improved economic outcomes at lower costs. Recall the adaptive expectations argument that employment is affected by inflation only to the extent that inflation *differs* from what was expected. Under rational expectations, no *predictable* change in inflation can make the *expected* rate of inflation deviate from the *actual* rate of inflation (Baumol and Blinder, 1988: 364). Hence, according to the rational expectations economists, unemployment will always remain at the natural rate—except for random, and therefore totally unpredictable, gyrations due to forecasting errors. The implications of rational expectations for the conduct of macroeconomic policy are significant, for if expectations are rational, the inflation rate can be reduced without the need for a period of high unemployment because the short-run Phillips curve is vertical. Since Rational Expectation economists believe that inflation can be reduced without losses in output, they tend to be inflation-hawks and allies of the so-called bond-market vigilantes.

Financial market operators are said to influence policymaking through their ability to reward or punish governments for the policies chosen. As Woodall (1995: 15) points out, even if monetary policy remains effective, governments may feel they have lost autonomy because "they are shackled by investors who hold their currency, in particular bondholders." Although central banks can set short-term interest rates, they can no longer control long-term rates. The effect of a change in monetary policy on bond yields depends on bondholders' expectations of its impact on the economy. For example, if a central bank tries to loosen policy at a time when inflationary expectations are rising, its attempts will be partly neutralized by a rise in long-term rates. To a large extent, "central bankers must conduct monetary policy by influencing expectations" (Woodall, 1995: 15).

The nature of a bond is such that it offers a fixed nominal coupon value to the holder at specific future dates. However, its selling price can differ from its face value. When market interest rates change, the prices of bonds will change. More specifically, if interest rates rise, the prices of bonds will fall; if interest rates fall, the prices of bonds will rise. Hence, general interest-rate rises generate capital losses for bondholders; reductions in the rate of interest create capital gains for bondholders. The longer the term-to-maturity of the bond, the greater the possibility of capital gain or loss (Miller and Pulsinelli, 1985). Given a level of risk, the rate of interest on short-term bonds differs from the rate of interest on long-term bonds.

When financial asset-holders suspect a government's commitment to price stability, the dominant expectation is that market rates of interest will rise in the future. The interest rate hike represents increases in the political risk premium (i.e., political risk is the risk that a government will pursue policies that reduce the value of an investor's asset). Assume that an investor purchases a bond with a five-year maturity and an effective yield of six percent. If market rates of interest were expected to rise to nine percent gradually over the next five years, and if the investor tried to sell that bond in three years, he or she would sustain a capital loss. If all yields on bonds from one year to five years are the same, rational investors expecting higher market rates of interest in the future will attempt to sell their longer-term bonds to avoid the anticipated capital losses as market rates rise. Higher market interest rates increases the opportunity costs of holding money for transactions purposes. As a result, individuals and firms will make fewer transactions, thereby slowing down overall economic activity in the country. Reduced economic activity leads to higher unanticipated inventories, and thus layoffs of workers.

In a world of capital mobility, financial asset-holders can reduce the political risk of inflationary policies by transferring their capital to countries with more inflation-conscious government. Governments that pursue price stability are rewarded with infusions of capital, while governments prone to bouts of "macroeconomic populism" (Dornbusch, 1988) suffer the fate of capital flight. International financial integration has imparted a disinflationary bias onto central bankers.

The rules of fiscal policy have changed as well. But the effects have been more ambiguous than for monetary policy. In some ways, fiscal policymakers have been strengthened by financial innovation and by the expansion of international finance. In other ways, their power has been checked. Financial market operators encourage profligate governments to tighten their belts by demanding higher bond yields or depreciating the value of their currencies. At the same, though, the increased mobility of international capital has given governments more freedom to borrow when they had to finance deficits in their domestic markets. International capital has played a huge role in supplying the needs of the American government since the worsening of the country's fiscal deficit in 1980.

In a closed economy, if a government increases its budget deficit it pays higher interest rates to persuade domestic investors to hold more government debt (i.e., bonds). The higher interest rates, in turn, "crowds out" investment demand. But once governments have access to the global savings pool, they can borrow more cheaply because even a small rise in interest rates will immediately attract overseas funds (Woodall, 1995: 15). On a world stage, larger budget deficits will push up real interest rates, but the domestic penalty is now smaller. It is no coincidence that public-sector debt in industrial states has increased sharply: during 1974-94, total net public-sector debt as a percentage of GDP in the OECD economies has risen from 15 percent to 40 percent (Woodall, 1995: 15). The budget deficit as a percent of annual GDP among G-7 states has increased from 0.9 percent in 1947-67 to 5.2 percent in 1981-87 (Nau, 1990: 374).

As in the monetary policy case, the influence of structural arrangements and their political effects must be considered. Under the Bretton Woods regime, fixed exchange rates and restricted capital flows exerted discipline on macroeconomic management. There it was seen that the impact of official transactions on reserve levels would force policy adjustment. Before reserves were exhausted, governments had to tighten fiscal policy in order to reduce the current account deficit. International capital mobility removed that constraint. As Meerschwam (1991) explains, fiscal authorities in one state could now decide to pursue a politically-popular domestic expansion program, financed through heavy international borrowing. Through this program of borrowing, the authorities cause large and persistent deficits on the current account, which are mirrored in large and persistent foreign capital inpayments. Unlike the situation where authorities are concerned about depleting its foreign reserves in defense of a fixed exchange rate, in this case they are not forced to change their macroeconomic policies—at least not in the short-to-medium term. Although the current account deficit means that liabilities are incurred that will have to be paid off in the future, politically undesirable adjustments of domestic policies can be postponed as long as international markets finance domestic policies. For example, the worsening of the United States current-account balance from a surplus of $1 billion in 1980 to a deficit of $160 billion in 1987 was mirrored by the growth of foreign inflows of capital (Crook, 1992: 33). "Monetary and fiscal authorities [were optimistic] that policy independence would prevail once new international institutional arrangements freed them from foreign reserve constraints in setting optimal domestic policies" (Meerschwam, 1991: 44).

But this optimism proved to be misplaced. Even in a world of flexible exchange rates and capital mobility, the external sector—this time in the form of financial asset-holders' assessments of a state's credit risk—plays a role in domestic policymaking. International financial integration allows a government's creditors (i.e., domestic and foreign holders of the state's currency and bonds) to "pass a vote of no-confidence in its policies" (Crook, 1992: 34). "After indulging governments for years and allowing them to build up debts relatively painlessly, [financial asset-holders can] suddenly decide enough is enough and turn into disciplinarians, demanding a fatter premium to compensate for the risk of default or higher inflation" (Woodall, 1995: 16). Failure to receive higher premiums (i.e., higher rates of interest on government bonds) can lead to capital flight, as investors move their money abroad. In such a case, policymakers only manage to procrastinate over unpopular adjustment decisions; they cannot avoid them permanently.

UNHOLY TRINITIES AND THE PRICE OF INDEPENDENCE

The changes in the international financial regimes, such as the shift from fixed to flexible exchange rates, and the reemergence of international capital mobility, changed the relationship between states and financial asset-holders. From the Depression until the early 1970s, states held finance in a national prison, not permitting financial asset-holders the opportunity to hedge political risks created by state macroeconomic policies. As long as these risks remained manageable, in the high-growth environment of the 1950s and 1960s, financial asset-holders were not pressed into challenging the existing state-imposed capital control regime. As price stability eroded, domestic growth slowed, and interest differentials between nationally-denominated assets grew, the costs of the capital control regime became unsustainable. Incentives for financial innovation to circumvent the controls grew. As states dismantled the disciplinary structure of fixed exchange rates, the political risks of high inflation soared. Financial asset-holders, long held under the thumb of states, began to exercise both "exit" and "voice" strategies in order to enhance their autonomy from states.

Today, some financial analysts warn that the relationship is now reversed, with governments now the captive of the financial asset-holders. As Mundell (1962, 1963) have explained, policy autonomy costs more in terms of lost exchange rate stability as international capital mobility increases, due to current- and capital-account effects. Even states with clear expansionary preferences would be expected to choose policy mixes that reduce the political risks to asset-holders' expected rates of return. Evidence from the OECD shows that governments with large fiscal deficits, large current-account deficits, and a history of high inflation now pay a penalty in the form of higher real interest rates (Woodall, 1995: 17). This "unholy trinity" (i.e., the dilemma that governments cannot simultaneously achieve the objectives of exchange-rate stability, capital mobility, and monetary policy autonomy) has become a staple in international economics.

I would, however, add an "unholy trinity" of my own, which in its own way has become as great a dilemma as the first. That is, governments can no longer command credibility of policy (in the form of lower long-term interest rates) and macroeconomic policy autonomy, in the face of international financial integration. The reason is simple. Policy autonomy creates incentives for governments to practice deception, and in a world where financial asset-holders have access to the same information as governments, state attempts at deception will result in political-risk diversification strategies, such as currency substitution. These diversification strategies manifest themselves in the form of higher long-term interest rates. Financial asset-holders demand greater accountability from their governments, and governments would be wise to deliver. Accountability includes transparent policymaking, where asset-holders can plainly see the implications of policy on their rates of return. Stubborn state attempts to hang on to declining autonomy will only result in greater uncertainty in the markets—an uncertainty that will keep political risk premiums high. This chapter stressed the power of financial asset-holders as the new disciplinarians in evaluating national macroeconomic policies. While much of the analysis of this study focuses on the changes that international financial transactions have wrought on national policymaking autonomy, changes in national financial markets since the early 1970s were no less dramatic. Indeed, the international financial integration that has constrained policymakers has altered the relationship between governments and domestic financial institutions as well. Domestic financial intermediaries, facing competition from overseas sources of credit as well as price-related financial innovations designed for a high inflation environment, sought to renegotiate the terms of the deal that they had struck with their states decades earlier. The following chapter will explore changes in the bargain that financial institutions have made with their governments.

NOTE

1. Indeed, I argue that ideological shifts are structural explanations in themselves, in that doctrine determines what policy options are even considered.

CHAPTER V

Renegotiating the Bankers' Bargain

> Thus have the fears of the older generation of central bankers been vindicated. Certainly it is no coincidence that this whole cycle started at a time, 60-80 years ago, that also witnessed the advent of suffrage in many democracies. This placed political leaders under enormous pressure to supply social services to the newly enfranchised electorates. Initially, the response was to subject banking systems to controls designed essentially to facilitate the supply of credit that the governments did not raise through taxation. In the long run, however, the markets themselves were the prime beneficiaries of governments' need for credit. The gold standard was aristocracy's way of keeping the financial markets in their place; democracy has yet to find a substitute (Pringle, 1992: 107).

The period since the early 1970s has been one of unusual stress and turmoil for international finance and domestic financial markets the world over. In the 1980s, many states modified the system of regulating their financial markets, including both banks and securities markets (Cerny, 1993). The dynamic behind these changes, which often cut across traditional political cleavages, was a complicated blend of different but interrelated political and economic factors. First, an ideological backlash against state economic interventionism in general became the central characteristic of conservative politics, especially in the form of Thatcherism in Britain and Reaganomics in the United States. Second, there developed in the 1970s a widespread perception that the welfare state and Keynesian demand management had reached the limits of effectiveness and were leading to a vicious circle of stagnation and inflation—a perception shared by significant elements of the Left as well as the Right. Finally, the pressures of a world economy characterized by increasingly complex and volatile international capital flows—and the impossibility of insulating national economies at both macroeconomic and microeconomic levels—forced states to experiment with a variety of policies, from neomercantilism to promoting even further liberalization, designed to improve their competitive advantage in a more liberal world. Finance was therefore at the very heart of the "competition state" (Cerny, 1993).

In many ways, finance has "come into its own" as a central issue of national policymakers in both the industrial and developing worlds. With the new and enhanced status of finance has come a new fear—a fear of the repercussions of unconstrained capital markets wreaking havoc upon economies and laying waste to existing socioeconomic orders. To be sure, the unleashing of financial power has called into question the feasibility of the type of macroeconomic policymaking that had served as a hallmark of postwar industrial development. The years of limited capital mobility, and government-directed allocation of credit, have given way to a market-driven allocation process.

Why this has occurred, and the implications of this sea-change on the way economic entities—individual, corporate, and state—are organized, are the subject matter of this chapter. This Brave New World of international finance is made possible by a new round of technological and financial innovation, partially an unintended effect of past government policies, and partially the creation of a new relationship between state and market in response to change. The limited capital mobility of the 1945-70 period was an aberration along the road to ever more integrated regional and global capital markets. The success of the capital controls of that time was due to the confluence of three streams: (a) the political decision of leaders of the industrial world to cooperate in order to avoid a repeat of the devastating Depression of the 1930s in particular, and the socioeconomic costs of the vicissitudes of the business cycle in particular; (b) the political decision on the part of American leaders for their country to become the world's central banker—the underwriter and lender for the world economy; and (c) the state of technology and industrial development, which allowed for large bureaucratic entities to organize, plan, and execute policy on a national level.

Since 1970, these three factors have changed. The disinflationary bias of the Gold Standard, which led to exaggerated business cycles and the sacrifice of national policy goals to the defense of the currency, gave way increasingly to the inflationary bias of the post-World War II period. Inflation, not depression, became the key concern of governments by the 1970s. Just as the 1930s' political coalitions were built to reflate the economy, the coalitions built in the late 1970s—that came to power in the 1980s—were dedicated to bring inflation to heel. The increasing stress of economic leadership on the United States in the 1960s gave way to the suspension of the gold-exchange standard in 1971 and creation of the floating rate currency "non-system" in 1973. I say non-system, for industrial state leaders were determined to create new fixed and limited-flexibility currency schemes (the Exchange Rate Mechanism of the European Monetary System being just the latest). However, efforts to recapture the government control of the Bretton Woods era have failed due to important shifts and innovation in technology and finance. The nearly 100-year secular trend toward greater efficiency gains through corporatization, reached its zenith in the 1950s. Until that time, bureaucratic entities could rationalize the industrial process. Because production reached the mass scale in the 1910s with Fordist production operations, large-scale organizations were used to allocate resources—material, human, and capital—to where they were needed. Standardization of both product and process lent themselves to bureaucratic organizing techniques.

The Second World War was the start of a new innovation cycle. New products, and improvements on old products, came on line. Innovation challenged the standard format of the industrial enterprise, and stimulated a new round of entrepreneurial capitalism, particularly in the United States. The effects of the changed industrial environment did not become apparent until the 1970s, when the economic downturn exposed the weak underpinnings of Fordism. Combined with the end of the fixed exchange rate system and new capital mobility, new financial instruments were created in order to deal with greater uncertainty.

Acting separately, innovation, technology, and regulatory reform would each have spurred rapid financial change during the 1980s. But they came together, and interconnected, each multiplying the effects of the others. As a result, there has been little time for the capital market, or the governments that regulate it, to adapt. Given that both are moving into uncharted waters, the transition to a new world of finance

is likely to be hazardous. Mistakes have been made, and no doubt more
will be. The stable postwar industrial world had ended—and with it the
arrangements governing the relationship between states and financial
markets, known as the bankers' bargain.

A SYMBIOTIC RELATIONSHIP

Territorial states and financial markets have had a tenuous, though
mutually profitable, relationship throughout history. Since the first
"financial transformation" of the late eighteenth and early nineteenth
centuries, government intervention in the operation of financial markets
has been driven by the imperatives of the territorial state and the state-
based international system (Cerny, 1993: 52). The first imperative has
been the consolidation and expansion of the state apparatus itself,
which has required secure sources of capital, especially during periods
of fiscal crisis. The development of nationwide banking systems greatly
enhanced the potential power of the governments of these territorial
states, enabling them to borrow on a vastly greater scale—a power used
mainly to wage wars of historically unprecedented cost.[1] Financial
markets benefited from their ties to the state, for the state offered
protection of profitability for bankers and other financial
entrepreneurs—mainly through the granting of segmented market
monopolies—and enforcement of contracts. Thus, governments have
promoted and guaranteed domestic banking systems and, in a more
uneven way, securities markets. Indeed, government demand for
finance, especially to cover growing budget deficits, is still a major
factor in the expansion, as well as the regulation, of markets.
Increasingly, governments turned to central banks as instruments
through which they hoped to centralize the control of credit and gain
privileged access to it. Central banks then became important mediators
in the political relationship between the market and governments.

The second imperative has been economic competition between
states themselves, which has required the expansion of national wealth
more generally and the development of new production and
consumption processes. Thus, governments have provided direct
finance to industry through subsidy, procurement, and public
ownership. They have attempted indirectly to channel private sources
of finances to selected sectors, and manipulated monetary and fiscal
levers. And they have supported the development of "finance capital"

or "organized capitalism" in the era of corporate integration characteristic of the Second Industrial Revolution (from the late nineteenth to the middle of the twentieth century).[2] Different national systems of regulation have generally consisted of policy measures and enforcement structures that represent varying balances between the above goals. These balances reflect the interaction of three main dimensions of differentiation between states: endogenous state capacity, or the ability of particular states to intervene effectively; the nature of national economic structures; and the degree of vulnerability of the national economy to transnational market (and other economic and political) forces and pressures. Essentially two competing models of capitalism have emerged—relatively open, market-driven systems and relatively closed, state or corporate-driven systems—although these analytical distinctions blur somewhat in practice (Cerny, 1993: 53). To distinguish between the two systems, it is important to focus on the process by which savings are transformed into investments and then allocated among competing users (Zysman, 1983: 55).

The first type has tended to be characterized by active financial markets and a diversified banking system combining to provide relatively short-term credit with a view to financial returns. Under this "capital-market" system, resources are allocated by prices established in competitive markets. The second type, often called "strategic" or "developmental," has tended to be characterized by structures that give a greater developmental role to long-term debt rather than equity or short-term debt, and which integrate industrial and financial decision-making under the aegis of structured linkages between the state, the banks, and extended corporate networks. Under this "credit-based" system, critical prices are either administered by government or set by large financial institutions. It is often argued that the character of the spread of modern capitalism is the result of the leading position, during key phases of capitalist development, of certain states characterized by capital-market financial systems, especially Britain in the nineteenth century and the United States since the Second World War. The role of finance is crucial. The stability of the production and trading system under the gold standard was guaranteed by the dominance of London as a financial and commercial center (rather than by Britain as the industrial "workshop of the world"), by the willingness of the British state to back up its financial institutions, and the willingness of British individuals and institutions to export capital. In turn, the stability of the post-World War II period was guaranteed by American support for the Bretton Woods system and the dollar-exchange standard, along with a willingness to alleviate the postwar dollar shortage (Cerny, 1993: 53).

Robert Pringle (1992) refers to the terms of the economic and political relationship between financial institutions and the state as the "bankers' bargain." He argues that a rough balance of power was maintained in which each side had its recognized sphere of influence—the state exercised control of monetary and economic policy while extending limited support to the banking system, whereas the banks secured freedom to exercise their business judgment and competitive impulses, subject to close official regulation. The premise of this chapter is that the current bankers' bargain, forged in the depression years of the 1930s, has been under pressure for the past twenty years. The reason for this upsetting of the state-market relationship has been the vast expansion in the power of financial markets. Much of this expansion has come with the rise of globalization of borrowing and lending, which has reduced the dependence of markets on the state. Likewise, states' control over the allocation of finance for economic policy purposes has been weakened. Market processes have contributed to the inexorable erosion of the effectiveness of policy instruments. The increasing financial sophistication on the part both of individuals and firms—driven by fundamental changes in the structures of international production and financial intermediation—has undermined the possibility of discretionary policy changes.

What most upset the equilibrium between financial and political interests was the policymakers' realization that, although they had extended further privileges to the financial sector, they had not gained greater policy autonomy. On the contrary, market processes contributed to the inexorable erosion of the effectiveness of policy instruments. To take one example, exchange rate "overshooting" in the volatile foreign-exchange market persuaded many governments to dedicate monetary policy to exchange rate stabilization, which meant that it could not be used for other purposes (Pringle, 1992: 92). More generally, many of the difficulties facing both monetary and fiscal policy can be traced back to increasing financial sophistication on the part both of individuals and firms, and to their ability to "see through" discretionary policy changes, due partly to growing familiarity with financial market processes.

Although several forces have been behind the increasing influence of financial markets, two have been particularly strong: first, the interaction between political and financial interests (the politicians' desire to underwrite new programs interacting with the profit motive of financial entrepreneurs); and second, new interests generated by social changes which have introduced, in each decade since the First World War, a new generation of customers with rising expectations of political and financial services. The point is that an increased supply of political services required financing, and an increased supply of financial services required government support. As barriers broke down in the tightly controlled national financial systems, both issuers and investors discovered new choices. And as financial product market segmentation eroded, price competition increased among close substitutes, which diminished the value of traditional relationships that had long served to tie issuers, investors, and intermediaries together (Meerschwam, 1991: 2-3).

A BARGAIN STRUCK

Since the development of deposit banking, the classical gold standard stands as the only regime to have imposed tight constraints on both governments and markets (Pringle, 1992: 93). In Chapter II, I discussed international monetary regimes. Here, I will discuss how those regimes affected domestic state-financial relations.

The gold standard operated from about 1880 to the outbreak of World War I in 1914. An attempt was made to reestablish the gold standard after the war, but failed in 1931 during the Great Depression. Today, there are vague discussions of reestablishing the gold standard, but it is unlikely that this will happen. Nevertheless, there is a fixation with the precious yellow metal, and supporters of return to gold talk of the halcyon days of the gold standard. The appeal of the gold standard can be traced to the belief that it provides price and exchange rate stability (Eichengreen, 1985).

Under the gold standard, each national government defined the gold content of its currency and, according to the "rules of the game," passively stood ready to buy or sell any amount of gold at that price. Since the gold content in one unit of each currency was fixed, exchange rates were also fixed. This was called mint parity. The exchange rate could then fluctuate above or below the mint parity (i.e., within the gold points) by the cost of shipping an amount of gold equal to one unit of the foreign currency between two monetary centers.

The exchange rate was determined within the gold points by the forces of demand and supply and was prevented from moving outside the gold points by gold shipments. That is, the tendency of a currency to depreciate past the gold export point was halted by gold outflows from the country. These gold outflows represented the deficit in the country's balance of payments. Conversely, the tendency of the country's currency to appreciate past the gold import point was halted by gold inflows. These gold inflows measured the surplus in the country's balance of payments. Since the deficits were supposed to be settled in gold and countries had limited gold reserves, deficits could not go on forever but had to be corrected quickly.

The adjustment mechanism under the gold standard, as explained by Hume (1752), was the automatic "price-specie-flow mechanism," which operated as follows. Since each country's money supply consisted of either gold itself or paper currency backed by gold, the money supply would fall in the deficit country and rise in the surplus country. As a result, the exports of the deficit country would be encouraged and its imports would be discouraged until the deficit in its balance of payments was eliminated. By linking domestic money supplies to gold flows (albeit with some central bank intervention) in all countries subscribing to the standard, sustained outflows of gold could be relied upon to contract the domestic money supply.

The price-specie-flow mechanism was an automatic adjustment process. It is triggered as soon as the balance-of-payments disequilibrium arises and continues to operate until the disequilibrium is entirely eliminated. For the adjustment process to operate, governments were not supposed to sterilize the effect of their money supply of a deficit or surplus in their balance of payments. By passively allowing the money supply to change for balance-of-payments considerations meant that governments could not use monetary policy for achieving full employment without inflation.

According to the "rules of the game" of the gold standard, governments of deficit countries were required to reinforce the adjustment process by further restricting credit (e.g., through increasing the interest rate), while governments of surplus countries were required to further expand credit. Thus, the rules imparted an disinflationary bias. However, Nurske (1944) and Bloomfield (1959) found that monetary authorities often did not follow the rules of the game during the period of the gold standard but sterilized part, though not all, of the effect of a balance-of-payments disequilibrium on the country's money supply. Michaely (1968) argued that this was necessary to moderate the adjustment process and prevent an excessive reduction in the deficit country's money supply and an excessive increase in the surplus country's money supply.

The above is how the adjustment mechanism was supposed to have worked under the gold standard. In reality, according to Taussig (1925) the adjustment mechanism worked much too quickly and smoothly and with little, if any, transfer of gold among countries. Taussig found that balance-of-payments disequilibria were settled mostly by international capital flows rather than through gold shipments. That is, when the United Kingdom had a balance-of-payments deficit, its money supply fell, interest rates rose, and this attracted a short-term capital inflow to cover the deficit.

The Bank of England reinforced this incentive for capital inflows by deliberately raising its bank rate (i.e., discount rate), which increased interest rates and capital inflows even more. Furthermore, the reduction in the British money supply as a result of a deficit seems to have reduced domestic economy activity more than prices, and this discouraged imports.

Not only did most of the adjustment under the gold standard not take place as described by the price-specie-flow mechanism, but if the adjustment process was quick and smooth, this was due to the special conditions that existed during the period of the gold standard. The pound sterling was the most important international currency and London the most important international monetary center. Therefore, there could be no lack of confidence in sterling or shifts into other currencies and to other rival monetary centers.

The Bretton Woods period provides the only example of an attempt to subject the financial markets and national governments to an internationally agreed set of rules and institutions. Certainly, the regime reflected American foreign policy and business interests, and was sustained by American power. Yet, at least an attempt was made to justify and legitimize the rules in terms of universally accepted "rational" norms. Through international financial institutions, governments of member countries were constrained by: (1) the commitment to a liberal, multilateral world economy enshrined in the articles of agreement of the International Monetary Fund (IMF) and the General Agreement on Tariffs and Trade (GATT); (2) the need to justify internationally any proposed change in the par value of a country's national currency; (3) the fact that exchange rate changes were fraught with political difficulties because any change hurt some sectoral interest; and (4) the program for removing the remaining trade and payments restrictions under Article VIII of the IMF. The instruments available to make these commitments effective in the markets included capital controls, credit controls, interest rate ceilings, fiscal policy, and limited credit facilities from the IMF. These instruments were effective only so long as financial-market activity was at a low level, domestic and international markets remained segmented, and such constraints on national autonomy were viewed as legitimate. While these conditions held, governments were in control, using central banks as the main institutional means of exerting such control.

This regime was weakened in both domestic and international dimensions by social changes and financial innovation. The 1960s saw the rise of a new class of internationally mobile individuals—notably international corporate executives and professionals—for whom it was increasingly a matter of choice where they called home. As these groups joined the ranks of the old rich, the pool of internationally mobile (and tax-avoiding) funds rose, swelled further by capital flight from developing countries. It was this pool that the new Eurocurrency markets would tap, from the early 1960s, in addition to the liquid funds of the corporations themselves. Exchange control became gradually less enforceable.

The growth of transnational corporations was spearheaded by US corporations, riding the great waves of American direct foreign investment, encouraged by the creation of the European Economic Community (now the European Union) in 1958. The 1960s also witnessed the expansion of American banking overseas on an unprecedented scale. Whereas formerly only a few American banks maintained a handful of foreign branches, mainly in London and South America, by the end of the decade they had scattered branches throughout the capitalist world, including many developing countries.

Governments continually attempted to reassert control, partly by direct action on financial flows and partly through the creation of swap lines between central banks to defend the dollar (Salvatore, 1990; Spero, 1990). But such policies, aimed at reasserting official control, only spurred further innovation. Everywhere market segmentation started to erode. In time, these market changes overthrew the postwar reliance on direct controls. Too many new and quite legal channels of financing were available. American controls did not succeed in their objective of preserving the existing monetary system; instead, they helped to establish the offshore markets, and they undermined the effectiveness of other countries' existing controls. This failure signaled not only the waning of American hegemony but also the passing of the era of government control over international finance.

The Bretton Woods arrangements eventually collapsed in the early 1970s because market growth created a new set of incentives: governments saw that they could do better outside the official system, i.e., they could borrow offshore on a very large scale, an option that was not available in the 1950s. As Meerschwam (1991) points out, the monetary and fiscal authorities had faith that policy independence would prevail once new international institutional arrangements freed them from foreign reserve constraints in setting optimal domestic policies. Thus, from the mid-1960s, the new international money markets granted President Johnson an initially ample supply of credit to finance the Viet Nam War, allowing him to avoid raising taxes. However, this growth of US government liabilities (from about $30 billion in 1966 to $60 billion in 1971) fueled a further rapid expansion of Eurodollar credit, which was then used to finance massive speculation against the dollar (borrowing dollars on the market and selling them spot). This speculation was a key factor in the collapse of the Bretton Woods system, with President Nixon's decision to suspend gold sales in August 1971 (Pringle, 1992: 97).

National policymakers decided to take the market solution to their payments woes. That is, by borrowing and moving to flexible rates, policymakers hoped to afford themselves greater freedom for policy discretion. They were to find out that they had in fact surrendered their freedom and, in some cases, their credit also. Finance, not government, was the real beneficiary of currency floating. Policymakers only managed to procrastinate over unpopular adjustment decisions, they could not avoid them permanently. The move to flexible rates was associated with a massive expansion of demand for financial intermediation and new financial services. This was for two main reasons. First, inflationary economic policies, previously held in check by fixed rates, were allowed greater scope and needed vast amounts of financing: floating by itself was found not to give sufficient autonomy. International credit also needed to stabilize exchange rates. Second, huge differences in expectations about exchange rate movements, linked to rapidly shifting inflationary expectations, entailed an immediate increase in risks of all financial contracts (especially long-term contracts). Suddenly, there was no international money, nothing that could serve as a standard of deferred payments (Kindleberger, 1984). So the markets got into the business of creating risks, or at least financing risk-taking, and at the same time providing new techniques for reducing these risks.

As more volatile and generally higher interest rates appeared, investors and issuers became more interest rate (price) sensitive. This change promised rewards to the financial entrepreneur and innovator that could devise financial products that took advantage of new attitudes, especially as capital began to flow ever more swiftly across international markets. In this environment, governments responded with further marketization moves. In the regulatory sphere, this process is usually labeled "deregulation." However, this term, as Cerny (1993) points out, has usually masked a complex process of regulatory change at several levels. For example, regulations cannot merely be removed. The very operation of market economies is dependent upon the existence of *a priori* rules, as well as of a range of mechanisms to deal with market failure. These rules concern property rights, contracts, currencies, and other basic elements embedded in the nature of the modern capitalist state. Changing regulations has sectoral, macroeconomic, and transnational effects far removed from the original intentions of policymakers. Consequently, regulatory reform has not simply resulted in a reduction of regulations or of the overall weight of state interventionism, but has generally led to a complex process of drafting new regulations. These new regulations, because they are untried and untested in practice, can not only be more onerous in their effects, but can entrench new vested interests, distorting markets still further.

Finally, regulatory reform really means the attempt by the state to impose upon market actors—and upon itself—new market-oriented rules. Small private capital markets do not become dynamic sources of efficient capital allocation overnight; indeed, regulatory reform may, especially in a more liberal world, force upon them a new vulnerability which can be highly detrimental to the existing financial sector, to industrial sources of capital, and to the state. Exposure to new winds of market change can require even more complex safety nets, especially in the form of prudential regulation (e.g., capital adequacy standards) or the extension of "lender of last resort" facilities to a range of newly-troubled financial institutions (e.g., as in the American Savings and Loan crisis).

During the 1970s, in the United States, a very tightly regulated financial market relaxed to provide increased freedoms as regulators lost control. This loss of control came about as international markets outside the jurisdiction of national regulators began to offer serious competition to the national marketplace (the growing Eurodollar deposit market, for instance, presented an attractive alternative to the price-regulated market for certificates of deposits). One reason for wanting to circumvent the regulators' control was a higher level of interest rates, accompanied by their increased volatility; this situation provided investors with a new incentive to shop for the best financial product prices. Interest rates themselves had risen more readily because the revised system of exchange rates gave policymakers the freedom to concentrate on domestic policy objectives, neglecting international accounts on the grounds that the flexible exchange rate would take care of them. When stiff commodity price shocks threatened to produce domestic recession, the domestic policy focus would lead to expansionary monetary policy, inflation, and higher nominal interest rates. And while the macro- and international economic changes helped break the regulated system, the new product and price freedoms offered financial firms new rewards and risks. It led some to embark on rapid growth strategies that now be regarded as ill-advised. In fact, spectacular failures resulted, as present problems in the American savings-and-loan industry testify.

Additional private and official demand for new financing created, in effect, a new banking system closely analogous to the development of domestic banking systems in the eighteenth and nineteenth centuries. Governments made no attempt to limit cross-border financial flows. Deficit countries borrowed heavily while creditor governments went on providing guarantees to private banks in the form of deposit insurance, export credit guarantees, and safety nets for all "big" banks.

TERMS OF THE DEAL

In response to new opportunities, financial institutions started to lobby for greater freedom to offer services internationally, a freedom restricted by remaining exchange controls and other restraints on openness. In both "capital market-based" and "credit-based" types of system, the main regulatory framework for financial markets as capitalism developed resulted from the desire of national governments to protect domestically-based institutions. Finance was widely seen as a vital strategic industry, too important, especially in the context of postwar macroeconomic management, to be left to the market alone. In the "capital market-based" systems of Britain and the United States, despite different mixes of statutory supervision and "self-regulation," financial regulation developed incrementally, generally as the result of market failures and exogenous shocks. The American framework, from the establishment of the Federal Reserve System in 1913 (the result of the Panic of 1907) to the post-Depression reforms, was a particularly *ad hoc* structure, reflecting the fragmented sovereignty of American bureaucracy as well as the diversified structure of the financial system itself (Cerny, 1993). In both cases, the main principle of regulation was compartmentalization. To prevent endogenous market failure, this involved the separation of different financial "markets" to prevent failure in one from creating a chain reaction through the others, as had been seen to happen in 1929. The types of compartmentalization, however, differed: in the United States, commercial banks were prevented from dealing in securities; in Britain, stockbrokers were prevented from trading on their own account, while "jobbers" (market-makers) were prohibited from trading directly with the public.

More widely, in the context of the Keynesian welfare state, governments established a set of buffer mechanisms to prevent exogenous shocks from setting off domestic contagion effects. Capital controls, interest rate controls and other monetary policy instruments, exchange-rate stabilization, lender of last resort facilities, and the like depended ultimately on the capacity of transnational regimes and the financial strength of the international "hegemon" to underwrite the liquidity and stability of the system. Wider financial stability, in turn, made it possible for governments to "fine-tune" national economies in order to maintain the economic expansion necessary to manipulate the levers of the welfare state. Maintaining and increasing the flow of credit to the economy enabled capitalist economies to go beyond the bounds of fixed capital and physical monetary reserves in expanding the production system in a way that was compatible with greater liberalism and interdependence in production and trade.

The postwar expansion of the welfare state, then, was dependent upon the maintenance of the financial regulatory mechanisms that had developed in reaction to the breakdown of the interwar international financial structure in the 1930s. However this was itself still dependent upon maintaining, protecting, and guaranteeing the nationally-based financial systems that had originated in the first financial transformation (Cerny, 1993: 55). This became increasing difficult to do, however, especially as those systems were more and more being called upon to perform transnational tasks in the rapidly expanding world of international integration of production and trade. Now the so-called "second financial transformation" of the 1980s and 1990s, if it is indeed a new financial revolution, is widely seen to be the consequence of this structural contradiction. Financial market regulatory reform is, then, a response to the inadequacy of such nationally-based regulatory systems to deal with the new internationalization of finance.

The main features of the pre-transformation market for financial services can be summed up in a few words: segments, control, relationships, and protection (Crook, 1992). Segmentation was long a fundamental element of the regulatory responses of different states to financial market failure. While the separation of financial powers largely stemmed from custom in Europe, it was codified in American law. Over the years governments strengthened the barriers between the segments, often in response to periods of financial instability. They wanted to make the financial system more predictable and safer. So they enacted rules that mainly said who could do what or where it could be done. This approach has been intended (1) to prevent failures in one sector of the market affecting other sectors (the economy as a whole), (2) to protect weak (or politically powerful) sectors of the market from destabilizing competition, and (3) to prevent conflicts of interest (including "insider trading") which might injure smaller, private investors and thereby damage business confidence. This was crucial not only to the American financial system, which was seen by New Deal policy innovators as being at the center of the process that caused the Depression of the 1930s, but also to the American-guaranteed welfare states elsewhere as they emerged from the Second World War.

Segmentation could operate at a number of levels: in terms of geographical or hierarchical limitations within a particular financial sector, as with the prohibitions on interstate banking in the United States; between different financial sectors, such as separating commercial banking and securities markets; between different functions within sectors, such as restrictions on "universal banking," the delineation of boundaries between brokers and market-makers, the requirement that different functions within firms be rigorously separated (that is, maintaining "firewalls") or polarization; or involving the protection of professional structures within each sector, especially the setting of minimum commissions but also other prudential regulations such as capital adequacy rules, prohibitions on manipulation of customers' accounts by brokers to their own advantage (including "front running" and "churning") and so on, tailored to the particular problems of each sector.

The essence of segmentation, of course, is the restriction of competition, and restrictions on competition only retain their efficacy when other market actors are bound by analogous restrictions or do not have the market power to challenge the restrictions. As Crook (1992), points out, this caused a problem. Markets divided by regulation tend, *ceteris paribus*, to give monopolistic power to favored suppliers; new would-be competitors are turned away. To deal with that power, regulators were obliged to control the industry. They did so by setting prices (notably interest rates), using quantitative restrictions (e.g., credit controls), and practicing what used to be called "moral suasion." There were few complaints. Privileged occupiers of a market segment could hardly expect to be left to themselves. Control was the *quid pro quo* for security.

This gave rise to another difficulty. Financial systems serve as gatherers and processors of information. In market economies, the main carriers of information are prices. In financial markets, it seemed, prices could not be left to do their job. Never fear: there was another way to gather information. Safe within their segments, firms developed specialist expertise. Above all, granted a more or less fixed set of clients, they developed relationships with their borrowers and lenders. While the rationale for financial intermediation is, after all, precisely that banks and other intermediaries know more about the creditworthiness of would-be borrowers than do savers, if "relationship-finance" worked as it was supposed to, the cost in economic efficiency of controlled and segmented markets would not be prohibitive. In return for that cost, the resulting system would be stable.

When other outlets exist for obtaining funds at lower margins or investing for higher returns, then the segmented sectors will be squeezed. Preventing their decline may require effective changes in the regulatory regime to avoid loss of competitiveness. That regime would, in theory, need to be made either more restrictive and/or more inclusive, the first in order to prevent what is sometimes seen as "free-riding" on the stability provided by the regime (and to protect the positions of existing institutions and state interests), the second to loosen the regime itself to force those institutions and interests to adapt to changed competitiveness conditions. Of course, the acceptance of some loss of competitiveness may also be an option, especially in the short term. But where loss of competitiveness is the result of longer-term changes in the exogenous structure of competitiveness—whether because of the growth of new institutional structures or financial innovations that exploit loopholes and/or develop new forms of business within the territory covered by the regime, or because of the impossibility of insulating domestic markets from changes abroad—then action in the form of deregulation will usually be unavoidable. And unless the state can change or effectively counteract the competitive conditions themselves, then an overly restrictive approach to regulation may well result in further competitive decline. The crucial factor is the mix of restrictive and market opening measures taken.

This results in a complex economic and political process of regulatory arbitrage in which the policy communities representing financial sector interests and the regulators themselves, in "competition state" fashion, seek to reform the regulatory regime in the light of the new conditions. The obvious danger is that the removal of restrictions on competition will lead to either (a) a new instability or volatility that undermines potential gains in competitiveness (chaotic competition) or (b) a new distortion of markets—or both. In the second case, the new situation may simply allow those market actors best placed to take advantage of the new structured action field to use their market power to restrict competition in different *de facto* ways, using new economies of scale and transaction cost advantages to entrench their dominance. What begins as opening can turn into closing. Structural changes in the American airline industry in the 1980s—after deregulation—are frequently taken as exemplifying this process. Thus deregulation has inevitably been accompanied by various forms of re-regulation (Cerny, 1993), aiming not only to impose (and reinforce) more efficient, transnationally oriented market-type behavior, but also to control new sources of market failure and new forms of market distortion.

The contract between governments and suppliers of financial services had another clause: the government provided protection from foreign competition. This was as indispensable as segmentation, regulation, and relationships. Financial prices and flows of credit could hardly be controlled if borrowers and/or lenders had easy access to other suppliers. Domestic financial firms would find themselves losing business to less-regulated foreigners. Domestic financiers expected secure profits in return for putting up with controls; if those profits disappeared, the deal would be off.

After 1945 no special effort was needed to give protection to domestic financial firms. Capital controls were already in place almost everywhere. The support they gave to the segmented and regulated structure of domestic financial systems was not their main purpose. Perhaps it was not even understood; governments had a simpler aim in view. As John Maynard Keynes said in 1944, in a speech about the international monetary arrangements that were to be established after the war:

> We intend to retain control of our domestic rate of interest, so that we can keep it as low as suits our own purposes, without interference from the ebb and flow of international capital movements or flights of hot money . . . Not merely as a feature of the transition, but as a permanent arrangement, the plan accords to every member-government the explicit right to control capital movements.

And that is what they did. The result was not only to give governments the firmer macroeconomic control that Keynes thought desirable, but also, as a by-product, to make feasible the deal struck all over the world between governments and suppliers of financial services.

BREACH OF CONTRACT

In the recent history of financial markets, the pattern has been one of "desegmentation," in order to allow national financial institutions, faced with loss of competitiveness, to resist, and this has required both deregulation and new regulation to deal with the changed policy environment. Beginning in the 1970s, and continuing at a much faster pace during the 1980s, domestic finance based on segments, control, relationships and protection broke down. Market segments have been overrun by newcomers. Domestic controls have been repealed or greatly reduced. Relationship-banking in narrow niches has given ground to "securitization" and other sorts of price-based finance. In the big economies, most capital controls have been swept away. Nearly everywhere else they have been eased, or will be soon (Crook, 1992: 10).

The growth in the 1960s and 1970s of the unregulated markets in London for loans and other financial instruments denominated in currencies other than sterling—dubbed "Eurocurrency markets"—has provided a familiar story in the literature on transnational regulatory change. These were vastly expanded: first as dollars spread abroad in the 1960s to avoid regulatory restrictions in the United States; next as the new regime of flexible exchange rates in the early 1970s required huge new private capital flows to hedge against changes in the value of currencies; and then as "petrodollars" were recycled through London, in particular, after the first oil shock of 1973-74. The Eurocurrency markets are usually cited as the single most important structural change, creating permissive conditions which in turn forced other financial markets to react to the new structures of competitiveness that emerged. The pattern of cause and effect is complicated. Several factors in the 1950s and 1960s—pressure from expanding American finance capital for more open financial markets, American expenditure abroad (both public and private), expansion of international trade in the 1950s and 1960s, and the growth of transnational corporations—all put the Bretton Woods system under strain. The Eurocurrency markets, however, brought all of these factors together in the mid-to-late 1960s, before the Bretton Woods system actually broke down, and then expanded dramatically in the wake of its collapse.

The impact of the Eurocurrency markets was twofold. In the first place, huge amounts of funds flowed through a relatively unregulated market, free, for example, from American and British exchange controls and domestic interest rate controls (which the British government avoided in order to maximize income to British institutions and maintain their traditional international role), at interest rates that were significantly more attractive than those available in domestic markets. This meant not only that the Eurocurrency markets were price-competitive, but also that they could attract the market actors (borrowers and lenders) with the greatest financial market power, including American commercial and investment banks, transnational corporations, governments seeking finance, large public sector firms, and one source of funds with unprecedented power, the member states of the Organization of Petroleum Exporting Countries (OPEC). Demand for sovereign loans from states with inadequate financial systems themselves, from the advanced industrial states to Third World countries seeking development capital, gave the structure the impression of both growing demand and relative stability. A second aspect of the Eurocurrency markets, however, was probably more important for the specific issue of desegmentation, and only came on stream with the Third World debt crisis of the 1980s and the drying up of international syndicated loans; this was the central role the Eurocurrency markets played in shifting the composition of financial exchanges away from loans to negotiated securities.

The trend toward desegmentation has been uneven. In the United States, basic legal prohibitions on interstate banking still exist and so do the restrictions on commercial banks trading in securities, but these have been largely eroded by the advent of money market funds and a whole host of exceptions and legal changes. The ability of American financial institutions to shift their operations abroad since the 1960s forced many early changes, and the strength of American investment banks, powerful institutions that grew up in the gray area between commercial banking and stockbroking, has been a key factor in levering change at the political as well as the market level. Although it is often considered that the erosion of the Glass-Steagall Act (that part of the Banking Act of 1933 that separated commercial banks' attempts to get into the securities trading) is the result of the commercial banks' attempts to get into the securities business, in fact much of the pressure comes from investment banks and other institutions that want to undertake traditional banking business in order to diversify their activities and develop into "financial supermarkets." In Britain, the "Big Bang" of 1986 basically removed a whole system of restrictions on the securities markets, but this was only part of the overall picture following the lifting of exchange controls in 1979, and credit controls thereafter, once again giving new opportunities to nonbank institutions as well as banks to engage in a wide range of financial activities. In the securities markets in both countries, closed self-regulation gave way to greater legal regulation, with the state pushing, as well as international competitive pressures pulling, the long-protected sector of equities towards greater liberalization.

In France, the state has taken a strong lead in undermining previous state-sponsored restrictive practices and in imposing desegmentation on other—often reluctant—market actors, both to counter the loss of market share to London and to gear up for the coming of the Economic and Monetary Union (EMU) by 1999. In Germany, where universal banking—no separation between commercial and investments sides of the business—was already the rule, geographical segmentation (rooted in the German federal system) effectively insulated the financial system from systematic pressures for deregulation until the early 1990s; however the power of the *Bundesbank*, the fact that there is a single regulator for both the banks and securities markets, and the dominant role of the banks in the securities markets themselves have in fact meant that there has been little hindrance to *ad hoc* changes in practice which have made Germany a powerful player, especially on the growing bond markets. But in the European Community generally, the growing 'freedom of capital movements may handicap more rigid systems of financial regulation by starving them of both borrowers and investors, as capital flows towards less compartmentalized centers such as London. And in Japan, financial institutions have been adapting not so much through deregulation at home, although regulatory reform has been gaining momentum in recent years, as through the capacity of the huge Japanese institutions, now dominant internationally, to operate in deregulated markets outside Japan.

Segmentation has traditionally meant that borrowers and investors have had to choose between markets which were normally characterized by higher returns and more risk, such as share markets, and those usually characterized by lower returns and less risk, such as intermediated loans. At the same time, as market actors have been restricted as to the particular "playing field" in which they were permitted to compete, there has been a secondary regulatory effect of making it easier controlling market distortions: fraud, unfair competition, monopolization, and so on are easier to detect in a smaller, more insulated arena. Desegmentation has meant that, while a wider range of institutions and market actors have been able to go after higher returns, it is more difficult to control risk. But it also becomes more difficult to control market distortions. This is why the most salient issue for the public that has arisen out of the desegmentation process—and apparently (but in many ways misleadingly) out of the deregulation process as a whole—has been that of "insider trading."

The second major change in transnational financial market structures has involved the twin processes of disintermediation and securitization. Although each might be seen to have some different dynamics, the main dynamic has been the intertwining of the two processes themselves. Disintermediation concerns either the slower growth or the fall in the supply of intermediated bank credit (essentially loans), caused first by the impact of negative real interest rates in the 1970s and then by the Third World debt crisis of the 1980s. Securitization involves the growth of negotiable securities issues and trading, especially in the 1980s. In effect, whereas loan finance was traditionally seen to be less risky even if generating lower returns (because the intermediary—a bank—with its diversified deposit base acted as a buffer against failure) and securities had higher returns but more risk, both elements seemed to move in favor of securities in the 1980s. Banks also needed to reduce their exposure to bad loans ("non-performing assets") not only by cutting back on loans in general, but also by finding new sources of funds when failures undermined investor confidence in the banks themselves.

Furthermore, securities had three major advantages over loans. In the first place, they could be packaged in a variety of new ways that increased both borrower and investor demand. As securities markets became more liquid—as buyers and sellers became more plentiful—primary issues could be tailored to a more segmented and sophisticated market. Secondary trading, too, could cover a much greater variety of instruments that might be matched to the specific requirements of a wider range of market participants, especially those with transnational linkages and market power. Second, they opened up new sources of finance for governments, especially the United States, but also Japan and France, which were dealing with rapid rises in national budget deficits. Finally, they could be traded more and more easily on the international level than ever before, especially given the rise of the Eurocurrency markets and deregulation of domestic securities markets (partly in reaction to Euromarket competition). Thus, securities became far more liquid than loans at the level of major institutions operating transnationally. Sovereign governments (including major public enterprises) and blue-chip firms, dealing only in very large volumes, stopped borrowing through banks and started issuing new debentures or shares (or mixtures of the two); firms could, in effect, lend directly to other firms, with banks and other institutions acting only as brokers and/or guarantors.

Meanwhile, of course, new financial institutions grew to meet the demands for specialization which these developments entailed: sometimes subsidiaries of the banks themselves, sometimes entirely new institutions, and sometimes the result of complex mergers and takeovers in the financial world, all being permitted in the desegmentation environment described above. These institutions were dependent not on a deposit base but on a new range of brokerage and market-making activities, raising funds on the markets themselves for customers and making profits from commission income and the spread between buying and selling prices rather than from interest income. Such institutional developments interacted with the process of desegmentation in a mutually reinforcing way, making new institutions into key market actors and decompartmentalization into what economists would call a "sticky" structural development: that is, one difficult to reverse. This of course does not mean that disintermediation will continue unchecked. Efforts by major states to control their budget deficits, the gradual unraveling of the Third World debt crisis (as banks attempt to cut their losses) and the volatility of some securities markets (as manifested in the October 1987 stockmarket crash) all fed into an upturn in traditional bank lending after 1988 and a certain stagnation on many securities markets, with the rising volumes and prices of the mid-1980s a fading memory. But this is unlikely to reverse the process overall, especially in the context of the 1990-92 recession with its combination of a "credit crunch" and falling demand for loans. One significant aspect of securitization in this sense is the way it has interacted with the process of financial innovation, the third major change in financial market structures.

To the question, "Which of these changes did most to promote the expansion of global finance?" The obvious, but incorrect, answer is the easing of controls on international capital flows (Crook, 1992: 10). To the broader question, "What was the most powerful force for financial change, domestically and internationally?" a similar answer might seem equally compelling: deregulation. On this view, governments chose to undo the financial order created in the 1930s through 1960s. That is, government policy, guided by the pro-market thinking that became fashionable in the 1980s, was the initiator. However, one reliable rule in economics is that systems of regulation that distort prices continually break down, whether governments like it or not. Distorted prices create shortages and opportunities for profit. To exploit these opportunities, people and firms find ways round the rules. As a result, deregulation is often no more than acknowledgment that the rules are no longer working. In such cases, deregulation is as much an effect as a cause.

If one were to look at the set of connections between international finance, trade, innovation, and regulatory reform, the two-way links between trade and finance would be clear enough. As trade expands, flows of finance directly associated with trade automatically expand too. At the same time, broader and deeper markets for international capital facilitate trade by giving would-be net importers better access to credit. So trade and finance are linked together in a multiplier process. Next, consider the links between finance and innovation. Financial firms, spurred partly by the profit opportunities that regulation creates, will innovate in ways that expand offshore finance. This is how the so-called Eurocurrency markets came into being in the mid-1950s. So innovation makes international finance expand. Then, as the volume of cross-border banking grows, domestic banks feel the heat of fiercer competition. This drives them to innovate again. A second multiplier is at work.

What do regulators make of all this? Their first instinct, most likely, is to resist the process by closing loopholes. American regulators tried to kill the Eurodollar market in its infancy, but failed (Hawley, 1987). In international finance, regulators are at a great disadvantage, because money is so slippery. Moreover, a third multiplier is working against them. Financial institutions in countries with heavy regulation see they are at a competitive disadvantage. So they lobby for deregulation. At the same time, with every expansion of international finance due to trade and innovation, new ways to evade regulation are revealed. In both ways, an expansion of global finance promotes deregulation. And self-evidently, to complete the circle, deregulation promotes the expansion of global finance. Note that the international financial system will be drawn toward more liberal policies even if governments are initially against them. To resist that liberal tendency, regulators would have to become ever more active and intrusive. If they fail, international finance grows—driving, as well as driven by, trade, innovation, and deregulation.

As it does so, bargains, like the one struck between governments and domestic financiers in the 1930s through 1960s, break down. Exposed to offshore finance, controls fail; without controls, the boundaries between market segments cannot be defended; and without segmented markets, relationship-finance gives way to price-based finance. In short, market forces break in and run riot. However, the above description is only of the basic mechanism acting to undermine the old financial contract. If there is nothing more to be said, those anti-market arrangements might have lasted much longer. There is, indeed, more to be said.

FINANCE'S NEW DEAL

Macroeconomic conditions in the 1980s—notably, the development of American macroeconomic policy in 1980-84, during the first Reagan Administration—might have been designed to stimulate the expansion of cross-border finance. The combination of loose fiscal policy (caused by tax cuts unmatched, in aggregate, by lower spending) and tight monetary policy (reflecting the Federal Reserve's determination to fight inflation) fueled domestic demand, raised American interest rates, and made the dollar appreciate. As Crook (1992: 12) points out, these changes helped the trend towards international finance in five ways.

The new mix of policies, first, caused the United States current-account balance to move sharply into deficit: demand at home went up, and the strong dollar made imports cheap. For the same reasons, the economies of Japan and Germany moved further into current-account surplus. This increase in current-account imbalances among the three biggest economies required a corresponding expansion of net cross-border flows of capital. In effect, Japan, Germany, and other countries with current-account surpluses lent the United States the capital it needed to pay off its excess of imports over exports.

Second, the dollar exerted a powerful influence in its own right. Its sharp rise in the early 1980s, and its fall after 1985, made exchange-rate volatility more of a worry to financial markets than it had been before. Interest in options, futures, and other ways of hedging against exchange-rate risk increased. New and better techniques were much in demand. The rise in dollar interest rates (from an average of 7.4 percent in 1975-79 to 12.1 percent in 1980-84) similarly encouraged innovation. High and variable interest rates made investors want cleverer ways to manage their financial risks. In this way, too, the 1980s provided a climate in which innovators thrived.

Third, the increase in interest rates and financial volatility added to the rewards that could be won by evading domestic regulation. Those rewards depend upon gaps between the price of capital in regulated domestic markets and the price in foreign markets. The higher the interest rates are, and the more interest rates and currencies move around, the greater the opportunities for profitable "regulatory arbitrage" are likely to be. And the more controls are evaded, the weaker the case for maintaining them becomes.

Fourth, there was technology. Cheap computer-power proliferated across the industrial economies, transforming dozens of industries, finance among them. Communications technology improved dramatically, too. Together, these made possible 24-hour financial trading and a vast range of new financial products for round-the-clock traders to buy and sell.

These new products and techniques also directly hastened the decline of relationship-banking. Advances in computers, together with tougher rules on the disclosure of corporate information, created a bigger role for global credit-rating agencies. The comparative advantage that banks used to have in gathering and sifting information was steadily being eroded. And as institutional investors became bigger and more powerful, their resources and connections allowed them to track corporate performance for themselves. Gradually, therefore, in their international operations, banks have become facilitators as much as intermediaries—arranging issues of securities, packaging and trading debt, providing lines of credit, and so on.

Advances in technology raise a number of hard questions for financial markets—including whether all the fancy new methods have added to or reduced the danger of instability. In the 1980s new technology reinforced the mechanism, already in place, that was promoting global finance.

Finally, there was politics. In the 1980s, Ronald Reagan, in the United States, and Margaret Thatcher, in Britain, led a shift to more conservative, less interventionist economic policies. Deregulation, and not just in finance, was in vogue. Mrs. Thatcher's government abolished foreign-exchange controls within days of taking office in

1979, partly to advertise the fact that Britain under the Tories would be open for business with the world, but partly also to proclaim that needless regulation of any sort would henceforth be under attack.

With the shift in economic thinking, financial regulatory reform has been the rage nearly everywhere in the industrialized world over the past twelve years. As the decade wore on, supposedly socialist governments challenged Mr. Reagan and Mrs. Thatcher in their deregulating zeal. Even Japan's government—in popular mythology, the die-hard controller of everything in sight—has liberalized its system extensively (Meerschwam, 1991).

The above depiction of the rise of globalization strongly suggests that international finance would have expanded quickly in the 1980s, even without the ideological push toward deregulation. The macroeconomic background, the spur of new technology, and the internal pressures for change that every price-regulated system faces, were not to be denied. These forces, indeed, go far to explain why the political urge to deregulate came when it did, and why resistance to it was so muted. They also explain why governments with no political commitment to deregulating (notably Japan's) ended up doing so almost as boldly as the zealots.

While regulatory reform did not singly cause the expansion of global finance, it was one factor among many—and was as much an effect as a cause. Once that is admitted, and national policies towards finance are relegated to a supporting role, it becomes easier to see that national financial systems have been, throughout, much more alike than they seem. The traditional model—based on segments, control, relationships, and protection—was in place everywhere, until the late 1960s. It began to break down in the 1970s. In the 1980s, the trend gathered pace and became irreversible. The story is as true for Japan, despite the bewildering hierarchy of its financial institutions, as for the United States.

This chapter has examined regulatory reform and innovation in the financial markets of the advanced industrial states. Prior to the mid-1970s, national financial markets were riddled with regulations and market conventions, which shielded deposit and loan rates from normal pressures of supply and demand. Both deposit and loan rates were set independently of market-determined rates, and were shielded from competition from Eurocurrency rates. By the 1990s regulatory reform had succeeded in freeing interest rates on deposits of firms and individuals. By the late 1980s, most OECD states had established markets in certificates of deposit with rates closely tied to those in the money market.

NOTE

1. Organski makes a similar argument in measuring the political capacity of states by their ability to extract resources from its citizens.

2. Gerschenkron (1962) made the argument that the later any given state's industrialization started after Britain's, the greater the degree of state intervention (and consolidation of sources of finance) needed to make industrialization successful.

CHAPTER VI

The Limits of Policy Autonomy

For a policy to prevail it must have power . . . it must obtain the compliance of those who really act in the economy (Gourevitch, 1989: 264).

The focus of this chapter is on the state's relation to transnational capital. In Chapter III, we reviewed how industrial states constructed an international monetary order after the Second World War that restricted international movements of domestic capital. Over time, this restrictive order brought these governments into conflict with an increasingly assertive group of transnational corporations, banks, and investors. In this chapter, we trace the political and economic priorities of industrial state governments as they confronted, first, the effects of parameter shifts in reaction to both a changed international monetary regime and commodity supply shocks in the 1970s, and then growing worldwide economic disorder, brought on in part by rapid transformations in banking and finance. In the process, I attempt to reveal the dynamic relationships among state actions in the global political economy, the political and economic activities of non-state financial market operators, and developments in global financial markets.

One clear, if unintended, effect of these state efforts to restrict capital movement was to encourage some dramatic innovations in international finance in the 1970s and 1980s that enabled capital to better elude state control efforts. The activities of non-state actors as constraints on national policymaking is the story about financial innovation and the creation of new markets in response to state-imposed restrictions. As Hawley (1987) reveals in his study of early

American government efforts to reign in the Eurodollar market, the effect of state control efforts was to stimulate market innovation, which diminished state capacity to accomplish these very goals.

Hawley's study is important in outlining four main conclusions on such state control efforts. First, the "interests" of transnational capital are complex and contradictory, and may not even be evident to corporate and financial actors themselves.[1] Second, the state plays a part in defining capital's interests in a process of interest mediation and formation, in which the ideology of state managers has a role. A third conclusion is that constraints are placed on the state by its particular economic, political, and military location in the world interstate system. Finally, there is a dynamic relationship between state intervention in financial markets and ongoing global financial innovation, which occurs, in part, to thwart state efforts at control.

These conclusions have relevance to the contemporary debate concerning the role of non-state actors, as well as the genre of literature broadly defined as "theories of the state," which posit some degree of state autonomy from capital. Katzenstein (1977), in his study of domestic and international influences on state foreign economic policies, notes that systemic explanations do not adequately explain why an international challenge elicits different national responses. "Today's international political economy remains unintelligible without a systematic analysis of domestic structures" (Katzenstein [1977], 1991: 188). His focus on the effect of second-image (domestic-level) structures on foreign economic policy complements the two other approaches used in this study. Chapters II and III used third- and reversed second-image analyses, focusing on different political, economic, and technological features of the international system that affect strategies of foreign economic policy. Chapter IV, by contrast, examined in detail domestic, bureaucratic factors and the policymaking process. As Katzenstein ([1977] 1991: 192) points out, "[a] focus on international developments is particularly useful for analyzing the range of choice of foreign economic strategies[;] an analysis of bureaucratic factors highlights the contingency of strategies . . . ."

MARKETS AND STATES: COMPETING LOGICS

Markets and states, despite elements common to each, operate according to different logics. States structure human behavior by a set of hierarchies, rules, and procedures that mobilize individual efforts toward a common goal. Markets are arenas for buying and selling in which individual activities are connected by conditions of supply and demand as expressed by price. Nonetheless, the fixed character of market arrangements for finance has a political significance similar to that of those enduring arrangements for political administration, which we call the state bureaucracy. Both financial systems and state bureaucracies are at once constraints on action and instruments of action. The institutional organization of markets and administration—on which different capacities government action rests—also influences the political conflicts about the purposes of intervention. The institutions of the economy and the structure of the markets influence both which interests find political expression and the forms of the conflicts that ensue. Since the different institutions of the economy do shape the actual redeployment of resources, which we have labeled industrial readjustment, they perform the political task of ordering social choices and outcomes. Moreover, these institutions are themselves the subjects of political controversy precisely because they constrain government action and shape the expression of political interests. These market arrangements, such as financial institutions and markets, are linked to the controversies of parties and government, both by their histories (the fights that have shaped them) and by the skirmishes that accompany their day-to-day operations. The emphasis on the influence that marketplace arrangements have on political conflict and policy distinguishes this interpretation of industrial change from more conventional accounts that focus primarily on political actors and institutions.[2]

To understand the adjustments that advanced states have made since the early 1970s, we must eliminate the artificial dichotomy that separates the study of markets from the study of politics. Though traditionally viewed as different means of coordinating activities, political command and market prices in fact melt together in the actual workings of the advanced economies. Market positions are a source of political power and government choices shape the operations of the market. Thus, any analysis must begin from the understanding that there are no markets apart from politics, that markets were in fact political creations, and that political life is entangled with the workings of markets and market institutions.

International financial markets are likewise shaped by politics and economics: "the basic laws of economics push relentlessly toward market integration and worldwide global economy, while the political process practiced by governments and other interest groups is expressed by constant jockeying for special economic privileges" (Agmon, 1985: 1). The forces of economic efficiency, which if successful will lead to the law of one price, will drive individuals and business firms toward an integrated world economy. In the rarefied world of the "invisible hand" of the market, all resources will be efficiently allocated, and decisions will be made in a rational economic way. Such allocation will probably result in specialization and free trade in factors of production, goods, and services.

The constant struggle of various interest groups to better their share of wealth and power results in government intervention and in the construction of barriers to the free movement of financial assets. The intervention of political forces and institutions makes it necessary to replace arm's-length market transactions with a negotiation process. The free market mechanism of the pure economic model is replaced by committees and officials who affect prices through regulation and negotiations.

Governments derive their economic power from four key sources: their ability to tax, to issue currency, to borrow, and to regulate financial markets (O'Brien, 1995: 150). These four functions have a substantial effect on all economic activity and are also the main sources for political risk. In three of those areas—taxation, issuing currency, and regulation—governments have traditionally held a monopoly position. In terms of borrowing power, governments hold a position of privilege derived primarily from the ability to issue the currency needed to repay debts—which really is the ability devalue the currency when debts become onerous. Open financial markets threaten those abilities. Financial market operators—both large institutions as well as individual investors—now have the option to switch to other tax jurisdictions.

The interplay between the facets of sovereignty and the basic economic forces, like the laws of demand and supply, determines much of what transpires in the financial markets of the world. Both current prices and transactions as well as the behavior of the prices in the future are influenced by political factors. The cost of money (i.e., the money market discount rate) in key financial centers reflects market expectations regarding the future value of that money. When, for instance, a government finds it difficult to borrow money, it is forced to raise the rate it pays for the money (i.e., the discount rate) to attract lenders. Thus, a rising discount rate for a state's money reflects a broad base of declining confidence in that state. Political risk stems from the uncertainty that is embedded in the process of decision making in political organizations and the impact that current and future decisions have on economic variables. As O'Brien notes, "printing money is still the legal privilege and monopoly of governments, but the standard to which governments are being held in term of the soundness of their currency is getting stricter. Those currencies that fail the test have to link themselves with stronger moneys . . . or their citizens will switch to an alternative" (1995: 150).

PARAMETER SHIFTS

Goertz, in his study of contexts in world politics, notes that "explanations which underline the relevance of context often stress the spatial and temporal connections of a phenomenon" (Goertz, 1994: 74). The financial liberalization process of the late 1970s and 1980s was part of a larger process of international adjustment and the enhancement of market efficiency. Drawing from the literature in urban political economy, which looks at the competition among municipalities for mobile capital resources, I will examine in this section the role of market structure in shaping policy outcomes among states. Like municipalities, states face a local market for public goods in which the polycentric structure of governmental arrangements can increase consumer choice and the level of competition bureaucrats face (Schneider, 1989: xi.). Increasing consumer choice and competition, for instance increasing the scope of investment portfolios for capital interests, can dramatically affect the ability of bureaucrats to extract resources from the states they rule. Moreover, states are increasingly limited in their ability to control the resources they desire and to achieve the patterns of growth they want. Capital mobility has transformed world market structure from a global oligopoly to a more globally competitive one.

The case for an emphasis on international structural factors in explaining macroeconomic policy is found in the broad economic, political, and ideological changes in the international environment during the 1970s and 1980s.[3] Goertz describes how diffusion models, which focus on the importance of outside factors in determining behavior, offer examples of explanations with such an emphasis. Whereas rational actor models focus on individual and group preferences in explaining behavior, diffusion models, similar to other structural models, stress the role of context—including prevailing belief systems—in setting the parameters that constrain choice.

The fact that acceptance of the gold standard "rules of the game" in the 1880s, of Keynesian demand management after the Second World War, and of financial liberalization and domestic regulatory reform in the 1980s first occurred in the dominant economic power and then diffused to other industrialize countries in a fairly short period of time provides evidence that using a structural approach may be fruitful in explaining these phenomena. The hegemonic stability thesis and the second-image reversed models also imply diffusionary processes, in which governing mechanisms developed in a dominant state are emulated by or imposed upon other states. But unlike diffusion models in general, these two are explicitly state-centric in centering the origin of change within relations among states.

The parametric model suggests that to understand the process of revolutionary change one must ask what are the constraints that usually succeed in impeding change in world politics. The parametric model takes elements of a state-to-state diffusion model and combines it with one focusing on the state's interaction with an international environment that is changing. In addition to this emphasis on state-to-state interactions characteristic of diffusion models, the parametric model focus on the interaction between the non-state actors and the power structures in which they act. The parametric model argues for certain ways of viewing the structure of the international system and its importance in explaining state behavior. It suggests that international financial integration occurred as a response to a changing international context. When certain structural constraints, such as the inability to safely diversify portfolio assets transnationally, weaken or disappear then capital mobility becomes possible.

The parametric model is similar to the "barrier model" outlined by Goertz (1994), where he explains explosive change through the analogy of breaking through barriers. While the parametric and barrier models contain elements of the diffusion and rational actor models, they stress two processes commonly left out of rational actor models. One is the dynamic of the learning process. If, for instance, the relationship between a government and financial asset-holders vary because of the regulatory environment, then both market operators or state officials must perceive, interpret, and learn about the arrangement, or regime, before their behavior changes. Taking Goertz's model one step forward, non-state actors are constantly adapting to the constraints imposed by states, ideology and technology.[4] Innovation rarely occurs spontaneously, but is a response to perceived need—such as a reduction in the autonomy granted by state authorities through regulation. In the process of adapting to an existing regime, non-state actors alter the regime when they expand the autonomy lost in the regime imposition.

Governments likewise respond to the erosion of the regime. Given that dramatic changes in the relationship between governments and domestic sectoral interests, or between the state system and transnational sectoral interests, are rare events[5] suggests that governments usually succeed in both maintaining control over non-state actors and containing their own interstate rivalries. This last fact that interstate rivalry is an element that enhances the autonomy of non-state actors should not be lost. It is such rivalries that lead to the breakdown of interstate collaboration on control regimes, which allows non-state actors to assert a greater degree of autonomy. Also, during rivalrous periods, governments are more likely to compete for the affections of non-state actors through the granting of concessions, such as greater autonomy or protection from market failure.[6] This scenario explains, in a vastly different manner, the state-to-state dynamic that the diffusion framework emphasizes. State policymakers learn by monitoring what other governments do and by trying out new policies themselves in response to constraints. As in the case of non-state actors, the constraints under which governments operate are not constant but changing. In the case of financial liberalization, the other advanced industrial states were very interested observers of the American and British regulatory reform efforts. In the case of the European Monetary System, other European policymakers studied the anti-inflation commitment of German monetary authorities. In both cases, when the followers adopted the policies of the pioneers it was partially because they had learned that the achievement of preferred outcomes could be achieved only at the cost of accepting the new state of affairs between themselves and finance capital interests.

The last point mentioned above relates to a second process that Goertz mentions as not being included in the rational actor perspective. This is the changing preferences of the actors. Models of revealed preference, which determine people's preferences from observing their behavior, assume that preferences will remain unchanged while we observe the behavior (Varian, 1989: 117). "One essential aspect of the explosive character of [structural change] is that at a critical point in the process policy goals change" (Goertz, 1994: 94). For example, it is the conservative, free market-oriented governments of United States and Britain that first pursued financial liberalization, but at the point when the process takes off left-of-center governments adopt new policies— often at great reluctance—as in the case of France. Part of the revolution is that left-of-center governments become convinced that they *should* permit capital mobility and contain inflation (e.g., Fitoussi et al., 1993, details the "competitive disinflation" policies of France after 1987). Goals and preferences are also transformed with the regime; it is not just rational calculation in a new situation.

The parametric model used in this study is thus interactive, in that governments and non-state actors react both to the existing structural constraint and to how other governments are faring in the same situation. When non-state actors expand their field of activity to the international level, they have greater opportunities to exploit weaknesses in an existing control regime. Likewise, while states have a collective interest in maintaining the control regime and the parameters that constrain non-state actors, they also have private interests in attracting non-state actor resources. It is these latter state interests that non-state actors exploit in order to expand the parameters of their own autonomy. Maintaining an international capital control regime is difficult because national market variations, changing technology, and political factors can combine to erode its effectiveness over time. Measuring parameter change is difficult because the implications of many small changes in the regime, and their cumulative effect, do not become clear until financial market operators challenge the regime constraint.

Regimes weaken and parameters erode because "essential structural components change" (Goertz, 1994: 97). In the case of finance capital, the end of price stability in the late 1960s signaled the denouement of Bretton Woods regime. The rise of the offshore Eurocurrency markets which introduced competitive pricing of financial assets, the end of fixed exchange rates which introduced greater volatility in markets, and the spread of technology and new financial instruments which developed in response to volatility, were all developments which, at the same time, flowed from lost price stability and contributed to greater uncertainty and still more change.

In addition to the variability of structural components, the regime is not uniform across space. Again, the international capital control regime provides a good example of how when a regime is composed of different parts, it gives way unevenly. Capital controls were lifted and financial market reform was undertaken at different times among advanced industrial states, with the United States and Britain leading and the others following. A key variable that can explain the temporal variability, along with "learning" mentioned above, is the domestic relationship between government and finance.

Because Britain in the nineteenth century, and the United States in the twentieth, were the dominant ("hegemonic") trading and investment powers of their respective ages, finance capital interests were granted greater autonomy domestically than their counterparts in Europe and Japan. According to Zysman (1983), because of their dominance, the British and American governments did not have the need to use state power at home to create competitive advantage in international markets. Both states maintained a capital market-based financial system with resources allocated by competitively-established prices. The regulation of financial market operators was of an "arms' length" variety. In such an environment, the parameters of activity for financial market operators were wider than in Europe and Japan, where either bank- or state-dominated credit-based systems were maintained. Under such systems, the parameters of finance capital autonomy were limited either by finance capital's tie to industrial capital or by direct state control. Limited autonomy meant fewer independent investment decisions by financial asset-holders and greater financial repression.[7] These consequences were tied to their governments' harnessing of relatively scarce finance capital in the pursuit of policymakers' preferred economic outcomes. As long as finance capital was relatively abundant, the dominant states could afford finance greater freedom.

According to the Heckscher-Ohlin theorem, factors of production (of which capital is one) flow from areas where it relatively abundant to where it is relatively scarce, where marginal return is greater. The numbers on pre-1914 British investment and postwar American transnational activity provide evidence supporting this proposition. According to Chase-Dunn (1981), the export of capital in pursuit of higher returns reduces the incentives to support economic nationalism on the part of national finance capital interests in the hegemonic states. Therefore, it should not surprise that financial liberalization efforts begin in these states. The decoupled relationship between finance and industrial capital in the United States and Britain, however, has sparked vigorous sectoral struggles.

For the other advanced industrial states, whose domestic financial markets were smaller, insular, and much more under state control or tied to industrial concerns, governments were able to temporarily resist the pressures for regulatory reform and liberalization. The more concentrated the control of credit, the longer a government was able to hold back the neoliberal revolution. Ironically, as Goodman and Pauly (1993) point out, among these states the presence of capital outflows may have extended the maintenance of controls. Policymakers of states with capital inflows, on the other hand, could see benefits from changing the control regime and allowing liberalization.

MARKET STRUCTURE AND POLICY CONSTRAINTS

The core characteristics of the competitive model for private goods are well known (Schneider, 1989: 5-6): the idealized model of pure competition in the market requires a variety of goods and a multiplicity of buyers and sellers. Within their budget constraints, buyers are free to purchase those goods that most satisfy their preferences and needs. Given multiple buyers and sellers, and given freedom of choice, the competitive marketplace is efficient, an outcome that is normatively desirable. However, efficiency in the private market is conditioned by, among other things, the number of firms, the degree of differentiation between products, and the ease of entry of new firms into the market.

The market for public goods is structured somewhat differently, in that it is definable by the interaction of governments. As in any market, there are buyers and sellers. In the market for finance capital, the "buyers" are the investors, either directly in financial exchanges or indirectly through the banking system, who chose to invest the in the state. These buyers choose to invest in specific policy mixes and then pay for their choice by the regulations they agree to follow, and the taxes they agree to pay to the government. While profit maximization can be assumed to be the overriding criterion in choice, other factors, such as government support for creditor claims, provision of banker safety net, and patriotism are also considered.[8] Whatever their preferences, investors face budget constraints. As rational consumers, finance capital interests want to invest in the policy mixes offered in the transnational market for finance capital at the lowest cost (i.e., least amount of regulatory restrictions and taxes). The "sellers" in this model of the public market are national governments. Within each national government, politicians and bureaucrats are the decision-makers with primary responsibility for assembling the particular package of profit opportunities and security of income offered by each state. States charge for the policy mixes they deliver primarily by levying taxes and imposing some restrictions on capital use (e.g., repatriation). As a whole, governments seek to provide profit opportunities for mobile "buyers," while keeping taxes and restrictions at a minimum.

The objective function of government can thus be expressed by a vector of concrete goals, like a three percent annual rate of growth in the GNP, or by a more general objective, like sustained growth with price stability. In most cases these objectives and the resulting policies do not coincide perfectly with the aggregate wants of the community over which the government has a jurisdiction, or with the preferences of the "representative resident." Therefore, individuals do not view the policies of the government as serving their own goals. As firms are vehicles to maximize the welfare of shareholders, there exists a potential conflict between the goals of the government and the corporate and investors' sector in a given economy. This potential conflict gives rise to political risk. Political risk is defined as the unanticipated changes in the relative prices of factors of production, goods, or services caused by the actions and reactions of governments and other political groups within and between states (Agmon, 1985: 7). These unanticipated changes can result from direct or indirect actions by political actors. They can be related to international struggle among territorial states or to the internal positioning of power groups within a certain country.

Governments affect relative prices by levying taxes, by transferring payments, and by regulations. Both financial assets and physical assets can be taxed. Physical and financial assets can be taxed by various governments in different locations. A given government can exercise its taxing power on local production, on incoming goods and services, on exports, and in some cases on assets located outside its own jurisdiction.

Inflation is another way in which governments affect relative prices, and is a major source of political risk. Inflation is a tax on money balances and on nominal contracts that are held by wage earners and by wage payers, borrowers and lenders, and sellers and buyers of many goods and services. Therefore, the tax base of inflation is usually broad and covers most facets of economic activity. Inflation results in the transfer of wealth from one group to another within a national economy. Traditional public finance and monetary economics views this transfer as one that goes from the private sector to the government. However, in a world that is fairly integrated, internal transfers by means of inflation in one country are affected by and have an effect on other countries as well.[9]

Once the inflationary process is set into motion, it develops a life of its own. The dynamics of inflation can be described and analyzed by two related phenomena: the actions and reactions of rent-seeking groups and the process of inflation avoidance (Agmon, 1985: 11). The two rather similar activities make the future rate of inflation dependent on the relative political power of different groups in the economy.

The concept of rent-seeking groups (Krueger, 1974) is an idea that can be easily applied to a variety of instances when politics and economics interact. Whenever a government restricts the otherwise market-oriented activity, there is a potential rent. The existence of a rent or even potential rent initiates action by rent-seeking groups. These groups may be organized or ad hoc. They may act as groups or loosely organized individuals. Rent seeking is an additional cost for the society in general. The cost is even higher when the mere activity of rent-seeking groups contributes to a higher level of uncertainty in the economy under consideration. The constant struggle among various rent-seeking groups and individuals creates a constant process of unpredictable changes in relative prices. A higher volatility in relative prices means higher risk. Political actors may be rent-seeking groups within an economy or rent-seeking governments in the international community. Unpredictable changes in the relative prices are an outcome of this political repositioning.

It is the differences in national policies that lead to political risk for investors. One way to deal with pervasive political risk is to avoid it. Because political risk is generated by governments, the simplest way to avoid political risk is to step outside the jurisdiction of a specific government or government in general. The relationship among the rates of inflation over time is an outcome of the phenomenon of currency substitution (Agmon, 1985: 9-10). In a perfectly integrated market all currencies are perfect substitutes. Barriers to trade in money introduced by various governments make national currencies less than perfect substitutes. The existence of the transnational market for financial services—e.g., the external currency markets mentioned in Chapter III—makes the internationally-traded currencies better substitutes than non-traded currencies. The external currency markets provide political risk reduction directly by allowing firms and individual investors to transact outside the jurisdiction of the major industrialized governments. The existence of relatively control- and regulation-free credit markets limits the ability of the governments involved to use monetary policy to achieve political and economic policy goals.

Given variation in investor tastes, as well as variation in regulations and taxes, the transnational market for financial capital operates through two basic mechanisms (Hirschman, 1970). First, investors can use "voice" to affect market choices. For example, they can become involved in political campaigns and lobby for changes in policy to reduce the restrictions on capital usage. Second is the "exit" option, which emerges from the actions of financial asset-holders, as they "shop around" between different governments to find the policy mix (that combination of the benefit of profit opportunities and the cost of regulation and taxes) that most closely matches their preferences. It is the mobility of finance capital—investors' ability and willingness to exit from a state with an unsatisfactory policy mix to locate in a more satisfactory state—which drives the transnational market for finance capital.

The products, or policy mixes, offered for "sale" in the international market for capital consist of the services national governments provide, such as a growing and stable economy providing profit and employment opportunities. National governments should be viewed as "managers" and not the direct providers of many of the services they offer. As such, a state organizes and supervises the provision of public goods and services, but the actual provision is the work of financial asset-holders, who purchase government debt. To the extent that governments can induce financial asset-holders to provide capital at low cost, such arrangements actually increase the freedom of government to assemble efficient policy mixes by selling debt at low real interest rates. Governments charge for providing a profitable environment by levying taxes and imposing certain restrictions on the usability of capital. Sources of competition in bidding for capital come from other states and the international markets that are under the control of no one state (e.g., the Eurocurrency markets). Lacking world government, the fragmentation of authority does not allow for control of capital as in the case of national markets.

Tiebout (1962), writing on urban political economy, sought to define a local market for public goods based on the interaction of diverse municipal governments; and he sought to show how competition in this market could increase the efficient provision of local public goods. Expanding the focus to the international level, Tiebout's model can be useful in analyzing the international financial market.

Tiebout started with several simplifying assumptions. In his model, metropolitan space was presented as an undifferentiated plane across which residents were assumed to have virtually unlimited mobility (Schneider, 1989: 12). Residents were further assumed to have varying "tastes" for public goods. Combining variation in preferences with high mobility, Tiebout argued that the existence of numerous local governments could simulate an efficient local market for public goods in which metropolitan residents "shop around" to locate in a community where the service/tax bundle offered by the local government most closely approximated individual preferences. While this public market did not generate all the efficiency gains of the private market, Tiebout demonstrated the importance of "exit" as consumers expressed their preferences through location decisions across multiple local governments providing diverse product mixes. One need not make too great a logical leap in applying these assumptions to the case of finance in an international market.

The Tiebout market increases efficiency in two ways. First, given increased choice between various communities (or states, in the case of international finance), consumers (investors) can maximize the match between their preferences and the actual goods and services provided by their municipality (state). The existence of multiple governments, providing differentiated policy mixes, allows investors to "vote with their funds," moving capital across states to locate in the specific state whose policy mix most closely resembles their preferences.

Furthermore, this polycentric model predicts that competition between municipalities (states) will encourage the efficient provision of government services.[10]

Tiebout's model is built on the concept of citizen/consumer sovereignty and is driven by their mobility. My model of the political economy of transnational finance is built, likewise, on the concept of citizen/investor sovereignty and is driven by the mobility of their finance capital. Government policies are essentially given, for while in a purely competitive market sellers (in this case governments) have interests and develop strategies to achieve their goals, their success is constrained by the freedom of buyers to choose between highly similar products offered by a large number of sellers. By extension, in my formulation of the globally competitive market for financial capital, governments are relatively passive: as a consequence of their sensitivity of investor interests and the substitutability of alternate locations, competition in the transnational financial capital market limits the freedom of governments as sellers of public goods.

However, for fear of taking an analogy too far, there are certain structural characteristics of the transnational market for finance capital which distinguish it from the private market: shopping between national governments is more difficult and involves greater risks than choosing between two hardwares. As a consequence, the independent role of governments as producers is enhanced. This is largely due to the fact that national governments are spatial monopolists. States "own" a piece of territory and consumers (investors) can "purchase" the policy mix offered by a national government only by locating (investing) within its boundaries. Consequently, the decision to invest in a national policy mix occurs through the locational decisions of investors: the transnational market operates as invested interests shop around.

It is here that Frieden's distinction between industrial and financial capital becomes important. Most assertions of full international capital mobility refer to international transfers of financial assets, especially bonds and bank claims. Equity markets appear to be far less integrated, and other forms of capital even less so. Inasmuch as capital is specific to location, increased financial integration has only limited effects on policies targeted at particular industries. Given territorial monopoly, investors in the national policy mix face a much more limited choice among the already assembled policy choices offered by states.

Given the imperfectness of competition and given the nature of the policy mixes which national governments offer, the international market for financial capital is a market in which national governments have the freedom to design policy mix alternatives: e.g., budgeting for public services can be regarded as strategy chosen by states; changes in interest and exchange rates are others. Again, I borrow from the urban political economy literature by examining Peterson's (1981) work, which specifically links fiscal policy to strategies for growth. Peterson's argument hinges on the concept of a benefit/cost ratio relating the benefits of local services to the local tax bill. By explicitly including service cost considerations into locational decisions, Peterson extends Tiebout's model of the market and focuses attention on the strategic implications of budgeting.

Cost considerations are major factors in locational choices because governments vary not only in the kinds of services they provide but also in the tax levels and regulatory restrictions they impose to support their services. According to Peterson, an existing market for public goods is characterized by variation in the benefit/cost (service/tax) ratio offered by local governments. Given such variation, his specific argument is driven by the benefit/cost ratio experienced by above-average-income residents and by the businesses which strengthen the local tax base and reduce the taxes levied on present property owners.

Extending Peterson's model to the international arena, one can imply that governments that consistently offer poor benefit/cost ratios to investors (i.e., lower overall returns on assets given the taxes on profits and restrictions on capital use) will be unable to attract desirable new capital and may witness the flight of existing capital. This erodes the state tax base, which in turn leads to higher taxes and restrictions in relation to economic performance levels. Returns on financial assets can be reduced due to either anemic real economic growth or high inflation.

For Peterson, local budgetary politics are driven by the need of municipalities to avoid the negative consequences of a declining benefit/cost ratio. He divides municipal expenditures into three categories: developmental, allocative, and redistributive (Schneider, 1989: 18). The classification of specific municipal expenditures into these categories is determined by the effect any particular service has on the benefit/cost ratio of an above-average-income resident of a community. Thus, Peterson links budgetary politics and the politics of growth.

Specifically, developmental policies provide infrastructure necessary to support further growth, particularly economic development. Because these "investments" reduce the costs of doing business in a specific location, they improve the benefit/cost ratio experienced by mobile and desirable capital, and promote further growth in wealth. At the other extreme are expenditures for redistributive functions, such as social welfare and restrictions on capital mobility, which provide benefits to lower income individuals and owners of immobile factors. Governments that engage extensively in redistributive activities will present an unattractive benefit/cost ratio to desirable, mobile, fiscal resources. Finally, allocative policies are the "interaction" functions of government—such as general administration—that are largely neutral with regard to benefit/cost considerations.[11]

The Peterson model converges with much of the recent work of Frieden (1987, 1988, 1991). Frieden (1991) examines the policy preferences of various socioeconomic groups toward financial integration. He emphasizes the differential effects of the increase in capital mobility and focuses on questions concerning which actors are better (or worse) off after financial integration than before and how the various actors can be expected to respond politically to this change in economic environment. Frieden argues that over the long run, international financial integration tends to favor capital over labor, especially in developed countries, but in the shorter run—which is more relevant to politics and policies—in the developed world, financial integration favors capitalists with mobile or diversified assets and disfavors those with assets tied to specific locations and activities such as manufacturing or farming. Therefore, international financial integration increases the influence of capital by making it easier for owners of financial assets to take them abroad in response to national policies they do not like. This, Frieden argues, drives a wedge between two camps—the first consisting of the financial sector, owners of financial assets, and integrated transnational firms, all of which have gained with financial integration, and the second consisting of firms specific to a particular industry and location, all of which have been harmed by the generally increased competition for loanable funds.

By exploring what high levels of financial integration imply for the policy preferences of economic interest groups in regard to such other issues as macroeconomic policy and the exchange rate, Frieden attempts to show how various interest groups are expected to behave in this environment. He argues that international capital mobility tends to remake political coalitions by way of its impact on the effects of national policies (e.g., the political division between producers of tradable goods and producers of nontradable goods and services is likely to become more important, as are distinctions between internationally diversified and undiversified investors), and that financial integration has implications for the distributional effects, and therefore the politics, of national policies. While a clear prediction is for conflict between "integrationist" and "anti-integrationist" forces, the political debate has not been and will not be restricted to policies directly concerned with increasing or retarding international capital mobility.

ACTORS, INTERESTS, AND CONSTRAINTS: BRINGING POLITICS BACK IN

The previous section described the international market for financial capital. In this market, owners of financial assets are the buyers or investors of the services and policy mixes offered by national governments, which are the sellers. The "sell" decisions of national governments are dominated by the interests and actions of bureaucrats and politicians, which are both driven and constrained by the mobility of resources.

Any complete model of political actions must take into account that the market for public goods (i.e., such as finance capital) may be more similar to a regulated oligopolistic market than it is to a purely competitive one. The market for finance capital is also driven by a political economy linking the structure of government to decisions about services, taxes, and regulation. The desire to maximize national economic wealth is the key ingredient of this political economy. Emphasizing this link integrates the "voice" and "exit" dimensions of the market for finance capital. This extension ties economic resource mobility, which is central to the competitive model, and the world of political demand resulting from the need to maximize the tax base (i.e., national wealth).

This section examines in greater detail the incentives and interests of the actors in the national market, showing how goals and strategies are rooted in the characteristics of the market as outlined in the previous section. Borrowing again from the urban political economy literature (Schneider, 1989), as well as the work on "invested interests" by Frieden (1987, 1988, 1991), I discuss the interests of four sets of actors (finance capital, industrial capital, labor, and government) whose actions drive the national market, assessing the degree to which their interests are homogenous, and identifying the source of conflict between them. Some cleavages are internal to any given set of actors: for example, the interests of capitalists will differ depending on the relative capital mobility and sector specificity. Other conflicts occur between sets of actors: capitalists and labor may disagree over the desirability of future economic growth or over the optimal funding for government social welfare services.

Despite multiple lines of cleavage and conflict among actors in the market, there is at least one interest upon which consensus is more easily achieved—the desire to increase the fiscal wealth of the nation. This shared interest derives from the structural arrangements of the national market for capital, in which the relationship between profit opportunities and tax rates is directly tied to the strength of the national tax base.

The decisions of both state policymakers and non-state actors, as well as exogenous factors (e.g., technological and attitudinal changes) outside immediate government control combine to create international structures and set the parameters of state and non-state actor (i.e., agent) autonomy. The constraints on government policymaking involve a mix of structural components and the policy decisions of leading powers. The structure constrains choice by delimiting what is considered possible and what is not. But "what is possible" changes. Parameters shift as do the individuals that confront them. Thus it is neither completely the exogenous effect of the parameter shifts nor the endogenous interactions of states facing them that promotes rapid change. In level of analysis terms it is neither the state level nor the system level, but rather their interaction, which explains rapid change.

Rosenau (1990: 144) notes that "the conceptual and methodological consequences of the decision to treat agent and structure phenomena as interactive are not to be underestimated. Inquiry would certainly be much easier if one or the other level could be treated as a constant." If, for example, the actions of national policymakers could be assumed to be so totally a product of the parametric constraints as to be undifferentiated from one another, a wide range of conceptual complications would be bypassed. "Allowing for significant variability at the agent level, however, necessitates inquiry into the perceptions, intentions, and many other psychological mechanisms through which individual orientations are translated into action or reaction. Likewise, to proceed from the premise of interactive variability at both levels is to require concern with autonomy, consensus formation, intergroup bargaining, and other sociopolitical mechanisms through which agent actions are converted into structural policies."

One way to examine the distributional costs of international financial integration is to look at increased capital mobility from the standpoint of investors facing portfolio decisions, whom it must help (Frieden, 1991: 434). It can hardly be bad for capitalists to have more investment options than before, which is what capital mobility gives them. By the same token, increasing the options of capital presumably reduces those of labor by making it less costly for capital to move rather than accede to labor demands. The wider choice of investments open to asset-holders increases their influence on governments, labor, and industrialists. The 1980s may have indeed seen a secular shift in response to increased capital mobility, in which governments all over the world were forced to provide more attractive conditions for capitalists. Such conditions include everything from lower wealth and capital gains taxes to relaxed regulation of financial activities and labor relations. In a world in which financial capital moves freely across borders, it is difficult for one country to insist on stiff capital taxation when other countries are removing or reducing it. Inasmuch as this effect holds, increased financial integration implies an across-the-board, lasting increase in the social and political power of capital.

States are increasingly under pressure in this age of enhanced capital power. The basic goal of national policymakers is to increase the flow of funds into government coffers to support their manipulation of monetary and fiscal levers without increasing the taxes investors must pay. There are several strategies that can ease the national budget constraint without increasing the direct taxation of financial asset-holders. Two specific strategies are: (1) the "competitive state" model, of increasing state efficiency through regulatory reform, to provide investor profit maximization; and (2) the "developmental state" model, of strengthening the national tax base.

According to its proponents, regulatory reform increases efficiency by expanding the range of potential suppliers of financial services. Competition among them, including private firms accustomed to "the rigors of the private marketplace," supposedly leads to greater efficiency in the provision of national public goods. Deregulation has been a popular concept since the 1980s, and was a major component of Thatcherism in Britain, and Reaganomics in the United States. Since the early 1980s, continental European, Antipodal, and Latin American countries have jumped on the deregulation bandwagon. To the extent that deregulation increases efficiency, it should appeal to capital asset-holders. Financial services firms will support deregulation if it increases their opportunities to do business with government, but bureaucrats will not necessarily share their enthusiasm, to the extent that better efficiency measures increase the information available about the operation and costs of government programs, bureaucrats lose one of their major sources of power—the control over information. Bureaucrats will oppose deregulation if it reduces the size of their agencies.

While regulatory reform can be expected to evoke powerful opposition from entrenched bureaucratic interests, the desire to increase the national tax base is more consensual. Because states with a strong tax base have a greater capacity to deliver services at moderate tax rates, this is the strategy perhaps more ardently pursued by capitalists—and, indeed, other actors in the state. Tax base maximization can be accomplished in several ways, but the most common is to control the entry and exit of capital and to promote economic development.[12]

Industrial capitalists will favor controls on the exit of finance capital and other national policies that reduce their cost of financing. Forcing financial asset-holders to invest in industry at a return below the existing market rate generates a fiscal dividend to industrial capitalists: since a firm's cost of financing is a direct function of the price of capital, financial asset-holders investing at below market rates of return contribute more money to national capital formation. This transfers wealth to industry and shifts national costs from industrial to financial capitalists. While this strategy is appealing to both government and industry, it is limited by the number of financial asset-holders and their willingness to invest in "expensive" industry in any given state. Only attractive states, with high profit opportunities, can successfully pursue this strategy. Investors may turn instead to economic development as a means by which to diversify and strengthen the national tax base. To the extent that business growth produces a net fiscal surplus, economic development increases the price of capital for industry: the costs of development are shifted from financial asset-holders to industry and its workers. Indeed, this strategy has become extremely attractive to national governments in recent years, and may actually be the dominant approach to tax base enhancement. The capital asset pricing model, described in the previous chapter, explains the investors' incentives in diversification.

Financial asset-holders invest in a country for a variety of reasons, some of which might be adversely affected by economic growth. They may prefer price stability that makes high rates of economic growth unlikely. If it affects the price stability for which they chose that country, investors will oppose certain economic growth policies that would otherwise be fiscally productive (the image of the pessimistic bond-holder, who delights in bad economic news and shivers in good, should spring to mind). This conflict can place investors in opposition to the "growth machine"—the usually dominant coalition of actors in states who pursue economic growth.

If capitalists can generally agree on the need to improve the fiscal base of the state, increasing the level of profits and services in relation to tax and regulatory costs, there will nonetheless be disagreements over the desirable profit, service, tax, and regulatory levels. There are two lines of cleavage differentiating the way in which capitalists evaluate the relative value of national services and the relative pain of national taxes. These lines of cleavage distinguish the interests of finance capitalists and sector-specific (industrial) capitalists; and of owners of mobile and relatively immobile capital.

Finance capital more directly face the costs of national taxes than does sector-specific capital. For the typical investor, the national tax bill is concrete, and increases in income and capital gains taxes are direct and palpable. In contrast, the income tax costs of government subsidization and other services are more diffuse for the industrialist. Since the implicit cost of government services (e.g., subsidies, procurement, etc.) to industry are not separately enumerated in tax calculations, their impact can be hidden. If the demand for investment capital is similar to the demand for private goods, then higher prices decrease demand. Thus, if the industrialist's "fiscal illusion" dilutes information about the true costs of government-allocated investment, industry will demand more investment than investors are willing to commit to.

Capital interests are also affected by the mobility of capital in the state. In order to extract a fiscal dividend, government and industry will try to limit exit of finance capital. Because macroeconomic policies can transfer wealth from financial to industrial interests, fiscal dividends emerge in the relationship between capital that remain in the country.

An overriding goal of policymakers is to stay in power. Policy goals can be accomplished only by remaining in office. Obviously, to remain in office policymakers must attract enough votes to win election. National policymakers increase the likelihood of winning election by promoting sustained economic growth with relative price stability for their constituents. But the benefits of this strategy are realized only if taxes are kept low. Thus, policymakers benefit from improving their state's tax base, since this allows more demands to be satisfied within a given tax rate.

The interests of policymakers in improving their state's benefit/cost ratio may align them with financial interests: i.e., to the extent that economic development improves the national tax base, it can help incumbents win reelection. Some analysts argue that policymakers have become too pro-finance, granting concessions in excess of returns to the national electorate. This "critical" perspective raises an important question: how long and how far can a government deviate from the interests and demands of national invested interests? The answer may largely determine the degree of freedom that policymakers have in formulating national macroeconomic policies.

There are compelling reasons to believe that the freedom of national policymakers is limited. The transformation of the national and the international economy imposes certain limits on the success of national policies in maximizing the national tax base. At least since the 1960s, innovations in telecommunications technologies have allowed finance to elude the grasp of governments. While national governments seek to increase their own rate of growth, and control its composition, ultimately exogenous economic forces limit what any individual state can do.

Of the multiple lines of conflict dividing the actors in my model of the politics of international finance, I focus on those which hinge on the demands of governments for more resources. The bureaucratic quest for resources is thus the mainspring for the subsequent analysis of the national resource allocation process. I postulate that a fundamental conflict emerges as bureaucrats use their control over information to manipulate the design of policy and to control consideration of policy alternatives. Control over information allows bureaucrats to demand national budgets larger than the level desired by other actors in their state.

To recapitulate, bureaucrats demand large budgets because they have few incentives to minimize societal inputs into their bureau's production process. According to Niskanen (1971), because a successful bureaucrat will exact more money from the state than objectively required by others, the level of government expenditures for the provision of investment capital and services in relationship to demand is central to this argument. While bureaucrats prosper from their budget maximizing behavior, bureaucratic "profits" or "rents" come at the expense of financial interests: since the successful exercise of bureaucratic power shifts resources away from goods preferred by others, monopolistic bureaucratic outputs are, by definition, not optimal.

It also follows that the ability of national bureaucrats to exact larger budgets from their states will be inversely related to the degree of competition in the national market for investment capital. To see this, imagine a global market in which there is only one world state. Citizens and politicians, who have their preferences for national expenditures, will find it difficult to gather information about alternative investment vehicles and input costs. In this restricted environment, bureaucratic control over information is maximized and the ability of other national actors to gather information about the true costs of government services and alternative policy choices is low. Citizens and investors will find it difficult to monitor and control bureaucratic budget proposals and agency performance. At the other extreme, in a market with perfect information, the power of bureaucrats is reduced, because its source has been eroded. Of course, perfect information never exists. But the national costs of gathering information can vary widely and these costs can be radically lower in a state where citizens have access to the financial markets of other states with different policy mixes.

Finance—the control of credit—is the facet of structural power that has perhaps risen in importance more than any other in the past quarter century and has come to be of decisive importance in international economic relations and in the competition of corporate enterprises. It sometimes seems as if its complex manifestations are too technical and arcane to be easily understood. Yet its ability to determine outcomes—in security, in production, and in research—is enormous. The example of the "investment strike" is a case of structural power at the state level, uniquely available to financial asset-holders, that works primarily through the market mechanism (Gill and Law, 1988). An investment strike refers to the refusal of asset-holders to invest in a particular jurisdiction in order to induce a change in government policy. Whereas a reduced willingness to invest for productive purposes usually comes about gradually, the supply of finance to governments through purchase of government debt may decline very rapidly. This might result in the state being unable to finance its current activity unless it raises the rates of return for financial asset-holders who invest in the state.[13] Thus capital, particularly finance capital, has the power to indirectly discipline the state. In so far as many of the top financiers, transnational bankers, and mutual fund portfolio managers have access to government leaders, this indirect power may be supplemented by direct lobbying, and "gentlemanly arm-twisting" (Gill and Law 1988: 87). However, such arm-twisting is secondary to what can be termed the "power of markets," notably the financial markets. This power constrains the participants in the market, including the government when it needs to raise finance for its activities. In this sense, given certain social and political conditions, markets can have a certain autonomy.

Internationally, financial confidence in government increasingly depends on financial asset-holders' evaluation of state macroeconomic policies. Ideas about "sound finance" and "fighting inflation" constrain governments. As such ideas spread from one country to another, the pursuit of such policies is likely to attract more foreign capital. The response of firms to such policies and other determinants of the investment climate is often gradual, and spread over a number of years. By contrast, financial asset-holders can react to government policies, or expected policies, much more rapidly than owners of productive (industrial) capital. With the liberalization of capital flows between the advanced industrial states (and the emerging-market less developed countries) the reaction of financial capital interests need not be one of postponement of investment (as in an "investment strike"). Instead, huge sums of money can quickly flow out of a country to more attractive havens. The result of this can be a balance-of-payments crisis (dramatic depletion of foreign reserves) under fixed exchange rates, or a foreign exchange crisis (dramatic fall in the exchange rate) under flexible exchange rates. A falling exchange rate brings with it increased risks of rising inflation, especially for a small, open economy. Hence the international mobility of financial capital can swiftly force governments, which deviate from policies seen as suitable by financial market operators, to change course. For example, governments may be forced to raise interest rates, tighten monetary policy, and thus impose economic austerity measures to offset a currency, or payments, crisis. This is precisely what occurred in France in the now famous "Mitterand U-turn."

Competition between states can also increase pressure for efficiency and responsiveness. Politicians and citizens must retain fiscally desirable resources; if these resources leave a state, politicians face reduced chances for reelection and citizens will face higher taxes and regulations. Where there is choice internationally across states with alternative investment/tax mixes, the pressure on citizens and bureaucratic sponsors to control costs and to increase efficiency of government production will therefore be higher. This in the end may be the greatest constraint that financial asset-holders impose upon policymaking.

NOTES

1. That is, while transnational capital interests desire the freedom to transact globally, they also desire a stable investment climate—an attribute of a successful intergovernmental management of potential financial crises.

2. Political parties are identified by their ideological and policy positions on the role of state intervention in the market economy

3. Examples include the global trends towards regulatory reform, enhanced central bank credibility, and the shift toward anti-inflation policies.

4. A principal feature distinguishing the "quarternary (knowledge-based) economy" is movement away from habit toward adaptive learning by previously passive citizenries. When states impose strictures on certain activities, non-state actors adapt by innovating to circumvent those strictures. While such adaptive behavior is not limited to the denizens of quarternary economy—witness the endless examples of underground economies throughout

the Third World—information technologies greatly enhances citizens' adaptive power.

5. There have been only four international monetary regimes over the past century: classical gold standard (ca. 1870-1914); interwar gold-exchange standard (1924-31); Bretton Woods gold-exchange standard (1945-73); flexible-rate "non-standard" (1973-). Changes in the international monetary system were occasioned by, sequentially, the First World War, the Great Depression, and the unilateral American decision to end dollar-gold convertibility under conditions of declining confidence and rising inflation.

6. Andrews (1994) points to competition as an example of the structural power of international financial integration. I would further add that political multicentricity weakens the probable success of coordinative ventures to control non-state actors.

7. The degree of financial repression can be measured by differences in interest rates on same-currency-denominated assets in national and offshore markets prior to the abolition of capital controls.

8. In all cases the percentage of investor portfolios held in the equity of national companies exceeds the state's percentage of global market capitalization.

9. As we saw in Chapter 3, the French used this argument forcefully in the 1960s, complaining of the American "exorbitant privilege" in exporting its inflation to other countries through the exchange rate system.

10. The regulatory reforms and the elimination of organizational rigidities currently going on in Europe in anticipation of the single market reflect this.

11. I am reminded of Lowi's (1964) typology of government actions—regulatory, redistributional, and distributional. I borrow the term "interaction" from Zimmerman's (1987) modification of the Lowi article.

12. This explains the Bretton Woods era policy penchant for capital controls and financial repression. States were supported in these efforts by industrial capital-owners, who preferred the retention of state macroeconomic policy autonomy.

13. The alternative—resorting to monetary inflation to reduce the real value of its debt—would, from the standpoint of finance capital, cause the "investment climate" to deteriorate further, thus prolonging the investment strike.

CHAPTER VII

Conclusion

Over the course of writing this thesis I became increasingly interested in major trends that may change America and the world over the next two decades. Paul Kennedy's book, *The Rise and Decline of Great Powers*, spoke to a generation of American scholars who saw their country in the throes of a steady, if not precipitous, decline. Though the book did not begin the declinist debate, it soon took center stage as the focal point of the declinist argument. Not since Henry Luce's "The American Century" has a tome generated such discussion among both policymakers and policy laymen. Both books are about hegemony— that elusive trait of some great nations who achieve a temporary dominance in the international arena. According to the hegemonic stability argument, such a dominance is needed to facilitate a smooth functioning international financial system, which allows for global growth and prosperity. Only such a dominant state can supply the necessary international public goods to dampen the self-seeking behavior of other states. The lack of such an international system leader inevitably leads to the breakdown of the liberal order, and the reemergence of a Hobbesian world of all against all. For Charles Kindleberger, Britain in the nineteenth century and the United States in the twentieth have filled that role. Thus, the putative decline of American hegemony is not just a matter of concern for Americans, but for all those who have benefited from nearly fifty years of almost uninterrupted economic growth and prosperity.

The 1970s saw the close of a period of American dominance in mass-manufacturing industry. The spread of manufacturing capability to war-ravaged Europe and Japan, and, later, the newly industrialized countries of the "Third World" gradually reduced American

competitiveness in mass manufacturing industry. The rise of
protectionist sentiment emanating from the declining industry sectors,
and their workers, has been one of the major changes to be taken
account of in developing American foreign economic policy. In Europe,
the 1970s created an unemployment problem from which the Continent
is yet to recover. Efforts such as the European Monetary System
(EMS), the Exchange Rate Mechanism (ERM), and the Economic and
Monetary Union (EMU) are all aimed at jump-starting moribund
economies. Japan's spectacular economic successes have not come
without a price. The rapid accumulation of Japanese wealth has not
come with anything close to a requisite increase in investment
opportunities. The closed and regulated Japanese financial market has
caused capital to both go abroad and to artificially inflate Japanese-
domiciled assets. In the case of the former, increased Japanese foreign
investment has sparked resentment. In the case of the latter, overpriced
domestic assets created a "bubble economy" that finally burst, leading
to a spectacular sixty percentage point drop in the Japanese stockmarket
in 1990-92.

The debate about decline centers on two critical concerns: (1) the
nature and extent of the decline of American hegemony; and (2) the
stability of the liberal international economic order. Technological
innovation and the maintenance of a dynamic society are essential
components to the maintenance of hegemony. However, because of the
diffusionary process of hegemonic growth (i.e., it serving as the growth
pole for the world), the hegemon loses its "first producer" advantages
as new areas of growth, providing higher rates of return on investment,
emerge. Other states may "free ride" on the hegemon's provision of
international public goods (e.g., free trade regime) to extract resources
for state development. These late developer neo-mercantilists soon
become competitors to the lower value-added industries of the
hegemon. Over time, these late developers, through aggressive use of
Kaldorian[1] strategies and technology transfers, may achieve economies
of scale and competitive advantage in higher value-added production as
well.

It is labor, the least mobile and relatively scarce factor of
production, that suffers first from the decline of hegemony. Labor
mobilizes to demand protection from late developer exports and
restrictions on the mobility of capital. But capital mobility is
heightened by the duality of world economic integration and world

political fragmentation. Therefore, restrictions on capital mobility and, thus, control of the diffusionary process, can only come about if: (1) states band together to impose multilateral regulation of capital movements (which is highly unlikely and prone to free riding behavior); or (2) the world economy disintegrates. Therefore, as would logically follow, declining hegemons, whose governments are under pressure from labor and declining industry capitalists, are likely to shift to unilateralist policies to exploit their deteriorating but still dominant position. Other economic powers increasingly resent being forced to subsidize the declining power and respond with unilateralist policies of their own. Trade and other economic warfare ensues, plunging the world economy into depression and competing economic nationalisms.

With the stakes of the hegemonic argument laid out, the question remains, however, as to what extent the United States is declining. Much of the declinist argument rests upon three factors: (1) the decline of the United States share of world product (from 50 percent in 1947 to 20-25 percent today); (2) the rise and persistence of the American trade deficit (itself being treated as a measure of loss of American "competitiveness") and the budget deficit; and (3) the decline of American manufacturing prowess and technological innovativeness (due to low savings, poor worker education, lack of industrious values, etc.).

Declinism has entered the political arena dramatically in recent years. Bill Clinton's successful 1992 presidential campaign was based upon a portrayal of an America left behind by more energetic competitors. Robert Reich (1990) decried the lack of a skilled workforce "to meet the challenges" of a coming century of change. Ross Perot (1993) talked about the sinking manufacturing base of the American economy, which "provided the foundation of the middle class." Steven Schier (1992) bemoaned a "decade of deficits" and warned of needed fiscal belt-tightening, that may reduce future standards of living. "Competitiveness" has become a buzz-word, evoking the need for government, corporations, and labor to "pull together" for a national effort at renewal. The question remains, however, whether viewing the nation as America, Inc. (in a battle for market share with Japan, Inc. and Europe, Inc.) is the right perspective.

In the contemporary world economy, as Laux (1989) points out, competition takes place not only between firms for sales, but also among states competing for production sites. "Now that production and financing are organized on a worldwide scale, state intervention in the space called the 'national economy' acquires particular political urgency for the advanced industrial countries" (Laux, 353). Ever since the end of the Second World War, when governments in Europe and North America adopted the broad principles of Keynesianism, politics and political economy have become one. Governments attempt to achieve the levels of investment, employment, and technological capability required to generate the revenues—both public and private— sufficient to guarantee nationally-defined norms of social welfare, and thus electoral survival. Their tasks are now immensely complicated by the reorganization of production on a global scale, a process initiated by large transnational firms, by rapid technological change, and by the rise of the newly industrialized countries (NICs) in the developing world.

Nowhere is this transformation in the contemporary world economy more apparent than in the tremendous growth in the nature, dimension, and scope of international financial transactions. This revolution in global finance stems from a set of interrelated factors: a) the progressive deregulation of financial markets—both internally and externally—in the advanced industrial states; b) the globalization of financial markets; c) the introduction of an array of new financial instruments allowing riskier and larger financial investments; and d) the emergence of new players, particularly institutional investors, in the markets (Cosh, Hughes, and Singh, 1992: 19).

The transformation of financing activities from segmented national debt and equity markets to a truly global financial market is promoting continuing and growing competition both domestically and internationally. During the early 1980s stockmarket boom, American financial firms expanded to pursue opportunities abroad, establishing facilities and market presence worldwide. In turn, foreign banks and securities houses, attracted by the size and stability of U.S. financial markets, built a major cross-border presence to help meet the growing demand for international investment diversification.

The international integration of financial markets has altered the context of national industrialization around the world. The fundamental challenge to the development of a world economy is the conflict between the economic benefits of integration and the political interests of individual states. Economic power, which was concentrated in the United States, has been diffused through commercial applications of technology and rapid growth of foreign trade and investment. Despite movement toward an integrated world economy, turmoil remains, for integration brings with it distributional consequences that can only be addressed in the political arena. To date, the integration of economic interests has not been matched by effective political processes needed to balance competing priorities.

Changes in the world economy are revising the ground rules of economic policymaking and recasting the roles played by governments in international economic relations (Laux, 1989: 353). The territorial state has been reconstituted as a "national economy" and is now but one among a set of actors, including large firms and banks, seeking control over financial resources. While evolving interdependence has improved total economic growth, by increasing foreign trade and investment and domestic efficiency, the intensity of competition and the ripple effects of cyclical expansions and recessions have disrupted national economies and eroded political power. The resulting loss of independence has tempted many governments to intervene in the international markets to protect powerful domestic interest groups. For national capitalists, short-term investments in domestic financial markets or foreign investments often provide higher, lower-risk returns than investments in long-term industrial expansion. Yet inducing nationals to invest in long-term industrial projects at home is among the most urgent tasks facing national governments (Maxfield, 1990). The rise of international markets curtails state capacity for this task. Frustration over declining state capacity to induce and guide industrial investment lay behind the decision to reform national financial market regulations. Regulatory reform is an effort to implement policies that would increase the competitiveness of the given state's financial markets in an integrated global financial market.

INTERNATIONAL TRADE AND FINANCE: PIERCING THE VEIL

One of the central objectives of the field of international political economy in the last twenty years has been to introduce insights from the field of world politics into the study of global economic relations. Although this effort has been largely successful in the study of international trade, much less attention has been focused on the financial sector of the global economy (Helleiner, 1992). Seemingly highly technical and arcane, the study of international finance has been left to specialists in international economics, financial journalists, and international financial practitioners.

The relative neglect of international financial issues must be seen as a serious misallocation of academic resources within the field of international political economy. Billions of dollars of capital flow across borders on a daily basis. Periodic "currency crises," in which slight differentials in interest rates—or the perception of future changes in interest rates—occur which set off panic with political repercussions for a government whose currency, and, by inference, whose credibility, is being attacked. As financial markets have become increasingly internationalized, the study of global finance has become central to our understanding of the workings of the global political economy in the late twentieth century. Money and finance are of central and primary significance for a genuinely theoretical and analytical understanding of both world politics in general, and international political economy in particular. In the words of Jeffry Frieden (1991), international finance has become "the pivot around which the world economy twists and turns, and it affects politics and economies in every nation." This study is intended to be added to a small, but growing, group of literature to fill that gap in the field.

It has become increasingly obvious that our understanding of the economic and political forces determining domestic and international monetary policy is seriously incomplete. While political scientists have done little to elucidate the mysterious world of international finance, economists have done little research on the nature and extent of the politics of economic transformation. Until recently, few political economists focused on the actions of political coalitions that have led to changes in financial policy. Gowa (1983) highlighted the role played by domestic political forces in the American decision to end dollar convertibility into gold. This action reflected the subordination of international concerns to domestic objectives. Zysman (1983) pointed out that an examination of national financial structures can illuminate both government economic strategies and the political conflicts that accompany industrial change. The particular arrangements of national financial systems limit both the marketplace options of firms and the administrative choices of governments. Simmons (1994) showed that, taking the international environment as a given, domestic structures can act as intervening variables in determining the selection of adjustment strategies.

The difficulties of the 1970s were not simply the result of recession or of an OPEC-sponsored jump in oil prices. A profound economic transition was underway in Western industrial countries, one that involved basic changes in the goods that were produced, how they were made, and where they were made. The economic deterioration and transition began to provoke political reactions and contribute to shifts in who governed. Given the assertion of financial interests against state power and regulation, and the desire of governing elites themselves to conform to the dictates of world financial markets, it is my contention that macroeconomic policy procedures and the policy coalitions that form them are crucial intervening variables between international financial markets and the state's capacity for macroeconomic management.

The preceding chapters represented an attempt to clarify the nature of the structural constraints and examine their importance for macroeconomic policy in the major industrial countries. However, in acknowledging the existence of such constraints, I did not wish to lend the impression that they *determine* any set of policies. Structural constraints set the parameters of action from which a wide range of choice is available for policymakers. This study examines the nature of political constraints imposed by changes in the international financial order. That is, the increase in international capital mobility has imposed constraints on the policy autonomy of sovereign states. The analysis used in this study has been influenced by Gourevitch's notion of "second image reversed," which emphasizes the role of international factors on the shape of domestic politics. To be sure, the degree of systemic-level influence is dependent on the relative size of the domestic economy in question, with larger economies being able to withstand—or at least moderate—the systemic level-induced pressures for convergence in macroeconomic and financial policies.

The issue of convergence is an important one. Convergence is used here to describe the process of financial market liberalization that has been taking place in all advanced industrial economies since the early 1980s, rather than the result of conscious political collaboration. As the leading financial powers moved toward liberalization, competitive pressures for similar moves developed in mid-sized states, which faced the prospect of capital loss and reduced investment opportunities.

To argue that financial liberalization is the result of a systemic-level process, I had to demonstrate that such a liberalization was not a predicted outcome given the domestic predilections of governments in power at the time of the effort. While certain market-oriented governments, such as Thatcher's in Britain, came to power with the express intent of liberalizing the rules for international (and domestic) financial transactions, the same cannot be said for the socialist governments of Australia, New Zealand, Spain, and France. Indeed, the French case reveals the resistance, and eventual capitulation, of a mid-sized state effort to maintain policy autonomy in the face of overwhelming systemic-level pressure.

Thus, while this study principally dealt with the effects of the system on domestic policy choice, it acknowledges that ultimately it is domestic policies that affect the pace of change. Furthermore, to speak of systemic-level influences requires that I denote their sources, which rests in the policy changes of economically dominant states. Because such states wield inordinate influence on the structural and behavior dynamics of the international system, they act as leaders in generating important international trends. When those trends are consonant with the preferences of important social groups, the effect can be a powerful one. That is, governments pursue international financial policies for domestic political reasons having to do with the policy preferences of important social groups. The policies of the economically-dominant states influence the international financial system that, in turn, influence economically mid-sized and smaller states.

An important consequence of this study is that it suggests that the conventional notion of "hegemony" is not a requirement for the maintenance of an open international financial regime. In the new era of world politics, the information asymmetries that once allowed states to stay ahead of their publics no longer exist. Information technologies have expanded the number of relevant actors involved in the decision-making process. When an issue area is considered arcane, states increasingly defer to non-state actors with "expertise." Formerly passive sub- and non-state actors are now mobilized to adapt and circumvent state policy directives that are at variance with their self-interest. The activities of these non-state actors influence what policymakers view as the range of the possible.

Earlier in this work I argued that financial capital is most advanced in economically dominant states. To the extent that non-state actors exercise influence, they will push the state toward liberalization. Thus, when a regime reflects the preferences of these important non-state actors in the issue area, it becomes self-sustaining. This is because regimes are collaborative mechanisms for reducing incentives to cheat. In the financial arena such "cheating" would be liberalization, which would make certain markets more attractive to mobile capital than others. The acceptance of liberalization as the rule, rather than as the activity to be curbed, obviates the need for mechanisms to control cheating. Furthermore, governments themselves have an incentive to liberalize if such liberalization will increase the supply of capital to the state. That is, states in the 1980s decided to sacrifice direct control over (decreasing amounts) of capital in order to attract more. Scholars of urban politics will not be surprised by this. In a world of increased competitiveness for scarce resources, states (like cities) reduce restrictions on capital use and mobility in order to become more attractive havens. In the process, the sitting governments (both conservative and left-of-center) can claim success in generating wealth and jobs in the country.

Though from an objective standpoint there are benefits and costs in adopting any one policy, different political communities have different preferences. Therefore, what are acceptable costs on the part of one community may be unacceptable to another. The type of international monetary and financial regime and the presence of economic change exercise tremendous influence on the determination and success of domestic macroeconomic policies.

GLOBALIZATION AND ITS IMPACT ON POLICY

In this study, the defining aspect of rising international financial integration is the more frequent ability of investors in one country to choose financial products for their portfolio that are denominated in foreign currencies or issued in foreign markets. To the extent that financial markets are integrated and transactions costs are low, private investors will circumvent national boundaries to maximize the utility gained from investment. Securitized funds in 1990 crossed national borders at a rate of $12 trillion a year, compared with world trade in goods and services valued at only $5.2 trillion a year and US GDP of $5.5 trillion (Zeigler, 1990: 7). Though accurate figures are difficult to obtain, in 1994 the world foreign exchange market was reckoned to turn over the equivalent of $1.3 trillion per day (Woodall, 1995: 10). Yearly transactions in the London Eurodollar market, virtually unregulated by public authorities, by the late 1980s represented over 25 times the value of world trade (Walter, 1993: 197). Investors' decisions about what financial products to include in their portfolios depend—*inter alia*—on relative returns adjusted for inflation, expected exchange rate changes, taxes, and risk (Maxwell, 1990: 4).

The growth of international financial markets has been accompanied by new ways of understanding the world economy (Schor, 1992). The extent of financial integration has a major bearing upon both the effectiveness of monetary policy in any one country and the extent to which individual countries are able to pursue a monetary policy strategy independently of that of other countries. Increasingly, monetary policy has had to be framed within the constraints imposed by a high degree of financial integration in the world economy (Llewellyn, 1980). This development sets the past decade apart from the Bretton Woods era, when Keynesian economics were pursued. The fundamental principle underlying the Keynesian approach was the need for governments to carry out macroeconomic policy at a national level, and the importance of an international system of financial management that facilitated such policy. In particular, the unrestricted international movement of capital was seen as being incompatible with effective policy and hence prosperity.

The Great Stagflation of the 1970s discredited much of traditional Keynesianism. In particular, government efforts at macroeconomic "fine-tuning" yielded diminishing, and then negative, returns. Global financial neoliberalism emerged as a new doctrine that stressed the futility of international financial regulation and discretionary macroeconomic policy. Neoliberals contend that national governments or even international regulatory regimes neither can nor should control the flow of capital across borders, and hence cannot regulate interest rates, fix exchange-rates, or pursue macroeconomic policies that are in conflict with the "dictates of the international market."

The policymaking elites in the advanced industrial states have embraced neoliberalism, marked by trends toward reforming the regulation of national securities businesses and financial liberalization. While these trends meshed well with the free-market orientation of American and British elites in the 1980s, other industrial-state governments followed, either out of genuine enthusiasm for regulatory reform or fear of being left behind the more dynamic markets.

Cross-border financial flows and financial liberalization have had an impact on the stability of the world economy. Corporations now scour the globe for funds at the lowest cost, and investors shop around the world for the highest returns on their savings. Both corporations and investors engage in increasingly more sophisticated transactions that present both greater profit opportunities and greater risks. Massive pools of short-term hyper-mobile speculative capital have raised the specter of the casino with its attendant potential for destabilization (Strange, 1986). To the extent one assumes that financial markets are less than perfect, international financial integration can lead to a divergence between private and public welfare. Financial transactions, motivated by short-term considerations, can force prices of financial products above their public value—determined by long-term profit and risk assessments.

These developments were in no small part occasioned by the deterioration of the system of international monetary regulation. The Bretton Woods regime, which managed international financial relations after the Second World War, collapsed in the early 1970s. Its key components—fixed exchange rates, limited capital mobility, and restricted international linkages—had provided a degree of certainty in international financial relations and thus allowed for national regulation. Although based on American economic dominance, the Bretton Woods regime contributed to the viability of nationally-based macroeconomic autonomy (Schor, 1992: 2).

The demise of the Bretton Woods regime has called into question the feasibility of national regulation. Flexible exchange rates have resulted in currency market instability, while the decline of American power and leadership has led to the problem of achieving policy consistency in a more pluralistic state system. The growing complexity and uncertainty of the world economy have made it essential for governments to cooperate in formulating their macroeconomic policies. To be sure, the world economy is one of an increasingly integrated capital market alongside continued political fragmentation. As long as capital can flow relatively unimpeded across borders, international investors and transnational corporations will benefit from access to higher rates of return, while governments will continue to compete for the allegiance of national and international funds. Without cooperation, successful adaptation of the international economic system to changing developments is unlikely. However, the very fact of globalization of financial markets has made such cooperation more difficult to achieve (Webb, 1994). To paraphrase Aronson (1977), without understanding the roles and relationships of the major actors in the global financial system, sensible policies and policy changes are impossible.

POLICYMAKING AND FINANCIAL ORDERS

This study emphasized the role of economic policy choices in shaping international outcomes of wealth and power. The cycle of dominance and decline of great powers is not just a consequence of uneven patterns of growth and technological change. It is also a consequence of policy choices that spur growth, change technology, and alter circumstances.

After World War II, the United States and other industrial countries made specific economic policy choices that radically altered prevailing circumstances of soaring inflation, rapid nationalization of industrial assets, and bilaterally-managed trade. They created a liberal international economic order that emphasized stable prices, flexible domestic markets, and freer trade (permitting fixed exchange rates, which became the hallmark of the system). Under these policies, for the next two decades world industrial production and trade grew faster and inequalities between industrial and developing countries narrowed more sharply than in any previous historical period since the industrial revolution.

Markets work as mechanisms for narrowing policy differences in a pluralistic and complex international economy, however, only if they are circumscribed by a broad consensus among participating countries to keep markets open (i.e., avoid protectionism), maintain stable domestic prices (i.e., prevent wildly fluctuating exchange rates), and encourage flexible domestic markets (i.e., reallocate resources to meet international competition).

Henry Nau (1990), in a discussion of choice in setting the international economic agenda, stresses the key role of policy ideas that cut across national perspectives, political parties, and special interest groups—and ultimately shape or fail to shape the consensus that creates international markets and institutions and permits them to function efficiently. These ideas originate in the major participating countries in the "nexus of nongovernmental institutions that surrounds domestic bureaucratic and international institutional decision-making processes."

Ideas compete in this nexus to shape social views. These views then permeate, through political coalitions and elections, more immediate policymaking processes at both the domestic and international levels to influence choices about national purpose and economic efficiency. This "nexus of nongovernmental institutions" can be defined as think tanks, major universities, leading business organizations and corporations, as well as influential academicians that inform the policy debate. Haas (1992) refers to such groups as "epistemic communities." As a result, a larger consensus among nongovernmental institutions enables pluralistic policymaking organizations to work. Without it, domestic as well as international policymaking would grind to a halt, stalemated by unconstrained rivalries and a special interest-group perspective that sees all policy choices and outcomes as a matter of winners and losers and no solutions that serves the interests of many groups. The ability of epistemic communities to set the policy agenda and the range of choice among competing alternatives confers upon them structural power.

Ideas do not emerge in a vacuum. They are influenced by circumstances and interests; and to affect policy, they have to meet a certain test of public acceptance and succeed in mobilizing political and ultimately bureaucratic forces. The policy ideas that epistemic communities and state institutions hold and express help in themselves to shape public understandings of options. Moreover, translated into policies, ideas have to yield results.

Nau further speaks of a "Bretton Woods triad" consisting of: 1) moderate Keynesian fiscal and monetary policies to ensure stable domestic prices and thereby stable international prices or exchange rates; 2) reduction in trade barriers and foreign exchange restrictions to promote freer trade, comparative advantage, and, hence, competitive and more efficient use of domestic and international resources; and 3) limits on non-economic motivated intervention by governments in the workings of the domestic market so as to facilitate a flexible flow of labor where it is needed, the movement of capital resources into new and more innovative enterprises, and a stream of new products uninhibited by arbitrary regulation of individual sectors—all of which helps to control current account imbalances through a reallocation of domestic resources, instead of through inflation, frequent exchange rate changes, restrictions on trade and foreign exchange, or unconditional external borrowing.

Structuralist studies argue that the Bretton Woods policy triad and market mechanisms were not enough to stabilize contemporary world markets, given new circumstances of highly mobilized and speculative capital flows. But capital flows, while many times larger than trade flows, are not unrelated to real economic developments in domestic markets. Much of the volatility of capital flows in the 1970s, 1980s, and 1990s, it can be argued, was due not to new circumstances but to prevailing policies of deregulating global financial markets while re-regulating domestic and trade markets. More flexible money moved around in more inflexible product markets, exacerbating exchange rate and other instabilities. Restoring stable and flexible domestic markets may go a long way toward restoring stable international markets and reducing speculative capital flows.

EVALUATING HEGEMONIC ARGUMENTS

In this final section, I would like to review a rather illuminating exposition on the future of the international monetary and financial regime. The trend toward a less regulated global financial market is almost certain to continue. This has profound implications for the sustainability of any state's economic dominance. According to the hegemonic stability argument, the lack of a dominant country to act as the manager of the world economy will lead to the latter's demise as unilateral policies will prevail over the collective goals. Much of this argument follows logically from the political economy of trade, where hegemon-led collective action has been seen as necessary for the maintenance of an open, liberal international trade regime. Unilateral action, by contrast, has been seen as having a neomercantilist "closure" effect. Many international political economy scholars, influenced by the emphasis in the field on trade, assume that the same dynamic is at work in finance (Cerny, 1994). In the financial issue area, however, the converse would seem to be the case. Hegemon-led collective action is necessary to control financial flows, since financial asset-holders would use exit strategies to circumvent any individual state's controls. Furthermore, given the mobility of capital, the natural predisposition of states as competitors is more likely toward a more liberal regime. Thus, unilateral action has the effect of liberalizing the world financial system. Therefore, it can be argued that a hegemonic order is not needed to maintain openness. Quite the contrary, a hegemonic order is needed if regulation and control are the intended outcomes.

This reformulation of the hegemonic stability argument flows from the discussion in Chapter I concerning regimes created to solve the dilemmas of common interests and common aversions. The Bretton Woods financial control regime was established to coordinate state action to avoid financial capital mobility, which was viewed at the time as a potentially ruinous occurrence. Keynes was quite explicit at the Bretton Woods conference about the need to control financial market operators and nationalize capital. Policymakers had come to believe that open and unregulated international financial markets (1) have an inherent tendency to be volatile and destabilizing and (2) financial asset-holders would drain funds from industrial investment and trade. Short-term financial flows, in particular, were motivated by speculative rather than productive reasons and had to be curtailed. Finance, if allowed to roam freely, would destabilize the real economy, leading to major economic dislocations, if not a return to depression. Worldwide economic growth and prosperity through national demand management policies required a closed, not an open, international financial regime. The adoption of the Bretton Woods capital controls convention among advanced industrial states allowed the mutual aversion, financial instability, to be avoided.

By the 1970s, however, new techniques emerged in a world of adjustment. Information technology allowed financial asset-holders the means to escape the bounds of national restriction. The rise of offshore markets gave them a place to exit. As some states opted unilaterally to liberalize their financial markets, they created pressure on others to do the same. Financial asset-holders, whose investment criteria were based upon risk and reward, rather than winning political constituents, became far more efficient allocators of capital than policymakers. Regulatory reform and liberalization of financial flows, while enhancing the position of states where financial capital interests were most developed, also tended to shift financial decision-making from the state to financial asset-holders. Finance capital mobility constrains national policymaking autonomy because it weakens the ability of states to extract resources from financial asset-holders, who now have the ability to hedge political risk through currency substitution. Globalized production predicts to a battle among states for sites, similar to the battle among cities in the United States for investment.

The discussion so far suggests that the behavior of states will be relatively unimportant in determining the future of global finance. Does this mean, as one set of authors recently concluded, that further "internationalization is irreversible" (Banuri and Schor, 1992)? There is an important threat to the open and liberal order which has not yet been discussed -- an international financial crisis of major dimensions. Its importance comes from the way it would alter both market and state behavior towards a more closed pattern of financial relations. The most important change would be on the market side. The experience of several international financial crises in the past two decades, as well as that of 1931, demonstrates that market operators tend to retreat to the safety of domestic markets during, and in the wake of, such crises. The international banking crises of 1974, for example, dramatically shook the confidence of market operators in foreign exchange markets and the Euromarkets, and the volume of activity in both sectors dropped sharply. The stock market crash of October 1987 also caused a considerable retreat, albeit temporary, from the Euromarkets and cross-border investment positions. In general, the relative unfamiliarity of foreign markets and the currency risks involved in international financial holdings combine to discourage investment across borders in a crisis.

Reinforcing this market action, there are three ways in which states might change their behavior in the face of a major international financial crisis (Helleiner, 1992). First, if the crisis is severe, it might encourage states to introduce a system of extreme exchange controls. This was, for example, the case in 1931 when the enormous capital flight from Japan and central Europe led these countries to judge that the costs of introducing such controls were overshadowed by the benefits. Second, a crisis could lead states to intervene more substantially in their domestic financial system to offset the instability caused by the crisis. Such intervention domestically would indirectly aid initiatives to control international finance by diminishing possibilities for market avoidance and innovation. Third, states might be encouraged to cooperate in controlling financial movements. By bringing economic disruption and instability *simultaneously* to each major state, a major international financial crisis might provide the catalyst to encourage collective action aimed at controlling financial movements.

This combination of possible market and state responses to a major global financial crisis suggests that it is these crises, rather than piecemeal unilateral departures from liberal rules, as in the trade case, which pose the greatest threat to open and liberal financial relations. Why do such crises occur? There is considerable agreement that financial markets are endogenously prone to experience periodic crises as a result of imperfect information and the mobile, liquid nature of finance. This does not mean, however, that international financial crises should be seen as inevitable. There are generally held to be three ways for states to reduce the risks of their occurrence. First, a stable international macroeconomic environment should be maintained in order to minimize the risk of a crisis deriving from the "real" (industrial) economy. Second, regulation or supervision of international financial activity will help to minimize the tendency of financial systems to experience endogenously produced crises. Finally, in the event of a crisis, financial runs can be prevented from getting out of hand if an international lender of last resort exists to extend emergency credit.

The role that states have to play in maintaining an open international financial system is thus not so much that of maintaining liberal rules, as suggested by international political economists in the trade field, as that of managing inherently unstable market conditions. Indeed, it was exactly this kind of role which Kindleberger's original formulation of the hegemonic stability theory pointed to. While the theory's proponents from the discipline of world politics have focused on the need for a hegemon to stop states from breaking liberal rules, Kindleberger's concerns have been focused, in the tradition of Bagehot and Keynes, on the need for a hegemonic power to manage unstable markets. As he notes, states are needed to provide "the public good of stability that the private market is unable to provide for itself."

Financial analysts and policymakers are concerned over the newfound autonomy of financial market operators—the barbarians at the gate—who may overturn economic stability in their wake. Susan Strange (1986) used the casino metaphor to describe the activities of currency speculators and holders of bond derivatives. Indeed, as Woodall (1995) notes: "much of the paranoia surrounding the increasing power of [financial asset-holders] is based on the popular notion that, thanks to the fancy new instruments and huge trading volumes, exchange rates and bond yields are becoming ever more volatile. " Compared with the Bretton Woods period, exchange rates and bond yields are more variable, but as my discussion in Chapter IV showed such instability is a reflection of politically-induced risk. That is, governments can reduce volatility by practicing more consistent policies that will not roil the market, putting at the risk the values of asset-holders' wealth.

What are the prospects of states acting in a fashion that prevents a crisis? Kindleberger has argued that a hegemonic state is needed to prevent such a crisis because of collective action problems involved in maintaining financial stability at the international level. While his concern is mostly with the state-as-lender-of-last-resort function, collective action problems also bedevil global macroeconomic diplomacy as well as regulatory and supervisory discussions. The importance of a hegemonic state is not that it has enough power to provide unilaterally the three functions necessary for maintaining stability, but that its central position will give it a special interest in acting as the leader.

By the late 1970s it was already clear that, although the United States retained the most powerful position in the global macroeconomy, it had lost its ability unilaterally to produce a global economic expansion. Not only was the United States unable to persuade its allies to cooperate in its "locomotive" strategy to bring the world out of the recession of the early-to-mid-1970s, but also by 1978-79 for the first time in the postwar period the United States was forced by external pressure to curtail its own unilateral expansion. The resulting U.S. austerity program, induced by Volcker's tight monetary policy, played a major role in bringing on the international debt crisis. In this way the decline in American capabilities in the global macroeconomic sphere led directly to an increase in international instability as hegemonic stability theory predicts. While the United States was able to recapture temporarily a leadership position in macroeconomic affairs with its unilateral expansion after 1982, by 1985-87, it was forced once again into greater macroeconomic cooperation with its allies by external pressures. Indeed, as before, an increase in international financial fragility—in the form of the October 1987 and October 1989 stock market crashes—accompanied this decline in American power as global market operators worried about the success of such cooperation.

If states, even a hegemonic state, can no longer control the activities of financial asset-holders, they should be more attuned to the incentives that drive those activities. Financial asset-holders sought greater autonomy from the dictates of state policymakers in order to reduce the political risks to their wealth portfolios. Risk is reduced through diversification of assets. The surest way to reduce political risk is through currency substitution, through which foreign currency-denominated assets are substituted for domestic currency-denominated assets that may be depreciated by government policies (e.g., inflation-inducing easy monetary policies, regulatory restrictions on asset use). Asset-holders assess risk by demanding interest-rate premiums on assets. For example, higher assessed risk leads to higher bond yields. Risk assessment requires information, and it is in providing this "commodity" that governments still have a role to play in determining economic outcomes. Because financial crises come from inaccurate information on political risk, the better the information that governments can provide to financial asset-holders, the better the financial asset-holders are able to foresee trouble on the horizon and assist all governments in the achievement of mutually-preferred economic outcomes.

NOTE

1. Named after economist Nicholas Kaldor, these strategies are based upon "learning-by-doing" development. The state aids in the development of the nation by targeting certain "strategic industries" and restricting competing imports into the country until the domestic industry has achieved scale economies.

Bibliography

Agmon, Tamir (1985). *Political Economy and Risk in World Financial Markets.* Lexington, MA: Lexington Books.

Alesina, Alberto and Lawrence W. Summers (1993). "Central Bank Independence and Macroeconomic Performance: Some Comparative Evidence." *Journal of Money, Credit, and Banking* 25 (May 1993): 153-162.

Allison, Graham (1969). "Conceptual Models and the Cuban Missile Crisis." American *Political Science Review,* 63 (September): 689-718.

Andrews, David M. (1994). "Capital Mobility and State Autonomy: Toward a Structural Theory of International Monetary Relations." *International Studies Quarterly* 38 (June): 193-218.

Aronson, Jonathan (1977). *Money and Power: Banks and the World Monetary System.* London, U.K.: Sage.

Bank for International Settlements [BIS] (1994). *64th Annual Report,* 13th June. Basle: Bank for International Settlements.

Banuri, Tariq, and Juliet Schor [eds.] (1992). *Financial Openness and National Autonomy: Opportunities and Constraints.* Oxford, U.K.: Oxford University Press.

Bloomfield, A. I. (1959). *Monetary Policy Under the International Gold Standard: 1880- 1914.* New York, NY: Federal Reserve Bank of New York.

Bryant, Ralph C. (1987). *International Financial Intermediation.* Washington DC: Brookings.

Calleo, David (1987). *Beyond American Hegemony.* New York, NY: Basic Books, Inc.

Calverley, John (1995). "The Currency Wars," *Harvard Business Review* (March-April): 146-147.

Cashman, Greg (1993). *What Causes War? An Introduction to Theories of International Conflict.* New York, NY: Lexington Books.

Cerny, Phillip G. (1993). "The Deregulation and Re-regulation of Financial Markets in a More Open World," in Phillip Cerny (ed.), *Finance and World Politics: Markets, Regimes and States in the Post-Hegemonic Era.* Aldershot, U.K.: Edward Elgar.

Cerny, Phillip G. (1994). "The Infrastructure of the Infrastructure? Toward 'Embedded Financial Orthodoxy' in the International Political Economy," in Ronen P. Palan and Barry Gills (eds.), *Transcending the State-Global Divide: A Neostructuralist Agenda in International Relations.* Boulder, CO: Lynne Rienner.

Chase-Dunn, Christopher (1981). "Interstate System and Capitalist World Economy: One Logic or Two?" *International Studies Quarterly* 25: 19-42.

Cooper, Richard [1968] (1991). "National Economic Policy in an Interdependent World Economy," in George T. Crane and Abla Amawi (eds.), *The Theoretical Evolution of International Political Economy: A Reader.* New York, NY: Oxford University Press.

Cosh, Andrew D., Alan Hughes, and Ajit Singh (1992). "Openness, Financial Innovation, Changing Patterns of Ownership, and the Structure of Financial Markets," in Tariq Banuri and Juliet B. Schor (eds.), *Financial Openness and National Autonomy: Opportunities and Constraints.* Oxford, U.K.: Oxford University Press.

Cox, Robert (1987). *Power, Production, and World Order: Social Forces in the Making of History.* New York, NY: Columbia University Press.

Crook, Clive (1992). "Fear of Finance." *The Economist* Survey (September 19th): 1-48.

Dam, Kenneth (1982). *The Rules of the Game.* Chicago: University of Chicago Press.

Dornbusch, Rudiger (1980). *Open Economy Macroeconomics.* New York, NY: Basic Books.

Dornbusch, Rudiger (1993). *Policymaking in the Open Economy.* New York: NY: Oxford University Press.

Eckes, Alfred E., Jr. (1975). *A Search for Solvency: Bretton Woods and the International Monetary System, 1941-1971.* Austin, TX: University of Texas Press.

Eichengreen, Barry (1989). "Hegemonic Stability Theories of the International Monetary System," in Richard N. Cooper, Barry Eichengreen, C. Randall Henning, Gerald Holtham, and Robert D. Putnam (eds.), *Can Nations Agree?* Washington, DC: Brookings.

Fagerberg, Jan, Adne Cappelen, Lars Mjøset, and Rune Skarstein (1990). "The Decline of Social-Democratic State Capitalism in Norway." *New Left Review,* 81 (May/June): 60-94.

Feldstein, Martin, and Charles Horioka (1980). "Domestic Saving and International Capital Flows." *Economic Journal* 90 (June): 314-329.

Frankel, Jeffery A. (1992). "Measuring International Capital Mobility: A Review." *American Economic Review* 82 (May): 197-203.

Freeman, Chris (1988). "Diffusion: The Spread of New Technology to Firms, Sectors, and Nations," in Arnold Heertje (ed.), *Innovation, Technology, and Finance.* Oxford, U.K.: Basil Blackwell.

French, Kenneth R. and James M. Porterba (1991). "Investor Diversification and International Equity Markets." *American Economic Review* 81 (May): 222-226.

Frieden, Jeffry A. (1987). *Banking on the World: The Politics of American International Finance.* New York, NY: Harper & Row.

Frieden, Jeffry A. (1991). "Invested Interests: The Politics of National Economic Policies in a World of Global Finance." *International Organization,* 45 (Autumn): 425-451.

Gerschenkron, Alexander (1962). *Economic Backwardness in Historical Perspective.* Cambridge, MA: Harvard University Press.

Gill, Stephen, and David Law (1988). *The Global Political Economy: Perspectives, Problems, and Policies.* Baltimore, MD: The Johns Hopkins University Press.

Gilpin, Robert (1981). *War and Change in World Politics.* Cambridge, U.K.: Cambridge University Press.

Gilpin, Robert (1987). *The Political Economy of International Relations.* Princeton, NJ: Princeton University Press.

Glynn, Andrew (1986). "Capital Flight and Exchange Controls." *New Left Review,* 155: 37-49.

Goertz, Gary (1994). *Contexts of International Politics.* Cambridge, U.K.: Cambridge University Press.

Goodman, John B. and Louis Pauly (1993). "The Obsolescence of Capital Controls? Economic Management in an Age of Global Markets." *World Politics,* 46: 50-82.

Gourevitch, Peter (1978). "The Second Image Reversed: The International Sources of Domestic Politics." *International Organization,* 32 (Autumn): 881-911.

Gourevitch, Peter (1986). *Politics in Hard Times: Comparative Responses to International Economic Crises.* Ithaca, NY: Cornell University Press.

Gowa, Joanne (1983). *Closing the Gold Window: Domestic Politics and the End of Bretton Woods.* Ithaca, NY: Cornell University Press.

Haas, Peter (1992). "Introduction: Epistemic Communities and International Policy Coordination." *International Organization,* 46: 1-35.

Haggard, Stephan, and Robert R. Kaufman [eds.] (1992). *The Politics of Economic Adjustment: International Constraints, Distributional Conflicts, and the State.* Princeton, NJ: Princeton University Press.

Hall, Peter A. [ed.] (1989). *The Political Power of Economic Ideas: Keynesianism Across Nations.* Princeton, NJ: Princeton University Press.

Hawley, James P. (1987). *Dollars & Borders: U.S. Government Attempts to Restrict Capital Flows, 1960-1980.* Armonk, NY: M. E. Sharpe, Inc.

Helleiner, Eric (1992). "States and the Future of Global Finance." *Review of International Studies,* 18: 31-49.

Helleiner, Eric (1993). "When Finance Was The Servant: International Capital Movements in the Bretton Woods Order," in Phillip G. Cerny (ed.), *Finance and World Politics: Markets, Regimes and States in the Post-Hegemonic Era.* Aldershot, U.K.: Edward Elgar.

Helleiner, Eric (1994a). *States and the Reemergence of Global Finance: From Bretton Woods to the 1990s.* Ithaca, NY: Cornell University Press.

Helleiner, Eric (1994b). "From Bretton Woods to Global Finance: A World turned Upside Down," in Richard Stubbs and Geoffrey R.D. Underhill (eds.), *Political Economy and the Changing Global Order.* New York, NY: St. Martin's Press.

Hirschman, Albert O. (1970). *Exit, Voice, and Loyalty: Responses to Decline in Firms, Organizations, and States.* Cambridge, MA: Harvard University Press.

Kapstein, Ethan B. (1989). "Resolving the Regulator's Dilemma: International Coordination of Banking Regulations." *International Organization,* 43 (Spring): 323-347.

Katzenstein, Peter J. [1977] (1991). "Domestic and International Forces and Strategies of Foreign Economic Policy," in George T. Crane and Abla Amawi (eds.), *The Theoretical Evolution of International Political Economy: A Reader.* New York, NY: Oxford University Press.

Kennedy, Paul (1987). *The Rise and Fall of the Great Powers.* New York, NY: Random House.

Keohane, Robert O. (1980). "The Theory of Hegemonic Stability and Changes in International Economic Regimes, 1967-1977," in Ole R. Holsti, Randolph M. Siverson, and Alexander L. George (eds.), *Changes in the International System.* Boulder, CO: Westview Press.

Keohane, Robert O. (1986). *Neorealism and Its Critics.* New York, NY: Columbia University Press.

Keohane, Robert O. and Joseph S. Nye, Jr. (1977). *Power and Interdependence: World Politics in Transition.* Boston, MA: Little, Brown.

Kindleberger, Charles (1973). *The World in Depression, 1929-1939.* Berkeley, CA: University of California Press.

Krasner, Stephen (1983). *International Regimes.* Ithaca, NY: Cornell University Press.

Laux, Jeanne Kirk (1989). "The Changing World Economy: States in Competition," in Robert O. Matthews, Arthur G. Rubinoff, and Janice Gross Stein (eds.), *International Conflict and Conflict Management, 2nd. ed.* Scarborough, ON: Prentice-Hall Canada.

Lindblom, Charles E. (1977). *Politics and Markets: The World's Political-Economic Systems.* New York, NY: Basic Books.

Llewellyn, David T. (1980). *International Financial Integration: The Limits of Sovereignty.* New York, NY: John Wiley & Sons.

Loriaux, Michael (1991). *France After Hegemony: International Change and Financial Reform.* Ithaca, NY: Cornell University Press.

Luce, Henry R. (1941) "The American Century." *Society,* 31 (July-August): 4-11.

Marglin, Stephen A., and Juliet B. Schor [eds.] (1990). *The Golden Age of Capitalism: Reinterpreting the Postwar Experience.* New York, NY: Oxford University Press.

Marston, Richard C. (1995). *International Financial Integration.* Cambridge, U.K.: Cambridge University Press.

Massey, Patrick (1995). *New Zealand: Market Liberalization in a Developed Economy.* New York, NY: St. Martin's Press.

Maxfield, Sylvia (1990). *Governing Capital: International Finance and Mexican Politics.* Ithaca, NY: Cornell University Press.

McKenzie, Richard, and Dwight Lee (1991). *Quicksilver Capital: How the Rapid Movement of Wealth Has Changed the World.* New York, NY: Free Press.

Mearsheimer, John J. (1990). "Why We Will Soon Miss the Cold War." *The Atlantic* 266 (August): 35-50.

Meerschwam, David M. (1991). *Breaking Financial Boundaries: Global Capital, National Deregulation, and Financial Services Firms.* Boston, MA: Harvard Business School Press.

Miller, Roger LeRoy, and Robert W. Pulsinelli (1985). *Modern Money and Banking.* New York, NY: McGraw-Hill.

Millman, Gregory J. (1995). *The Vandals' Crown: How Rebel Currency Traders Overthrew the World's Central Banks.* New York, NY: The Free Press.

Nau, Henry R. (1990). *The Myth of America's Decline: Leading the World Economy into the 1990s.* New York, NY: Oxford University Press.

Niskanen, William A. (1971). *Bureaucracy and Representative Government.* Chicago: Aldine, Atherton.

O'Brien, Richard (1992). *Global Financial Integration: The End of Geography.* London, U.K: Royal Institute of International Affairs.

O'Brien, Richard (1995). "Who Rules the World's Financial Markets?" *Harvard Business Review* (March-April): 144-151.

Odell, John S. (1982). *U.S. International Monetary Policy: Markets, Power, and Ideas as Sources of Change.* Princeton, NJ: Princeton University Press.

Oye, Kenneth A. (1985). "The Sterling-Dollar-Franc Triangle: Monetary Diplomacy 1929- 1937." *World Politics,* 38 (October): 173-199.

Peterson, Paul E. (1981). *City Limits.* Chicago, IL: University of Chicago Press.

Polanyi, Karl (1944). *The Great Transformation.* New York, NY: Farrar & Rinehart.

Pringle, Robert (1992). "Financial Markets Versus Governments," in Tariq Banuri and Juliet B. Schor (eds.), *Financial Openness and National Autonomy: Opportunities and Constraints.* Oxford, U.K.: Oxford University Press.

Reich, Robert (1991). *The Work of Nations: Preparing Ourselves for 21st Century Capitalism.* New York, NY: A. A. Knopf.

Rogowski, Ronald (1989). *Commerce and Coalitions: How Trade Affects Domestic Political Alignments.* Princeton, NJ: Princeton University Press.

Rosenau, James (1990). *Turbulence in World Politics.* Princeton, NJ: Princeton University Press.

Ruggie, John Gerald (1983). "International Regimes, Transactions, and Change: Embedded Liberalism in the Postwar Economic Order," in Stephen D. Krasner (ed.), *International Regimes.* Ithaca, NY: Cornell University Press.

Salvatore, Dominick (1990). *International Economics, 3rd. ed.* New York, NY: Macmillan Publishing Co.

Schier, Steven E. (1992). *A Decade of Deficits: Congressional Thought and Fiscal Action.* Albany, NY: SUNY Press.

Schneider, Mark (1989). *The Competitive City: The Political Economy of Suburbia.* Pittsburgh, PA: University of Pittsburgh Press.

Schwartz, Herman M. (1994). *States Versus Markets: History, Geography, and the Development of the International Political Economy.* New York, NY: St. Martin's Press.

Simmons, Beth A. (1994). *Who Adjusts?: Domestic Sources of Foreign Economic Policy During the Interwar Years.* Princeton, NJ: Princeton University Press.

Singer, J. David [1961] (1994). "The Level-of-Analysis Problem in International Relations," in Phil Williams, Donald M. Goldstein, and Jay M. Shafritz (eds.), *Classic Readings of International Relations.* Belmont, CA: Wadsworth Publishing Company.

Spero, Joan Edelman (1990). *The Politics of International Economic Relations, 4th. ed.* New York, NY: St. Martin's Press.

Strange, Susan (1986). *Casino Capitalism.* Oxford, U.K.: Basil Blackwell.

Strange, Susan (1994). *States and Markets, 2nd ed.* London, U.K.: Pinter Publishers.

Taylor, Michael (1989). "Structure, Culture and Action in the Explanation of Social Change." *Politics and Society,* 17 (June): 115-162.

Tesar, Linda L. and Ingrid M. Werner (1992). "Home Bias and the Globalization of Securities Markets." NBER Working Paper No. 4218 (November).

Thompson, William R. (1988). *On Global War: Historical-Structural Approaches to World Politics.* Columbia, SC: University of South Carolina Press.

Tiebout, Charles M. (1962). *The Community Economic Base Study.* New York, NY: Committee for Economic Development.

Triffin, Robert (1960). *Gold and the Dollar Crisis: The Future of Convertibility.* New Haven, CT: Yale University Press.

Vernon, Raymond (1966). "International Trade Investment and International Trade in the Product Life Cycle." *Quarterly Journal of Economics,* 80: 190-207.

Wachtel, Howard (1986). *The Money Mandarins: The Making of the New Supranational Economic Order.* New York, NY: Pantheon.

Walter, Andrew (1991). *World Power and World Money: The Role of Hegemony and International Monetary Order.* London, U.K.: Harvester Wheatsheaf.

Waltz, Kenneth N. (1959). *Man, the State, and War: A Theoretical Analysis.* New York, NY: Columbia University Press.

Waltz, Kenneth N. (1979). *Theory of International Politics.* Reading, MA: Addison-Wesley.

Webb, Michael (1991). "International Economic Structures, Governmental Interests, and International Coordination of Macroeconomic Adjustment Policies." *International Organization,* 45: 309-342.

Webb, Michael (1994). "Understanding Patterns of Macroeconomic Policy Coordination in the Postwar Period," in Richard Stubbs and Geoffrey R.D. Underhill (eds.), *Political Economy and the Changing Global Order.* New York, NY: St. Martin's Press.

Wendt, Alexander (1987). "The Agent-Structure Problem in International Relations Theory," *International Organization,* 41: 335-370.

Williamson, John, and Marcus H. Miller (1987). *Targets and Indicators: A Blueprint for International Coordination of Economic Policy.* Washington, DC: Institute for International Economics.

Wilson, Harold (1971). *The Labour Government 1964-70.* Boston, MA: Little, Brown.

Woodall, Pam (1995). "Who's In The Driving Seat?" *The Economist* Survey (October 7th): 1-38.

Zevin, Robert (1992). "Are World Financial Markets More Open? If So, Why and With What Effects?," in Tariq Banuri and Juliet B. Schor (eds.), *Financial Openness and National Autonomy: Opportunities and Constraints.* Oxford, U.K.: Oxford University Press.

Ziegler, Dominic (1990). "In Search of the Crock of Gold." *The Economist* Survey (July 21st): 1-28.

Zimmerman, William (1987). *Open Borders, Nonalignment, and the Political Evolution of Yugoslavia.* Princeton, NJ: Princeton University Press.

Zysman, John (1983). *Governments, Markets, and Growth: Financial Systems and the Politics of Industrial Change.* Ithaca, NY: Cornell University Press.

Index

adjustment (in monetary regime), 48
agent-structure problem, 23, 36-40
Andrews, David, 124-125
Australia, 198
autonomy dilemma, 21

balance of payments:
  adjustment, 110-114
  autonomous transactions, 109
  capital account, 108-109
  current account, 108-109, 130-131, 159
  described, 108
  disequilibria in, 6, 14, 109-114, 130
  portfolio-balance approach, 111-113
  purchasing-power parity (PPP), 110
  trade-based (elasticities) approach, 109-110
Bank of England, 70, 74, 91, 94
Bank for International Settlements (BIS), 12, 117
"bankers' bargain," 22, 28, 140
banks, private, 97, 147-157
"Big Bang," 155

bonds, 111, 128-129
Bretton Woods arrangements, 23, 59, 79-84, 86
Bretton Woods era (period), 23, 55, 63-65, 86-90, 96-101, 143
Britain (United Kingdom), 11, 17, 34, 59, 66, 70-72, 75, 83, 91, 93-94, 105, 116, 122, 136, 148, 154-155, 171

capital controls, 7, 12, 64, 81, 92-97, 99, 118, 145, 170-171
capital mobility, 14, 17, 28-29, 33-34, 38, 64, 68, 83, 85, 115, 120, 123, 129, 136, 205
central banks, 71-74, 105-107, 115-116, 138
Cerny, Philip, 24
Clinton, Bill, 193
Cold War, 91, 98
collective action problem, 205-208
common aversions, dilemmas of, 46
common interests, dilemmas of, 46
communism, 66
competitive model, 178-183
competitiveness, 193